THE TENDER ART OF GRIEVING

THE TENDER ART OF GRIEVING

EMBODIED PRACTICES FOR LETTING GO & FINDING PEACE

AmarAtma Singh Khalsa

SHAMBHALA

SHAMBHALA PUBLICATIONS, INC.
2129 13th Street
Boulder, Colorado 80302
www.shambhala.com

Cover art: SY/Adobe Stock
Cover design: Daniel Urban-Brown
Interior design: Anna Becker

The information in this book is provided for educational and informational purposes only. Readers should consult with a qualified health-care provider or licensed therapist before making any decisions related to mental or physical health, medication, or therapeutic practices.

9 8 7 6 5 4 3 2 1

First Edition
Printed in the United States of America

Shambhala Publications makes every effort to print on acid-free, recycled paper.
Shambhala Publications is distributed worldwide by Penguin Random House, Inc., and its subsidiaries.

Library of Congress Cataloging-in-Publication Data
Names: Khalsa, AmarAtma Singh author
Title: The tender art of grieving: embodied practices for letting go and finding peace / AmarAtma Singh Khalsa.
Description: First edition. | Boulder, Colorado: Shambhala Publications, [2026] | Includes bibliographical references and index.
Identifiers: LCCN 2026002621 |
ISBN 9781645474951 trade paperback alk. paper
Subjects: LCSH: Grief
Classification: LCC BF575.G7 K5248 2026
LC record available at https://lccn.loc.gov/2026002621

The authorized representative in the EU for product safety and compliance is eucomply OÜ, Pärnu mnt 139b-14, 11317 Tallinn, Estonia, hello@eucompliancepartner.com.

This book is dedicated to the grief carried silently, longing for expression, and to the tender, voiceless places within you that yearn for compassion and validation. It is also dedicated to the body, the faithful keeper of breath and rhythm, whose quiet wisdom guides us through suffering and reminds us of love's enduring power. May we learn to honor you more deeply.

CONTENTS

Introduction 1

PART ONE:

Foundations of Compassionate Grieving 7

1. Start with Compassion 9
2. Reclaiming the Power of the Heart 16
3. Grieving in a Culture of Disconnection 32
4. How to Let Go 44
5. Embodiment as the Path to Peace 59

PART TWO:

Somatic Relief for Grief 71

6. Navigating Through Brain Fog 75
7. Managing Energy 87
8. Getting Better Sleep 100
9. Tending Digestion 110
10. Working Through Anger 122

11. Connecting with Sadness 134

12. Facing Anxiety 146

13. Honoring When You Feel Numb 160

14. Navigating the Abyss of Fear 177

15. Coming Up Against Guilt 194

16. Disentangling from Shame 207

17. Reconciling with Regret 224

18. Meeting Joy 236

19. Awakening to What Matters Most 250

20. Coming Alive Again 262

Conclusion: Living the Practices, Living the Love 278

Acknowledgments 281

Appendix A: Exercises by Chapter 283

Appendix B: Exercises by Method 287

Notes 291

Index 319

About the Author 331

THE TENDER ART OF GRIEVING

INTRODUCTION

It took me twenty years to understand that my pain was grief, ten years to figure out what to do with it, and more than eight years (and counting) to live and practice what I've learned.

I've been afraid of grief for as long as I can remember, though I didn't know that it was grief that had me so scared. *Grief* was a word we never used in my home. When I finally realized that grief was the undercurrent of my difficult youth, everything began to make sense. Still, it wasn't until my late twenties that I found language and context for the pain that had shaped my early life.

From the time I was three years old, I had recurring dreams of my father dying. Later came long days in the hospital while my grandmother recovered from heart attacks. I recall the hum of machines, the scent of antiseptics, the glare of fluorescent lights. Those early experiences made it hard for me to form attachments. If everyone I loved could disappear, why open my heart at all? The pain of loving and losing felt unbearable. My six-year-old mind wrestled with questions too big for its years: Why do people die? Where do we go when we die? What is the purpose of being here? My heart had no anchor and no words to describe the storm within.

When I was ten, the losses became tangible. After years of bullying and another move to a new town, I felt the weight of being "other." As a Punjabi Sikh boy in California, born in Canada, I carried traditions I didn't understand. Wanting to belong, I cut my unshorn hair, a sacred part of my Sikh identity. What I thought would help me fit in became its own series of losses: loss of identity, loss of culture, and, most profoundly, loss of innocence.

A year later, my grandfather died. He was my anchor. I lived in a multigenerational household with both parents working full time, which meant Darji, my grandfather, had been the steady presence that made me feel safe. He was the one who cared for me after school, sliced apples for me each afternoon, and sat beside me watching television—except when he watched *General Hospital* and *M*A*S*H*, which he rarely missed.

When he was gone, the ground fell out from under me. My family grieved, but silently. In our culture, death was not named aloud; it was taboo to talk about it. Outwardly, relatives offered food and company. But no one spoke of the pain. As a sensitive child, I felt like I absorbed what was left unspoken and carried both my grief and the unprocessed grief of those around me.

Not long after this loss, we moved again. For my father, the house was filled with reminders of my grandfather's presence. For me, leaving behind what little familiarity I had left was the breaking point. *Depression*, not *grief*, was the word used then. My high school and early college years were the hardest of my life. I lived like a shadow—functional on the outside, fractured on the inside. Shame from bullying became interwoven with grief, and self-criticism turned into self-hatred. I learned to suppress my feelings and perform that I was okay. This is what I was taught. Those closest to me, however, knew how deep the pain was. Panic attacks became normal as I tried to stuff it all down. I smiled and laughed, pretending everything was fine, while inside I was drowning.

Years later, when I began studying grief, I finally understood what had been happening. There was cumulative grief, the piling up of losses that were never acknowledged. There was intergenerational grief, the ancestral sorrow quietly passed through family lines. There was disenfranchised grief, the kind that goes unseen, such as identity loss, racism, and bigotry. And there was ambiguous grief, the kind that comes from losses without clear closure. All of these layers—both visible and invisible—pressed inward.

Unconsciously my body carried it all. Somatic grief, the grief that shows up in the body, took hold. I lost my appetite, battled stomach pain, and struggled to digest food. I was thin, anxious, and catabolic. I developed nervous habits, picking at my hair until clumps came out. By thirteen, alcohol and marijuana had become my way to numb pain I couldn't name.

What I couldn't process in mind or emotion, my body expressed for me. Eventually my body began to break down, and suicidal thoughts became more frequent. Just before turning twenty, and supported by my family, I took a leap: a three-month journey through southern Chile and Patagonia. Immersed in ancient forests and vast mountain ranges, I found a rhythm that matched my soul. I breathed mountain air, hiked for hours, camped under stars, and rose before dawn to greet the day with breath and meditation. Something in me began to awaken. Later that same year, I made the first of many consecutive trips to India, reconnecting to my Sikh roots and heritage.

It took years, and many tears, but slowly my body began to release. Movement and meditation became my medicine. Nature steadied me. Breath opened me. My body began to process the grief that had been locked inside for so long. It was my body that showed me how to heal.

Gratefully, grief came early enough that I could build my life around understanding it. In college I designed my own major—transpersonal studies—to explore spirituality, psychology, and religion. Later I earned a master's in Traditional Chinese Medicine (TCM), studying the body-mind connection through acupuncture. Alongside that training, I immersed myself in Sikh ministry, deepening my spiritual practice. Merging medicine and ministry, I entered chaplaincy and spent nearly ten years in end-of-life care. As one of the first board-certified Sikh chaplains in the United States, I brought a unique lens to the grieving process. As an interfaith chaplain, I sat with thousands of grievers—from children and adults to families, nurses, doctors, and other hospital staff—witnessing death, dying, and the love that endures beyond it. Those years taught me more about grief, love, and resilience than any book ever could.

Most of us are never taught how to grieve. Instead, we learn to push past our pain, stay busy, or keep up appearances. We pressure ourselves to "get over it," to perform being okay, to hide the ache and call it strength. These patterns of perfectionism or performance may help you survive for a while, but eventually they catch up to you. The body remembers what the mind tries to forget.

Over time, I learned that grief is not only universal but can also be expected. To live with emotional health and well-being, we must learn to face grief—past, present, and the inevitable losses to come. Grieving is an essential life skill that most of us are never taught.

Forged through the crucible of night calls, code arrests, and witnessing the rawest expressions of human sorrow, I began to see patterns emerge. As I was guided by mentors, collaboration, and the body-mind principles of Chinese medicine, new insights about grief formed in me. Grief shifted from something to fear or manage into a profound teacher—one whose wisdom invites us home to ourselves.

Eventually my work moved beyond the hospital. I began teaching, leading retreats, and offering coaching and education on grief and letting go. When I started sharing embodied and somatic practices online, I was moved by the response. It revealed how many people are yearning for grief-informed care and compassionate support. Over time, what I had been studying, practicing, and living coalesced into a framework: Compassionate Grieving—an integrative, body-centered, and spiritually grounded approach to grief in the modern world.

This book distills the important and relevant elements of the Compassionate Grieving model to help you make sense of and metabolize your grief. In it you'll find practices, breathwork, movements, meditations, and reflections that have brought relief and peace into my life and the lives of my clients. In writing this resource and companion, I gathered knowledge from many frameworks and traditions and wove them into a practical source for navigating one of the most universal and human experiences. Think of it as a guide you can return to whenever you need comfort, understanding, or a reminder that you are not alone.

Filled with stories, reflections, and gentle teachings, this book is written to feel like a compassionate friend walking beside you through the bewildering landscape of loss. Its purpose is to help you not get over grief but change your relationship with it—to hold it, soften around it, and even find love within it. Here you'll rediscover a sense of empowerment when you feel stuck or overwhelmed and begin to see that grief is about not only pain but also love, connection, and even the possibility of experiencing aliveness.

The book is divided into two parts. Part one lays the foundation, introducing the principles of Compassionate Grieving. You'll come to understand grief in its many forms—how it lives in your body, how it shapes your nervous system, and how you can begin to work with it rather than against it. Drawing from neuroscience, psychology, somatic therapy, Ayurveda, and Traditional Chinese Medicine, these chapters reveal how grief moves through the body and how the body itself can become the very place where healing begins.

You'll also find clear language that challenges how we've been taught to think about grief. Many of us were raised on myths such as "time heals all wounds," "stay busy and move on," or "letting go means forgetting." These cultural messages can make us feel as though we're doing grief wrong or that we should be further along than we are. This book invites you to unlearn those old paradigms and discover a more compassionate and body-centered way to heal.

Most importantly, this book is grounded in embodiment. In part two you'll learn more than fifty ways to release tension, create space, and find moments of genuine relief. These pages are designed to soften grief's sharp edges and bring moments of calm and clarity when the weight feels too heavy to bear. Each chapter explores a specific emotional landscape, such as anger, sadness, guilt, numbness, and anxiety, with simple embodied practices to help you learn to meet your grief in a new way—with tenderness and compassion instead of with resistance or judgment.

The goal is simple yet profound: to help you find peace within your pain, to remind you that grief can open you to deeper love, and to support you in discovering a more grounded, authentic way of living in relationship with loss.

People often ask what brought me to grief work. I sometimes joke, "I didn't dream of becoming a grief specialist at age twelve." But perhaps in some way I did. Perhaps that twelve-year-old boy, with all his pain and confusion, endured what he needed to in order to prepare me for this life of service. I'm grateful for the courage and conviction he carried through the darkest tunnels, guiding me toward the light. He's with me now as I write this, strong and mighty, sharing his wisdom and understanding with you.

I am grateful you are here, holding these pages in your hands. As you embark on this journey, here is my wish for you:

May these pages be a soft place for your heart to rest.
May your body find ease as you breathe, move, and open to what grief carries.
May your tears be honored, your silence respected, and your love remembered.
May you discover that within your pain lives the seed of deeper connection.
And may you never walk alone, for grief itself can become a companion, guiding you toward tenderness, meaning, and peace.

Let's begin together.

PART ONE

Foundations of Compassionate Grieving

1

Start with Compassion

I WANT TO BEGIN by acknowledging something important. In writing this book, my words may not fully capture the moment you are living inside of right now. If you are here, you are likely carrying a profound loss. That loss may come through death, divorce, a breakup, or the loss of a job or a life you once imagined. It may come from watching the fabric of society fray, feeling the weight of climate change, or sensing a world that feels increasingly unsafe and unsteady. You may be grieving something in the future, not yet here but already present in your body. Or you may be carrying grief that is ancient and old. Your grief may be abstract, as mine once was, filled with the loss of identity, meaning, or a sense of belonging—leaving you disoriented in this thing we call life. You may also be here as a friend or family member, wanting to understand more so you can be a caring and supportive human to someone you love. However you arrived, I am grateful that you are here.

Grieving may be one of the most challenging experiences of your life. Grief is no small thing, and please allow me to validate your experience. Grief has a way of breaking your sense of direction, unraveling your identity, and shaking your trust in what is stable and safe. It is heavy, disorienting, and sometimes feels impossible to carry. I want to name this clearly. Your pain is real. You are not imagining it, exaggerating it, or doing it wrong. Grief is not a mental illness. It is an emotional injury. It can ache in your bones, disrupt your sleep, and make even the smallest tasks feel monumental. If you find yourself struggling, please know that it makes sense. You are responding to something profound, to something powerful, to something that matters deeply.

And while I want to name the weight of this truth, I also want to recognize your courage. You are here. You are reading, breathing, and showing up for yourself in the midst of it all. That alone is extraordinary. It means some small part of you, even if it feels tired or weary, knows that this love deserves care and that tending to your grief is not a weakness but an act of devotion.

Compassion as Companion

Let us begin here, together, by creating space for compassion. You do not have to rush to feel better. You do not have to perform being strong. Compassion says you are allowed to be exactly as you are right now: raw, confused, angry, numb, or undone. You are not broken; you are human. This is the tenderness you start with, the truth that healing begins not by changing how you feel but by learning to hold what you feel with kindness.

In grief, compassion is not an idea or an emotion but rather an act of presence and tenderness. It is the willingness to stay connected to your pain without judging yourself, to let love reach where it hurts, to soften toward what feels unbearable. It begins when you pause long enough to notice your breath, your trembling, your exhaustion, and say to yourself, *This too belongs.* Compassion is the quiet strength that allows you to feel what you feel without needing to fix it or rush through it.

Compassion is grief's companion. It walks beside your sorrow, not above it. It recognizes that pain is not a problem to solve but a form of love that needs tending. When compassion meets grief, the war inside begins to ease. The body relaxes, the heart opens, and what once felt like too much becomes just enough to breathe through. Compassion does not erase the ache. Instead, compassion holds it with gentleness until the ache is felt, nurtured, and loved. In the presence of tenderness, tension and tightness can transform into something spacious and sacred.

To live with compassion is to honor the full range of your humanness: the tears, the fatigue, the longing, and the love that remains. It is the choice to meet your suffering with kindness instead of criticism, with curiosity instead of control. Compassion is not a strategy for escape or even avoidance; it is the ground that lets you stand amid heartbreak and still know you are whole.

In Compassionate Grieving, compassion begins with yourself. It is the willingness to notice your own hurt with kindness rather than judgment. When your mind says, *I shouldn't still be feeling this*, compassion whispers, *You're allowed to feel exactly what you feel.* This simple allowance begins repairing the inner fracture that grief often exposes—the split between what we feel and what we think we're supposed to feel.

Compassion also brings your body back into the story of healing. It is not merely an emotion or virtue; it is a physiological state of safety and connection. When your heart softens and your breath deepens, your nervous system receives the message that it is safe to rest, to weep, to open. Your body becomes a sanctuary again. This is also where the suffering in grief transforms—not by erasing pain but by metabolizing it through warmth, breath, and gentle awareness.

Compassionate Grieving is, therefore, not a method for getting over grief but a practice for being with it in a new way. It restores relationship toward wholeness with your body, with your emotions, and with the love that grief reveals. Compassion opens a doorway from resistance to reverence, from suffering to sacredness. In that openness, your heart remembers: Grief is a sign not that something went wrong but that something deeply loved is being honored.

Grief, a Story of Love

What if grief is not what you think it is? What if it isn't a sign that something has gone wrong but a sacred sign that something mattered deeply? What if there's something right with your grief, not something wrong?

For too long, we have been taught to fear grief as if it were the enemy of joy or the boogeyman hiding in the dark. But what if grief is not a monster to run from but rather something far more innocent, such as a messenger of love itself? What if your grief is a story of love simply looking for a place to land?

I believe we grieve in direct proportion to the love we experience. The greater the love, the greater the grief. When you allow this compassionate reframe, everything begins to shift. You no longer need to approach grief as a problem to solve or a wound to close or an emotion to bury but as a natural continuation of love's story. It softens the sharp edges of judgment and creates room for tenderness. This perspective doesn't make your pain disappear; it helps you recognize that you can carry this weight because you already know the power of love. It says, *Of course it hurts. Of course you feel this deeply. You loved greatly.*

You may have seen the quote that often circles around on social media sharing that grief is a love that has nowhere to go. I believe that grief is love *looking* for a place to go. Compassionate Grieving is the practice of creating banks for that river of love that no longer has a focus. Letting go is not about forgetting; letting go is about letting flow. Through the body, through the breath, and through the willingness to feel pain, it can find its way. This is how you give your love a direction again: You let it move through you instead of letting it get trapped inside you.

Grief longs for expression. It wants to be witnessed, spoken, and held. It does not want to be silenced, fixed, or hurried. It simply wants acknowledgment: *I see you. I feel you. You belong.* When grief receives that kind of compassionate attention, it begins to soften. What once felt unbearable begins to breathe. What once felt like breaking becomes an opening. This is how grief becomes a sacred invitation—when love and pain are allowed to exist in the same breath.

Befriending the Ache

If grief is love seeking a place to go, then befriending the ache is how you welcome it home. The ache you feel is not your enemy. It is not proof that you are broken or weak or that you're failing somehow in your grieving. The ache is love's echo reverberating through your body, asking to be met rather than managed. It lives in the tightness of your chest, the lump in your throat, the weight in your stomach. It speaks in sighs, tears, restlessness, and silence. To befriend the ache is to turn toward these sensations with compassion and curiosity—to say, *I see you; I will not abandon you.*

At first this may feel impossible. Every instinct inside you may want to run away, distract, numb, or busy yourself back into control. But if you can pause and breathe, even for a few seconds, you can begin to notice that the ache is not here to harm you. It is here to help you listen. It carries wisdom from the parts of you that still remember how to love. The ache is the language of the heart reminding you that something precious was lost—that you are still capable of loving even in that loss and that the feeling of loss is an expression of love itself.

Befriending the ache means creating safety for your pain to exist. You don't have to fix it or make it disappear. You simply offer it the same kindness you would offer a dear friend in sorrow. You can place a hand over your heart or on the place in your body where the ache lives and say softly, *I'm here. You can rest now.* In that small gesture, the nervous system begins to calm, the breath deepens, and the body starts to trust that it is safe to feel again.

This is the quiet miracle of compassionate grieving. When you stop fighting the ache and befriend it, grief changes shape. It becomes less like an intruder and more like an intimate teacher. You begin to sense that the ache doesn't need to be conquered—it needs to be companioned. Over time, you come to realize that the ache itself is not the absence of love but the proof of it.

The Sacred Unraveling

You may be standing at a threshold, a place between what was and what will be. You may feel like a caterpillar inside a cocoon, no longer who you were and not yet who you will be. This in-between place can feel uncertain and disorienting. It can feel like losing your shape, your footing, your sense of who you are. But what feels like falling apart is, in truth, the sacred beginning of transformation.

Inside the cocoon, a caterpillar does not simply grow wings; it dissolves. Once sealed in its capsule, the caterpillar's body begins to break down in a process called histolysis.[1] The structures that once defined its form soften and release. From that liquefied state, tiny clusters of cells called imaginal discs awaken.[2] These poetically named cells carry the blueprint for what is to come: wings, eyes, a new body.[3] During histogenesis, the butterfly is remade, cell by cell, from the very material of its own undoing.[4]

We praise the caterpillar for its innocence and glorify the butterfly for its beauty, but we rarely honor the sacred unraveling in between.

We forget that transformation requires surrender, that life remakes itself through loss. The melting, the waiting, the not-knowing, and the silence are not signs of failure. They are the alchemy of becoming.

The in-between is sacred ground. This is where the body's wisdom takes over. It remakes you not by bypassing pain or forcing change but by allowing dissolution to do its quiet work. The body knows how to rebuild from within. Cells are doing it all the time: You are being reorganized by something greater than your personal will.

The Body as the Ground of Becoming

Transformation is not exclusively emotional or mental; it is cellular, somatic, and embodied too. It lives inside your very tissues. In your cocooned season, you may feel undone or unrecognizable. This is not failure. You are not broken. What feels like breaking down may, in truth, be breaking open.

Breaking down and rebuilding can be holy work. You may long for transformation and to be on the other side of your grief but resist the messy middle of its unfolding. Much of this process happens in the dark, hidden from your own awareness. That does not make it wrong. It is the quiet work of your body, a sacred reorganization that happens beneath the surface, where consciousness and cells meet in renewal.

You may have been taught to conquer or control your emotions, to power through pain, to keep going when every part of you wants to rest. The body then becomes a workhorse that carries what the heart cannot yet release. Yet unprocessed feelings do not disappear; they settle into muscles, tissues, and fascia. Tension grows. Fatigue deepens. Your breath shortens. Even though research continues to reveal the inseparability of mind and body, you may still live as if the mind should lead and the body should obey. The truth is, your body grieves too.

Yet your body is also the fulcrum of release. When you allow it to rest, your mind begins to soften. The body becomes a compass that can guide you through grief. It holds an ancient wisdom that knows how to metabolize what you feel. Breath by breath, sensation by sensation, it helps you digest experience until meaning can emerge.

If grief is love seeking a place to go, then letting go is allowing that love to flow. Just as your digestive system knows how to absorb, assimilate, and eliminate, your emotional body also knows how to process grief. Learning how your body grieves teaches you how to grieve. When you nurture, honor, and listen to your body, you open a pathway to relief. It becomes your compass for healing and integration.

This mirrors the work of grief within you. Like the chrysalis, you may need to dissolve, not as a failure or collapse but as an act of sacred transformation. Grief initiates its own form of histolysis, where old identities and attachments loosen. And just as the butterfly's imaginal discs hold the code for new wings, your body holds the blueprint within the very ache of loss.

Your body is your companion and compass. It is the ground of becoming. It tells the truth about what is no longer working and what longs to be released. It is a sacred vessel through which transformation is felt, metabolized, and embodied. It invites you into the quiet intelligence of inner becoming.

The pulse of compassion lives in your very heart. Through each rhythm and beat is a quiet presence of care. If grief is love looking for a place to go, then it's the heart's knowing about how to create that flow. It takes the whole heart to love; it'll take the whole heart to grieve. It's the compassionate presence of the heart that guides our journey through grief.

2

Reclaiming the Power of the Heart

When I was working as a hospital chaplain, I noticed that before anyone spoke a word about their loss, the body had already said everything. Shoulders were collapsed, eyes were distant, breath was suspended. The body carried stories that language could not reach. Again and again, when someone reconnected with their breath or felt their steady heartbeat, even slightly, something softened. Grief did not disappear, but their suffering eased. What I learned at the bedside, and what both Traditional Chinese Medicine and contemporary research confirm, is simple and profound: The body is not only affected by grief; it participates in it.

Grieving is an emotional or psychological process. It is also profoundly physiological. The body is the fulcrum through which grief is experienced, expressed, and metabolized. When you abandon your body in times of loss—whether by numbing, tightening, dissociating, or staying only in your thoughts—grief grows heavier and more isolating. When you turn toward your body as a compassionate partner, grief softens. Your breath steadies your heart, your heart steadies your mind, and your mind can rest in the rhythms of the body's intelligence. What once felt like an overwhelming, emotional tidal wave collapsing over you becomes something manageable and bearable. In other words, centering your body as a companion in your grieving helps you feel larger in relationship to the emotional pain. Reclaiming your body and your heart as allies allows emotion to complete its natural cycle, shifting pain into presence and sorrow into tenderness. This is the tender art of grieving: listening to the wisdom of the body, allowing love and loss to coexist in the same heartbeat, and finding peace not by escaping grief but by inhabiting it fully.

For centuries, spiritual traditions have spoken of the heart as the seat of wisdom, the place where love and sorrow meet. Today, science is beginning to describe what mystics have long known: The heart is more than a pump. It communicates with the brain, influences emotion, and shapes how you experience safety and connection. When you align with your body's intelligence, healing becomes less something you force and more something you allow.

Even when you feel cut off from your body, it does not stop caring for you. With every heartbeat it nourishes you. With each breath it fills you with life. It digests your food, repairs what is worn, and quietly regulates the rhythms that keep you going. Even in desperation or numbness, a tender care works beneath the surface, asking only for a little recognition and kindness in return.

If you have ever loved an animal, you know this kind of love. Animals do not love with the mind alone; they love with their whole body. A dog waits by the door, tail wagging, jumping with delight at your arrival. A cat settles on your lap when your heart is heavy, nestling in with soft purrs. Their love is not expressed in words but through look, touch, personality, and body language. It is felt through presence, a fully embodied affection given by simply being with you.

Your body offers a similar loyalty. If the body had a voice, it might say, "I love you," "I love you," "I love you," with every breath and heartbeat. It rushes to protect you in fear and softens to hold you at rest. Yet for many of us, the body has become a stranger or even an enemy. We forget, blame, numb, shame, overwork, undernourish, or try to control it, ignoring its living intelligence.

This chapter explores the quiet miracle of how your body loves and holds you in grief. We will look at the embodied heart through three lenses: Western science, Traditional Chinese Medicine, and Ayurveda.

Each offers a way to understand how the body supports you and why grounding grief work in the body brings comfort, healing, and a sense of coming home to yourself. You will see how the heart, breath, and nervous system form a foundation for emotional healing, and how reclaiming the power of the heart reveals that your biology is on your side.

The Heart as the Center of Feeling and Flow

Love is not a metaphor. It is embodied. It is neurochemical, cardiovascular, and relational. Love lives and moves through the body. It is not only a feeling but a living process—a constant interplay of hormones, heart rhythms, electrical impulses, and chemical messengers. Most of this happens without your effort, yet you can influence it through how you breathe, move, and relate. When you hold someone's hand, breathe together, or sit quietly beside someone in grief, your physiology changes. Heart rates slow, blood pressure steadies, and a sense of safety returns.

To reduce the heart to merely an organ that pumps blood is to miss its wonder. The heart is not just a symbol of love; it is love in action. Every pulse, every contraction, every beat is a gesture of giving and receiving. It gathers and releases, receives and offers, again and again, like a sacred rhythm that mirrors the inhale and exhale of life itself. Through this rhythm nourishment flows, oxygen circulates, and renewal continues. In this way, the heart's work is not separate from love. It is the work of love, steady and faithful.

Your heart beats about one hundred thousand times a day and sends blood through roughly sixty thousand miles of vessels.[1] Most of this happens without your will or conscious effort. Without blood, there is no nourishment. Without nourishment, there is no life. Blood is a physical vehicle of love. It delivers, cleanses, and restores. Every 90 to 120 days, your red blood cells regenerate.[2] Within you there is a quiet renewal, like the cycles of the seasons.

But the heart does not act alone. It moves in reciprocity with the lungs. The lungs contain hundreds of millions of tiny air sacs called alveoli, where gas exchange takes place.[3] Together, heart and lungs form a beautiful synchronicity. The heart pumps blood to the lungs to be enriched with oxygen, which is returned to the heart and then sent to nourish the body. Blood and breath. Heart and lungs. Giving and receiving. Each inhale a beginning. Each exhale a letting go. This is not a competition. They move together in a choreography of care.

Have you ever seen a time-lapse video of fog flowing over a coastline? The forming and unforming fog looks like the breath, serene and calming. In the same way, the interchange between lungs and heart offers insight into emotional regulation and sensation.

This dance is a poetry of muscle and rhythm. It is the movement of love happening in your body. Understanding how your heart and lungs work is not just about learning anatomy. It is about remembering that grief is also a bodily experience. When you grieve, your physiology grieves too. The pounding heart, the shallow breath, the lump in your throat, the exhaustion after crying are signs not that something is wrong but that your body is participating in love's response to loss.

Sitting on her couch during one of our sessions, Marisa placed one hand on her chest and the other on her belly. I asked her to listen. Tuning in to her body at an emotional level was new. She had carried grief for years since her father's death. With the anniversary of his death approaching, she wanted to mark it differently than in the past, when the day often ended in exhaustion and an emotional hangover. As she settled, she was struck with awe. It felt like she was truly feeling her heartbeat for the first time, with presence and attention. Tears slid down her cheeks, not from sorrow but from gratitude. Simply noticing gave her the spaciousness she had been longing for, a love that opened her heart to grieving her father in the way she desired.

The Body's Harmonizing Orchestra

Between each heartbeat lies a subtle rhythm that reflects your emotional and energetic state. This rhythm is called heart rate variability (HRV), which refers to the variation in time between individual heartbeats, not just the rate of the beats themselves.[4] While it may sound technical, HRV is a sensitive indicator of how your nervous system is responding to life.[5]

HRV is regulated by the autonomic nervous system, your body's autopilot. Essentially your heart and breath quietly keep you alive so you do not have to think about it, while sending subtle signals to you about whether you are safe or under threat. Through these pathways, the nervous system regulates blood pressure, orchestrates hormones, balances temperature, adjusts muscle tone and posture, sets breathing rate, coordinates digestion, modulates immune and inflammatory responses, and rapidly assesses whether an environment is threatening or safe before you are consciously aware of it.[6]

Your body is constantly gathering information from within and generating sensations that let you know what is happening beneath the surface. That is why you might feel butterflies in your stomach before speaking in public, a dry mouth when anxious, cold hands when afraid, or a blush rising in moments of tenderness.[7] It is also why, when safety returns, you may feel a spreading warmth through your chest, an ease in your shoulders, or a softening in your belly. These subtle shifts are how your body communicates its inner state.[8] They are the language of the heart and nervous system working together to help you sense, respond, and find equilibrium again.

The autonomic nervous system has two main branches. The sympathetic nervous system mobilizes you for action. You may have heard of fight or flight—these are sympathetic nervous system responses. The parasympathetic nervous system restores balance through relaxation and repair. Think of them less as competitors and more as dance partners. In healthy flow, they collaborate, helping you respond to stress and return to balance. When they are in harmony, you can shift smoothly between action and ease, meeting difficulties that present themselves to you and calming down once they've passed.[9]

When the sympathetic system dominates for too long, you may feel restless, anxious, tense, or unable to sleep. Your heart might race, digestion may slow, and you can feel as though you are always on, even when there is no threat.[10] You may know this as feeling stressed. On the other hand, the parasympathetic system also has a protective shutdown when overwhelm is too great. Fatigue or low motivation is not caused by too much rest-and-digest activity. It comes from the body's freeze response, known as a dorsal vagal pattern, that lowers energy to help you survive emotional overload.[11] Both states are messages from your body asking for regulation and care, signals that it is time to restore rhythm between movement and rest.

Because the sympathetic nervous system is often chronically activated in modern life, many of us live in a near-constant state of activation, the body poised to act and react, even when there is no real danger. Over time, this can leave you depleted, anxious, or emotionally numb. To restore the balance of an overactive sympathetic system, practices that activate the parasympathetic system, which is primarily activated through the vagus nerve, become essential. Slow, rhythmic breathing, gentle movement, meditation, mindful walking, time in nature, soothing music, or simply connecting with someone who feels safe all help—each of these activities signals to your body that it can relax and let down its guard.[12] They help shift you from surviving to resting, from bracing to receiving, initiating what is often called the relaxation response.[13] As the parasympathetic system comes online, your blood pressure lowers, your breathing slows, your muscles release, digestion resumes, and your heart rate decreases.[14] These are not small acts. They are invitations for your nervous system to remember safety and to let grief move through discomfort rather than stay trapped inside. It is a state of repair.

While these descriptions make this process sound simple, your body is not a machine. It is a living organism that moves in rhythm and flow. As the sympathetic and parasympathetic systems take turns, their dance expresses itself through subtle variations in the timing between your heartbeats. This is your heart rate variability: the living conversation between action and rest, tension and release. While you may not perceive the milliseconds of change, you feel the effects in your emotional world.[15]

When HRV is supple, you experience resilience, or what I like to call "emotional buoyancy." Emotional buoyancy is the quiet intelligence that lets you meet moments of stress or sorrow without being pulled under the waves and drowned by your experience. In grief, buoyancy does not mean you stop feeling the weight of loss; it means you flow with the waves of grief rather than resist them. Emotional buoyancy is your ability to stay gently in flow with your grieving response.

When HRV becomes rigid, buoyancy is more challenging to experience. You may experience this as emotional drowning. You may feel as though you cannot catch your breath, that your heart is racing or heavy, or that life itself feels more fragile. This is not a failure; it is your body's way of signaling overwhelm; you have met your nervous system's capacity.

Terry came to me feeling on edge. She described herself as a Type A person. She was also a therapist who cared deeply for her clients and showed up reliably for her family. She exercised early in the morning, often waking up at five o'clock, loved coffee, kept full days, and rarely slowed down. She knew all the regulation techniques—she taught them. And yet, when it came to her own grief, she felt stuck in her head and overwhelmed by feelings that arose.

Over the years, Terry experienced many losses. Eventually the grief caught up with her, and she found herself crying uncontrollably and unable to make it stop. She used the words *emotionally flooding*. She asked how to get over her grief; but what was needed first was not more insight or effort but instead a way to recalibrate back to her body, shift the state toward the relaxation response, and provide a more flexible autonomic experience. As her nervous system began to soften and settle, so too did the experience of drowning. The waves no longer pulled her under; she was able to experience emotional buoyancy.

Grief and emotions are shaped by the condition of your nervous system. When it is rigid and wound tight, even the small emotions can feel unbearable, as if everything is falling apart. Where there is more flexibility, you can feel what arises without drowning in it. This gentle capacity to feel and move with emotion is a state of flow.

Have you ever noticed how nature moves in rhythm? Birds fly in synchronized patterns, schools of fish flow as if they're one organism, pendulums swing together, ocean waves align their crests before breaking on the shore. This is not coincidence; it is harmony at work. Nature organizes itself through synchronization. Your body, too, follows this same intelligence. Within you, this process is called entrainment.[16]

Entrainment describes how your biological systems—such as your heartbeat, breathing rhythm, brain waves, and even the oscillations of your cells—begin to move in harmony when balance is present.[17] It is as if your inner world is an orchestra: each system an instrument, each rhythm distinct yet connected, all guided by an invisible conductor. When these rhythms align, they create a song of synchronicity, a music of harmony and homeostasis.

The brilliance of entrainment is that your inner rhythms seek harmony. When you breathe slowly, your heart begins to follow that rhythm. As your heart settles, your brain and emotions respond in kind. Entrainment is your biology's way of remembering unity, nature's design for healing.

This concept is especially important when working with grief. It suggests that healing isn't just about "feeling better"—it's about restoring harmony to your inner orchestra. We experience this harmony as a sense of aliveness. Unprocessed or unfamiliar emotions can throw this orchestra out of sync, like a timpani struck at the wrong moment or a lingering note on the bassoon. Breathing becomes shallow, heart rhythms turn jagged, and the nervous system oscillates between alertness and collapse. The empowering truth is that HRV is not fixed—you can influence it.[18] The fluctuations between your sympathetic and parasympathetic nervous systems are responsive. Slow and rhythmic breathing, gentle movement, prayer, meditation, mindful rest, safe connection with another person, or even a moment of gratitude can increase HRV and support entrainment.

Each time you engage in these small practices, you are synchronizing with the wise intelligence your body already knows. You are reconnecting to life's natural rhythm of harmony. This is the physiology of emotion in action: your heart learning to listen, your breath learning to soothe, and your body remembering how to rise again after grief pulls you down. This is emotional buoyancy, the living pulse of resilience.

When you consciously slow your breath, soften your body, or rest in the presence of someone calm and attuned, your internal rhythms begin to entrain again. Your heart finds its music through rhythm. It does not operate independently of you. Through simple practices, you can modulate it and help your body return to a state of harmony, which makes emotional processing profoundly easier.

When this synchronization becomes steady and sustained, it gives rise to a new state called coherence. In this fluid rhythmicity between the heart, brain, and nervous system, your body begins to conserve energy, emotional regulation improves, and mental clarity becomes more available.[19] The HeartMath Institute describes heart coherence as a state of harmony between the heart, brain, and nervous system.[20] In this state, people often experience greater calm, intuition, stable energy, and emotional balance. Research shows that coherence is associated with higher HRV, lower stress hormones, a stronger immune response, and improved connection with others.[21]

Observing HRV is one of the ways you can witness this beautiful orchestra within. HRV measures the small, natural differences in the time between each heartbeat. These tiny variations, measured in milliseconds, reflect how responsive and adaptable your heart is.[22] Today, wearable devices such as an Apple Watch, Oura Ring, or WHOOP band can easily show you your HRV over time. It's quite extraordinary that we now have ways to observe emotional health, stress, vitality, and even spiritual well-being through these physiological signals. We no longer have to rely solely on faith or intuition to sense how our body is adapting to change. Science and technology now help us see it.

These small and seemingly insignificant variations between each heartbeat are one of the key physiological signatures of emotional flexibility and the body's ability to stay buoyant amid life's changes.[23] A higher HRV generally reflects greater balance and resilience in the nervous system, while a lower HRV can signal stress or depletion.[24] Even in grief, there is a quiet mechanism of harmony at work. Your body is always communicating how you are responding to distress while simultaneously seeking balance, guided by an inner template for recovery and renewal.

Your heart also speaks with the hearts of others. In the presence of someone safe and emotionally attuned, your nervous system can co-regulate with theirs.[25] Stephen W. Porges, a psychology and neuroscience researcher known for his development of the polyvagal theory, calls this part of our "social nervous system."[26] Your body listens and responds to the rhythms of another. This capacity is part of the physiology of empathy, compassion, and love. Safety is shared. Your body remembers how to breathe with another when words fall short. You may have felt it when you walk with a friend and your steps naturally fall into rhythm, or when you both say the same word at the same time and laugh, "Jinx!" Even more so when you are cozy on the sofa with someone you love, perhaps a beloved pet, and your breathing slows and synchronizes. These are simple expressions of social entrainment and coherence. In moments of emotional safety and intimate connection, oxytocin, the bonding hormone, often rises, which can lower blood pressure, ease pain, and increase a sense of security—another way natural rhythms of harmony and homeostasis take place.[27]

EXERCISE:
DEVELOPING EMOTIONAL BUOYANCY

Rest one palm gently over your heart and close the other hand into a fist, placing the knuckles on your spine at your lower back. Feel an equal weight of pressure between your fist at your lower back and the palm at your heart. Begin to breathe deeply and gently in your lower back and chest, consciously inhaling and exhaling slowly. Stay here for a few moments, resting your attention on this steady rhythm. Feel the rise and fall beneath your palm, the quiet intelligence of your body at work. With each breath, offer a silent recognition of appreciation for the natural harmony and brilliance beneath your hands.

When you include your body in the grieving process by slowing your breath, feeling your heartbeat, or honoring your body's subtle signals, you recognize you are not alone. Your body is helping you at profound levels, even when you cannot feel it. When the body becomes your partner in grief, the process becomes more easeful, more humane, gentler. It's the natural expression of embodiment. But when you feel disconnected from your body, your inner systems fall out of rhythm with one another. Energy that could support healing is spent managing disharmony instead.

The more you listen to your body's natural rhythms, the more you allow harmony to return. This is the quiet intelligence of love working through you, helping you find your way back to balance even in the midst of sorrow.

Emotions are a natural expression of life, not enemies to conquer. When you begin to understand the body's rhythmic intelligence, the way it synchronizes and seeks coherence, you realize that the body is never resisting your emotions. It is trying to help them move. The pounding heart, the shallow breath, the lump in your throat, and the exhaustion after tears are all signs of your body loving you the best way it knows how.

With small, steady practices, you can support that love and help it flow rather than resist it. You do not have to push through or hold it all alone. You can partner with your body and let it carry some of the weight. Grieving becomes less about endurance and more about allowing, less about control and more about connection, starting with yourself.

How the Heart Dances with the Brain

Your heart and brain are in constant conversation. Every moment, messages travel between them, shaping how you feel, think, and respond to life.[28] Research has shown that the heart carries its own network of neurons—a small intelligence within you that senses, remembers, and communicates.[29] You might say the heart has its own kind of knowing. It does not simply wait for the brain to tell it what to do. It listens, responds, and leads.

The vagus nerve, which helps regulate HRV, originates in the brain stem and connects your heart, lungs, and digestive organs.[30] It is the body's great communicator, carrying signals between the rhythms of your body and the centers of your brain that govern emotion and awareness. This nerve helps synchronize the heart and breath, supports the relaxation response, and allows a continual dialogue between the body and mind.[31]

When your heart rhythm is smooth and steady, and when HRV is supple and active, the vagus nerve sends signals of safety and calm to your brain. These messages reach regions responsible for emotional awareness, self-regulation, compassionate decision-making, and relational attunement.[32] In those moments, it becomes easier to think clearly, to listen deeply, and to act with kindness. When the heart is tense or erratic, when the sympathetic system is overactivated and HRV decreases, it can send signals of distress that make the mind race or the body brace.[33] What you feel in your chest is mirrored in your thoughts, and what you think is reflected back through your heart.[34] In other words, your internal state colors the meaning, narrative, and stories you make of what is happening.

For a long time, people believed the brain commanded and the body obeyed. We now understand the relationship is far more collaborative. In fact, most of the communication in the vagus nerve travels upward from body to brain.[35] So, the heart and body profoundly shape how the brain perceives and responds to the world. The researcher Bethany E. Kok calls this an "upward spiral," where safety and coherence in the heart invite wisdom and compassion in the mind.[36] This synchronization of entrainment between the heart and breath includes the brain. The harmonious state of coherence brings about mental clarity and physical calmness.

Think of this relationship between the heart and brain as a partnership built on trust. The heart listens to the mind, and the mind listens to the heart. When the two are in sync, you experience feelings of steadiness, clarity, and even kindness. Your body and mind biologically and rhythmically align in love.

This is not mind over matter. Nor is it matter over mind. It is a shared conversation, a nonhierarchical structure. The heart and brain are partners, not competitors. They're in the orchestra together, seeking synchronicity with each other. They feed off each other. They seek a dynamic dance of coherence. There is a heart intelligence woven into how you feel, relate, and heal.

What this really means for grief is this: Your body is already equipped to help you carry what feels unbearable. Grief does not have to be solved or silenced by the mind. You do not have to suppress or bury. You can be steadied and softened through the rhythms of the body. Each calm breath is your body's way of whispering, "You are safe enough to feel this. You are safe enough to love, even now." Trust the mechanism of entrainment. It's a natural phenomenon of synchronization.

The Heart in Traditional Chinese Medicine

Traditional Chinese Medicine (TCM), which has been working intimately with the body for thousands of years, offers a story of the heart that is intricate and poetic. If Western medicine is microscopic, TCM is macroscopic. In TCM, this story of love that dances between the heart and lungs also dances between the blood and *qi*.

One of the core concepts of TCM is that everything in nature, including the human body, is made up of yin and yang—complementary forces that exist in dynamic balance. Yin represents qualities that are cooling, still, nourishing, and receptive. Yang represents qualities that are warming, active, expansive, and expressive.[37] These two forces are not opposites but interdependent aspects of the same whole. Harmonizing yin and yang is central to any treatment.

Blood is considered yin, and qi is yang. Qi is the vital force, the breath of life. It animates the body and governs movement, immunity, digestion, and clarity. Qi uplifts, directs, protects, moves blood, initiates digestion, and awakens thought.[38] The lungs govern qi.[39] Through the breath, they draw in life force, refine it, and circulate it to nourish organs and tissue. The heart governs blood and is associated with *Shen*, the spirit.[40] It houses consciousness and identity. It is the ruler that governs by coherence. When the heart is calm, the kingdom is at peace. When Shen is settled, your mind is clear, your emotions are smooth, your sleep is deep, and your connection to the spirit is open.[41]

You might imagine the heart as the ruler and the lungs as its loyal minister, working together to keep life in balance like the sympathetic and parasympathetic systems in Western medicine. The interplay of qi and blood also mirrors emotional life. It is relational. It is the story of blood and qi, spirit and vitality, love and peace moving in synchrony. Qi gives energy, motivation, and movement. Blood gives warmth, intimacy, and the capacity to feel.

Yin does not cancel yang, and qi does not dominate blood. Balance is not a battle won. It is a conversation based on tending and befriending different parts of yourself. When these forces are in balance, your emotional life becomes more vibrant, connected, and resilient. Joy can arise naturally. Sadness can move through you without collapsing you into despair. Thoughts can flow without sending you into a frenzy. Stillness can be found without heaviness.

I have seen this gentle shift in real life, both in my acupuncture practice and in grief work. Anita joined one of my grief retreats not long after losing her dad. At first she was hesitant to try qigong, a TCM practice that combines movement and breathwork, unsure if it would help. She stayed with it and slowly began to feel the weight and tension lift from her heart and spirit. At the end of the weeklong retreat, tears in her eyes, she shared her gratitude for the relief she felt. "I do not feel toppled, and I still miss him, which I really love," she told me. For the first time, she sensed ease alongside longing, a joy within grief that made her whole face shine.

This kind of harmony, where qi and blood flow together, offers a body-based map for grieving. Sorrow can rest alongside peace. Grief can move as an expression of love without swallowing you whole. Uncertainty can be met with a deeper trust. What the mind experiences as paradox, the heart knows how to hold.

The Heart in Ayurveda

Ayurveda, a traditional medical system from India, is often called the science of life. Rooted in thousands of years of observation and a deep reverence for nature, it sees the body as a living expression of balance and connection. In this tradition there is a beautiful story about the heart. Within you is a gentle flame, a fire not meant to burn or destroy but to illuminate. This is called *Sadhaka Pitta*, a radiant inner light of insight, understanding, and love.[42]

Sadhaka Pitta resides in both heart and mind and serves as a bridge between them. It offers clarity, insight, spiritual understanding, and emotional intelligence, helping you make sense of what feels contradictory or overwhelming.[43] This inner flame is like your own candle in the darkness, quietly reminding you that your grief matters, that it is sacred and worthy of attention, and that you deserve compassion. It reminds you that while your mind seeks to understand pain, your heart can hold its meaning. The flame does not choose between feeling and thinking—it illuminates both so they can walk together.

At another retreat I met Lexi, who had lost her sister unexpectedly. Her mind kept replaying the details of her sister's final days while her heart ached with memories of her laughter. "I feel pulled in two directions," she said. "My head is tied to how she died and why she died, but my heart just wants to feel it." Through gentle breathing practices and reflection during the retreat, Lexi began to sense insights rising from the flame of Sadhaka Pitta. "For the first time," she whispered, "I do not feel torn apart. I feel like both belong, and I am at peace with that."

Ayurveda does not separate body, mind, and emotion. It speaks of an integrated intelligence that modern systems of medicine, with all their specialization, can overlook. The flame of Sadhaka Pitta clarifies the long-standing struggle between heart and mind. Through this lens, the inner flame helps dissolve conflict and competition and offers another view into the dance beyond duality.

Grief often convinces you that you must choose, that you can only feel one thing at a time. Yet the heart knows how to hold more than one truth—it can hold multiple truths at the same time. You can feel sorrow and still sense love. You can miss what is gone and still notice what is here. You can ache with grief and feel gratitude. You can cry and still laugh. You can feel uncertainty and still trust the next breath. These are not contradictions. Grief exposes the paradoxes of life; Sadhaka Pitta helps to reconcile the tension. They are invitations to remember that your heart is spacious enough to hold the fullness of your experience. In that holding, peace often arrives.

EXERCISE: EXPERIENCING THE AWE OF SYNCHRONICITY

Take a moment now to look around your room and sense yourself within the space. Feel your heartbeat and notice its rhythm. Place your hand over your heart. Notice its steadiness and constancy. Hold a moment of gratitude for all your heart is doing, all of it happening quietly and majestically at the same time. Allow yourself to feel awe for what your heart can hold and how it holds it. Let this be a moment of deep appreciation.

Welcome Your Heart and Body as Allies in Grief

The science and spirit behind your body's dance of love are profound. Your body is not a machine. It is a living map of interconnected relationships, a unifying force that guides your emotional world. Your heart cannot be reduced to a muscle pushing blood. Love moves through you in rhythm, in breath, in the pulse that quietly sustains your life.

Somewhere along the way, many of us lost connection to this quiet intelligence and drifted from emotional truth, much like I did in my youth. Yet your body never abandoned you. It knows how to hold grief and how to love through grief. It is neither a stranger nor an enemy. It is a constant ally. It nourishes you, steadies you with its rhythms, and holds you in the delicate dance between breath and heartbeat. Grief draws you into the heart. It asks you to confront your story of love. Your mind may struggle to comprehend grief's complexity, but your heart can hold it and help you navigate. That is the gift your body offers. Will you accept the invitation to enter your heart?

In the coming chapters, especially in part two, you will discover how your body tells you where grief lives if you are willing to listen. It will whisper where love needs tending, where balance is missing, and when rest is calling. Your body speaks in sensation through feelings, not usually in words. Listening to those subtle messages is the practice of interoception (which I'll talk more about in chapter 5).

Your heart is inviting you to listen in new ways. Welcome it as your ally. Let your body be included in your grieving, not set aside, not reduced to only mind or emotion, but honored as a whole living experience. This is how the journey of grief becomes easier, softer, and kinder.

The body does not divide itself into winners and losers. Within you, seemingly contradictory parts or dualities move like partners in a sacred dance. The heart does not fight the lungs, and love does not cancel grief. The brain and heart seek synchronization and harmony. They move together, holding you with rhythm and breath. This is a physiological phenomenon of love. It's a reclaiming of the power of the heart.

So let your grief breathe. Let it tell the story of your love. Trust your body to guide the grieving process. Your body knows how to love and find coherence, and that will be important to remember as we turn to the fragmented nature of grieving in today's world.

3

Grieving in a Culture of Disconnection

For centuries, Western culture has taught that thinking defines who you are. "I think, therefore I am," wrote the philosopher René Descartes in the seventeenth century. The modern world absorbed that idea, often mistaking intellect for identity and treating emotion as a flaw to be managed or a distraction to overcome. In that separation, known as Cartesian or mind-body dualism, you may have learned to live in your head while quietly abandoning your body, and to reason your way through pain rather than feel your way toward healing.

Perhaps the more grief-informed narrative is "I feel, therefore I am." Your existence is not proven by thought alone but sensed through the quiet pulse of your body's awareness. Feeling is how you know you are alive.

Yet in today's culture of disconnection, it can be difficult to feel safely. Grieving in this world can feel like walking through a gauntlet of expectations where intellect is praised, emotion is hidden, and tenderness is mistaken for weakness. You may find yourself trying to "get over it" or "stay strong" when what your body longs for most is permission to be felt, to breathe, and to belong again.

Disconnected from your inner world, you may contort yourself to fit a culture that struggles to be with difficult emotions. You learn to perform composure, holding it together on the outside while suppressing what aches inside. You smile when you want to cry, you stay busy when you need to rest, and you reach for control when what your body truly needs is care. In Ayurveda, this suppression is called *Prajñāparādha*, translated as "offense against wisdom" or "intellectual blasphemy." Over time, that performance takes its toll. The body keeps score, not to punish you but to remind you that what has been silenced still longs to be seen. In such a world, grief is often met with polite words and well-meaning platitudes instead of the honest presence your heart truly needs.

When Words Fall Short and Presence Matters

Arriving for the overnight shift as the on-call hospital chaplain, I received a page to visit the emergency department. Maria had just miscarried her first baby. She lay in the hospital bed, silent tears streaming down her face. Her husband could not be there because he had recently been deported to Mexico. Though her family had gathered earlier that day, by nightfall she was alone. The nurses asked me to sit with her.

As I listened, she repeated what relatives and friends had told her: "At least I am young, I can try again," and "God has a plan for me." I nodded gently and honored her words, but I could also feel the weight of those phrases settling into her body and mind. The story of her grief was already being reshaped by cultural narratives that asked her to suppress, minimize, and carry on. Knowing how this story unfolds, my heart sank for her internalized disregard. I heard the echoes of my psychology professors, "When you bury emotions, you bury them alive."

While her body was still aching from loss, the people around her were unknowingly urging her to push her feelings down. Their discomfort with her sorrow was clothed in well-intentioned words. Yet beneath those words, Maria was left alone with a grief that touched not only the loss of her baby but the absence of her husband, the fear for her future, and the ache of love with nowhere to go.

Maria's story reflects a sad reality of grieving in today's world: Our current cultural habits around grief and grieving separate us from our own heart and from each other. When grieving, we are shaped by not only the pain of our loss but also the ways we are discouraged from feeling and expressing that pain. At a time when we are already lonely and distressed, others' well-intentioned actions can exacerbate those feelings, leaving us feeling more isolated. In this chapter we'll look at the ways we derail ourselves and others from experiencing grief. Don't feel bad if you have done or said some of these things to yourself or others. Becoming aware of the habits is the first step to changing them.

It's often said that friends can become strangers and strangers can become friends during times of loss. This is because death and grief are profoundly uncomfortable—not just for those experiencing it but also for the people around them. Many of us were never taught how to navigate strong emotions, whether our own or someone else's. As a result, our society often lacks the emotional education needed for genuine compassion, care, attentive listening, and empathy. Where grief pulls you deeper into your feelings—an unfamiliar place for many—those around you may feel challenged by your sorrow. This discomfort can lead to misunderstandings, distance, or awkwardness. It's not that people don't care but because they simply don't know how to be present with sorrow.

Often, when people feel uncomfortable with your pain, their instinct is to try to fix it. They may offer quick solutions or tidy one-liners that, while well-intentioned, can be hurtful. You might follow along politely at first, but over time, these responses can leave you feeling infuriated, bewildered, and alone. The sociologist Darcy Harris describes this as a form of cultural oppression: Unspoken social rules prescribe how long and how openly we are allowed to grieve, which pressures mourners to hide pain so others are not uncomfortable. This can add shame to the burden of loss.[1]

Common well-meaning but painful platitudes include:

- Everything happens for a reason.
- They are in a better place.
- Time heals all wounds.
- It was their time.
- They would not want you to be sad.
- God never gives us more than we can handle.
- Be strong for your family.
- You need to move on.

- Stay positive.
- This too shall pass.

Anything that begins with "at least" is especially cutting. "At least you had time to say goodbye." "At least they lived a long life." "At least you can still get pregnant." While these statements may be factually true, they are often emotionally harmful. To avoid further hurt, you might start to hide your grief, pretend you are fine, rationalize your pain, or fit your feelings into others' expectations.

All of this can lead to a deep sense of isolation. If grief is love looking for a place to go and you are met with platitudes or an unlistening ear, it is natural to set boundaries. Not everyone deserves access to your story. The risk of putting up too many boundaries, however, is loneliness. Loneliness is not just an emotional experience—it's a physical one. Social disconnection activates the body's stress responses (the sympathetic nervous system), affecting the vagus nerve, lowering heart rate variability, and affecting downstream stress chemistry.[2] Loneliness and social exclusion also trigger specific brain regions involved in the processing of physical pain, including the dorsal anterior cingulate cortex and anterior insula.[3] In other words, isolation can literally increase physical pain.

Yet some people will meet you with presence and care, and you will be able to find coherence and co-regulation with them. Their body language and tone of voice will invite you in. They will maintain eye contact and show genuine interest, asking open questions and staying present with you in your vulnerability. These people are rare and precious.

I think of David, a neighbor of one of my clients who showed up at his door one day with soup. David didn't offer advice or share his own stories. He simply set the bowl down, sat on the couch, and said, "Tell me about her." For an hour, his friend wept and shared memories. There were no words of fixing, only presence. Such moments remind us that grief does not need to be solved; it needs to be witnessed.

Whether or not you have others in your life who can accompany you, you can learn to be present to your own grief. By allowing the love within your sorrow to guide you, you honor what is right about grief rather than what is wrong with it.

Six Invisible Rules That Shape Grief

Modern life often teaches us to value speed, productivity, and independence above all else. We are rewarded for pushing through discomfort, keeping up appearances, and moving quickly from one chapter to the next. This conditioning doesn't disappear when loss enters our lives—in fact, it often intensifies. The world keeps turning, and the subtle (or not-so-subtle) message is to "get on with it," to return to normal as soon as possible. We are left navigating an emotional obstacle course, trying to manage external expectations while also juggling our internal experience.

But grief doesn't operate on society's timeline. The pressure to resume business as usual can leave you feeling even more alone, misunderstood, or broken. You may notice these expectations coming not just from others but also from within yourself—a quiet voice insisting you should be further along, stronger, or more in control. In Compassionate Grieving, we name six cultural forces that commonly derail grief. They are so woven into the fabric of modern life that we may not even recognize them as obstacles. Yet they shape how we experience loss and how we allow ourselves to heal.

As you read through these, notice how often they show up around you—and within you.

1. **PRESSURE:** This is "grief on a deadline." It's the rush to "get over" your loss as quickly as possible. It's fueled by urgency. In the powerful desire to accelerate healing, it creates anxiety and activates the fight-or-flight response, flooding your physiology with stress hormones.

2. **PUSH:** This is the urge to power through pain instead of pausing with it. When you push past your feelings, healing is delayed and exhaustion deepens. Grief is never one-size-fits-all; you cannot force your feelings to fit like a square peg in a round hole. Everyone grieves differently, and when you try to control or contain that process, the body tightens. Inflexibility makes you brittle instead of resilient, often leading to sudden outbursts, irritability, or waves of overwhelm that seem to come from nowhere.

3. **PERFECTIONISM:** Perfectionism replaces compassion with comparison, making softness feel like failure. There is no prescribed "right way" to grieve, only your way. Yet perfectionism often seeps into sorrow, turning grief into another performance to get right. Self-criticism and unrealistic expectations feed feelings of inadequacy and failure. When it comes to grief, you don't know what you don't know, yet you may still hold yourself to impossible standards. Perfectionism strips away the kindness and gentleness that compassionate grieving requires.

4. **PRODUCTIVITY:** Grief isn't something you can check off a to-do list, and healing isn't measured by how much you accomplish. In the rhythm of hustle culture, you may hear familiar advice: "Just stay busy," "Keep yourself occupied," or "Distract yourself with work." Workaholism becomes the bait, pulling you away from what grief truly needs—rest, softness, and time. Many people are given only a few days to grieve before they must return to work and appear functional again. Productivity convinces you that stillness is lazy and rest is indulgent, when in truth, rest is sacred. It is the space where your body can begin to heal.

5. **PERFORMANCE:** This is the habit of putting on a mask of being "okay." Performance is the quiet act of holding yourself together so the world won't see you unravel. You say, "I'm fine," "I'm managing," "I'm okay," not because you are but because you feel you must be. This performance asks you to protect others from your truth, to make grief more palatable for those who cannot bear its depth. But every time you hide your pain, your body carries the weight of what's unsaid. Over time, that effort exhausts your spirit. Performance can rob you of the already limited vitality that you have.

6. **PRETENDING:** If performance is about making others comfortable, pretending is about protecting yourself from what feels too hard to feel. It's the subtle art of bottling emotions, holding everything in so you don't come undone. Pretending often happens

> because you were never shown how to move through big feelings safely. But those feelings don't disappear; they wait powerfully in the body for acknowledgment. The practices in the second part of this book are designed to help you meet those emotions gently and tenderly, so you no longer have to pretend, even with yourself.

Navigating this obstacle course with its hidden rules can leave you feeling like you're working hard but going nowhere. The sprint to the finish line paradoxically prolongs suffering, trapping you in cycles of exhaustion and self-doubt. Research confirms this: Avoidant coping in bereavement is linked to more severe and persistent symptoms over time, including higher rates of prolonged grief and post-traumatic stress.[4] In contrast, allowing yourself to approach your grief and make meaning from it predicts better adaptation and healing.[5]

I once worked with Claire, who returned to work just a week after her husband's sudden death. Her colleagues praised her for being so strong. She smiled and performed well, but two months later she contacted me—exhausted, bewildered, and looking for support. Her grief had not gone away; it had only been hidden under the mask of performance.

There is a different path, one that takes a compassionate approach and honors the slow, nonlinear nature of grief. It is the path we are exploring in this book and that we'll look at more in the next chapter on letting go.

Expanding Grief Literacy

Jenna first came to me for grief care because her brother had been killed in a car accident many years before. She'd been to support groups, trauma therapists, and counseling, yet she felt horrible and wanted greater support. As our sessions unfolded, she began sharing about her life outside of her brother's death, revealing other griefs that were present: her divorce, the job she had lost in the pandemic, a recent health diagnosis. One day she paused and said, "I think I have been carrying so much more than just my brother's death. It feels like I have this giant backpack on me filled with rocks I never named."

After doing this work for many years, I can confirm that almost all of us are carrying an invisible grief backpack. When there is a traumatic loss or an acute injury, it can be easy to point to the source of our grief. Death especially can eclipse most other griefs. But unnamed sorrows live in the body and heart, tucked into the many zippers and pockets of our metaphorical backpacks. Kenneth J. Doka, a grief researcher, calls this disenfranchised grief, when unnamed losses go unseen or unsupported by the wider culture.[6]

Many unnamed losses are not related to death and can take many forms: the pain of divorce or breakup, separation, estrangement, or family conflict; the upheaval of career changes, layoffs, retirement, or business failures; financial hardships; moving and losing a sense of home or community; health challenges such as chronic pain, autoimmune conditions, new diagnoses, fertility struggles, or disability; and the loss of friendships or a sense of belonging.

Some losses are abstract or intangible, such as the loss of identity, innocence, faith, safety, trust, or the future you once hoped for. There is grief in dreams deferred, in the life you imagined but did not receive, and the disorientation of major life transitions. Some losses are ambiguous—where there is no clear closure; or when someone is physically present but psychologically absent, such as with dementia. The family therapist Pauline Boss coined the term *ambiguous loss* to help name these complex, unresolved experiences.[7] There is also anticipatory grief, the sorrow that comes before a loss; intergenerational grief, carried across family lines; and collective grief, which emerges in communities facing trauma or injustice.

Death-related losses have their own layers. Whether the loss is recent or from long ago—whether it's a parent, sibling, child, partner, relative, dear friend, or animal companion—these bonds matter. The circumstances of loss vary, from sudden accidents to long illnesses, and grief often revisits on anniversaries, birthdays, and holidays; and at milestones such as graduations, weddings, or births.

Grief stays with you because love stays with you. The goal is not to erase grief but to transform your relationship with it. What intensifies suffering is not how much you still love the person or thing you have lost but the stigma, taboo, and narrow social expectations that surround loss. When we normalize the full range of losses and bring them into compassionate view, we begin to recognize grief is ever-present with life.

Creating greater grief literacy offers an opportunity to reduce isolation and expand your relationship to healing, especially when losses accumulate faster than they're being processed. In Jenna's story, she was grieving many things at once, each loss competing for attention as her body sought healing. Grief is, in a sense, opportunistic. When we suppress our responses to loss, the body stores them up; a future loss, perhaps a big one, can break open the door to all the previous unprocessed losses. It's important to know that grief is rarely one thing—it's often many things clumped together. This is what makes grief sometimes so painful. It's the current loss and the accumulated layers of losses hidden beneath asking for attention, all at the same time.

Take Jaime, for example. She had just accepted a new job, received a pay raise, and was moving to a more upscale part of the city. She was excited for all that was unfolding in her life. But as soon as she began packing, a heavy weight settled over her. A friend connected us, and we began working together to help her understand how this move had ignited so much despair. It became clear when we named it: Years earlier, she had gone through a divorce. She had lost a beloved dog, then a parent. She had moved several times, and her children had grown and left home. The move was not only a change of address; it unloaded an invisible backpack of accumulated losses.

Jenna's and Jamie's experiences are not unusual. We each have many losses in our life, and many of them go unrecognized and unassimilated until our body reaches a tipping point and can't hold it all any longer. When you push to move on or create a pressure to power through grief, what gets tucked away doesn't really go away. Out of sight might be out of mind for a little while, but as Dr. Bessel van der Kolk offered in his revolutionary book *The Body Keeps the Score*,[8] unresolved pain hides within the very tissues of the body.

The Powerful Impacts of Suppression

When you look closely, grieving in today's world mirrors the split between mind and body mentioned at the beginning of the chapter, only in community this shows up as a split between self and other. I separate from you because I am uncomfortable with your pain. I am uncomfortable with your pain because I am unfamiliar with it within myself. Having separated from that part of my humanity, I have no choice but to separate from yours.

This is an extra layer of pain that can get added on to grief. You feel not only the original loss but also the secondary losses of connection, community, and common humanity. Yet we do this to one another every day. The saddest thing is that you might also do this to yourself. You may separate from your own humanity, judging and shaming yourself for how you grieve, asking, *What is wrong with me?* Instead of softening into compassion, you tighten with self-criticism. The very places where love longs to flow—between us and toward ourselves—become blocked.

Yet grief is a universal response that expresses itself in many ways. It may not always be the trauma of death, but it is the ache of transitions, the sorrow of dreams that never came to pass, the sting of rejection, the disappointment of doors that closed, the longing for a life not lived. It's common to wonder, *What if I had taken another path? Who might I be now?* These unspoken griefs live quietly inside you, hidden even from yourself, deepening separation and isolation.

Emotional suppression breeds separation. Suppression creates invisible barriers, fragmenting the very parts of you seeking love and attention. It is woven into our culture and is why disconnection and loneliness are perpetuated in modern society.

Trauma and somatic researchers have shown that long-term suppression of emotion leaves deep imprints on the body as well.[9] When we habitually hold back tears, silence our anger, or numb our pain, the body doesn't simply forget.[10] Instead, it adapts to that emotional constraint by staying in a state of quiet tension. Over time, this chronic holding pattern amplifies stress throughout the system.[11] The body releases more inflammatory chemicals, known as cytokines, which are linked to fatigue, pain, digestive issues, and even lowered immune function.[12]

When emotional energy is blocked or avoided, the nervous system often remains in a subtle but persistent state of "on guard."[13] The fight-or-flight response becomes the body's default setting, even when there's no real danger present. Without enough opportunities to recover or feel safe, the autonomic nervous system becomes burdened. Heart rate variability tends to decrease, meaning the heart loses some of its natural flexibility to adjust to life's changes.[14] Vagal tone—a measure of how well the vagus nerve supports calm, rest, and connection—can also weaken. As this happens, neural pathways shift toward patterns of threat and protection rather than openness and connection.

This constant state of inner vigilance from suppression has cognitive effects too. The parts of the brain responsible for executive function—regulation, empathy, and perspective taking—become harder to access.[15] It's why, during times of deep stress or loss, you might feel foggy, irritable, or disconnected from your ability to think clearly. It's not a lack of willpower; it's physiology. Your brain and body are prioritizing survival over reflection.

When suppression becomes a normalized coping mechanism, when we've learned to push through rather than feel through, these physiological changes can eventually manifest as chronic conditions—persistent fatigue, headaches, tension, pain, or autoimmune issues.[16] The body begins to carry what the mind cannot resolve. Suppression aims to help you feel better; however, paradoxically, it tends to do the opposite. Buried emotions find expression through the body, sometimes as physical pain that seems to have no cause and doesn't show up on X-rays or scans, which can feel like chasing a ghost. Your activated nervous system keeps you in hyperarousal, shunting the wisdom and heart intelligence that arrive through the relaxation response. Your body calls for your attention as a companion to your grieving process.

For a griever, this means that the pain you feel in your body isn't "all in your head," which is what those with undiagnosable conditions are often told. It's your body's language. It's how your system tries to protect you from being overwhelmed. But what protects you in the short term can also limit healing in the long term. Suppression may keep emotions contained, but it also keeps the nervous system from completing its natural cycle of release and repair.

The good news is that this process is reversible. The same body that holds the residue of grief also holds the medicine for it. Gentle movement, mindful breathing, compassionate attention—these are ways of signaling to the nervous system that it is safe again. As safety grows, the fight-or-flight reflex can soften, inflammation can settle, and the body can begin to restore coherence. You begin to feel more energy, clarity, and emotional flexibility. Your body is not your enemy in grief; it's the instrument of your healing. It remembers what you've lived through and how to return to balance.

Grief, in its essence, is not trying to divide you. It is trying to draw you toward connection and cohesion. Beneath every sorrow is a deeper yearning: Be with me. Be with me in my humanity, be with me in my pain. It's through connection that healing arrives.

The divisions existing in the world today—whether social, political, or spiritual—carry threads of unacknowledged grief. These divisions may be reflected within your being when it comes to your own grief process. In that sense, the collective challenges are about not only conflict or misunderstanding but grief literacy. The radical act of grieving may in fact be a form of activism; healing as a process of social change. There is a need for new ways of honoring loss and letting it bring people together rather than driving humanity apart.

The body itself is a teacher of wholeness. Though made of many parts, it works in concert like a perfect symphony, managing countless reactions that allow you to see, smell, hear, touch, taste, walk, talk, and engage with the world around you. The body models integration. It does not pit one organ against another. Each plays its part within the larger whole. Neither grief nor your body is the enemy. What harms, however, are the cultural narratives of division that strip grief of its humanity and rob it of empathy, tenderness, love, and compassion. But these, like so many other ideas about grief, are false narratives. Grief, like the body, longs for integration rather than fragmentation.

Perhaps the most enduring myth of all is that healing requires a clean break—that letting go means severing what once mattered. In the next chapter, we'll gently unravel this idea and discover a more compassionate way to understand what it truly means to let go.

4

How to Let Go

AFTER DISCOVERING IN MY MID-TWENTIES that so much of my childhood pain was rooted in grief, I became determined to learn how to let go. That's what you're supposed to do, right? When you're grieving, letting go seems like the next logical step. And it's what well-meaning friends and family often encourage us to do. I spent many years wondering, *How do I move on? How do I get over this?*

I remember asking one of my mentors, "I carry all this pain—how do I let go?" She smiled gently, picked up a pen, and dropped it to the floor. "That's how you let go," she said. I couldn't have been more disappointed. At the time, her answer felt too simple, almost dismissive. But it reflected a common cultural narrative: Letting go is about dropping something, cutting it off, or severing it completely. Dutifully I tried to follow that model, attempting to release my grief as though it were an object I could set down and walk away from.

After years of feeling as though I was failing, I began to understand that letting go isn't a single act of release; it's a practice. Finding peace is active, not passive. It takes work. It's a digestion in which elimination is the final outcome, not the first. I learned that letting go isn't solely about releasing but discerning what to hold on to and why. These concepts dramatically changed my relationship with grief and letting go. True letting go isn't a rejection of grief; it's an opening, a softening that allows love to move freely again.

Three Common Misunderstandings of Letting Go

Drawing on years of personal experience and the many stories I've heard, I want to share three common misconceptions about letting go that can hinder the grieving process—and offer ways to reframe them with compassion.

Myth 1: Letting Go Means Cutting All Ties

People often say, "I've let it go" or "It is in the past," as if moving on is as simple as flipping a switch. But is it truly behind you? We are wired for connection, and attachment does not dissolve on command. Trying to sever ties with something or someone deeply meaningful isn't just unrealistic—it can deny the importance of a relationship that once gave you belonging. True letting go honors the bond even as you learn to carry it in a new way.

When I met Andrew, he had recently lost his wife of thirty-two years. "Everyone keeps telling me I need to let her go," he said, his voice catching on the word *her*. His wedding ring glinted faintly under the light as he fidgeted with it. "But how do you let go of half your life?"

He shared with me that their home was still filled with traces of her, such as her garden shoes by the back door, the scent of her favorite jasmine candle, and a handwritten grocery list still pinned to the refrigerator. He confessed that he sometimes still talked to her in the mornings, greeting her softly before making his coffee. Then, embarrassed, he added, "I know it's silly. I should probably stop."

What he didn't yet know was that his love wasn't the problem. His attachment was a sign of connection, not weakness. The task of grief isn't to erase these bonds but to integrate them. Letting go isn't about detaching from the person; it's about loosening the grip that comes from holding on too tightly to what can no longer be the same. That change is painful. That's grief. The love, however, remains.

Letting go is not a chopping block of detachment. It's a recognition that life is made through connections and bonds. Attachments are woven into your nervous system, muscles, and heart rhythms. The brain's reward system keeps attachments active, which is why the mind anticipates reunion even after loss.[1] Have you experienced this yourself? While I believe there is a phenomenon of continued relationship beyond death, the brain also relates to people as fixtures in your life just as commonly as knowing where a table is when walking in a dark room. Attachments are wired through neurochemistry. Your nervous system may swing from hyperarousal to collapse, your muscles may tense, and your heart rhythm will change, literally giving you heartache.[2] The same chemistry that fosters bonding also makes separation painful.[3] Emotional and physical pain share neural pathways, which is why grief often literally hurts.[4]

Daniel, whose younger sister died of cancer, once told me, "It is not just in my head. My body physically hurts." He couldn't understand why his body hurt so much physically. But what he was describing was grief's biology. His story shows that pain is the body's way of showing the depth of connection.

How can you let go when attachment permeates every fiber of your being? Instead of detachment, consider the idea of continuing to honor your bonds. Continuing bonds is a concept developed by the grief researchers Dennis Klass, Phyllis Silverman, and Steven Nickman that challenges the long-held notion that healthy grieving requires cutting emotional ties with the deceased.[5] Their research showed that grieving is better served by maintaining an ongoing, evolving relationship with the one who has died.

Maintaining a relationship with someone who has died is not a sign of being stuck but rather a natural way to live with love after loss.[6] In fact, these bonds often become the foundation of meaning and resilience. You might keep photos around the home, speak to them in prayer or quiet reflection, write letters, or celebrate birthdays and anniversaries. You might still say goodnight before bed or whisper their name in moments of joy or sorrow. These gestures are pathways toward healing. They allow love to continue flowing through a new form of connection, one that adapts to the reality of physical absence while honoring the eternal presence of love.

Continuing bonds theory emphasizes maintaining a symbolic and emotional relationship that helps you integrate the loss into ongoing life. The relationship evolves and can even grow as you carry the love forward while accepting that the person is no longer physically present. This process helps bridge the space between memory and meaning. Rather than letting go of your person, you're letting go into love and learning how to hold them differently, not less.

This perspective transforms the idea of letting go. Rather than forcing a separation, it invites you to let go of the pain of attachment while keeping the love alive. It allows the bond to mature into something spiritual, internal, and soulful. Death doesn't end the relationship; it changes the relationship. In this way, letting go becomes not about losing but about learning how to hold differently.

Lily lost her father several years ago and tried to push his memory away to cope with the monumental grief of losing not just her dad but her confidant and source of wisdom. In our sessions together, she shared how aimless she felt without his guidance. Rather than forcing herself to "let him go," we began to invite his memory into her healing process.

Slowly she started recalling moments when he had offered her sage advice or encouragement, letting those memories become touchstones rather than triggers. Over time, a new kind of relationship emerged, one that existed beyond his physical death. To her surprise, she realized she could still have a relationship with him; and in some ways, it was easier now. The old complexities of their father-daughter dynamic had softened, leaving only the essence of love and connection.

This brought her unexpected joy. By continuing her bond with him, she not only grieved his absence but also found a renewed sense of guidance and meaning. In remembering him this way, she discovered that love could remain alive even through loss. Her dad became a kind of guardian angel, a spiritual presence she could turn to in moments of uncertainty and fear. Through this renewed connection she found herself guided by his wisdom in ways that felt both familiar and new. What once felt like absence became presence—a quiet companionship that helped her move through life with greater trust and peace.

The grief researcher and neuroscientist Mary-Frances O'Connor reminds us that the brain does not erase attachments; it learns and updates.[7] Grief is the slow recalibration of brain and body to the reality that the person is no longer physically present, while the bond remains internally. You may still reach for the phone or set a place at the table. Memory, ritual, and meaning making will reshape the attachment so love is carried differently. Letting go is not forgetting—it is remembering differently, with tenderness and integration.

Myth 2: Letting Go Means Moving On

When you clean out a closet or give away the belongings of someone who has passed, it is easy to underestimate the meaning those objects hold. They are not just things—they store memories and pieces of their identity and your identity. When letting go is equated with moving on, it often feels as though you're being asked to forget. In grief, forgetting can wound the spirit. It can feel like a betrayal of love or a betrayal of your grief.

Consider Ana, who was leaving a twenty-year marriage. Well-meaning friends encouraged her to move on. When she boxed the last of the wedding china, her hands froze above the tape. Those dishes were a subtle yet present backdrop for conversations, holding decades of meals, laughter, and milestones. The memories raced through her mind as she placed the last bit of tape over the box headed to the donation center. Expecting one clean cut of detachment denied her history and humanity. For Ana, the presumed release of "things" was her way of letting go of twenty years of marriage. She believed that detachment would sever the pain as if it were a surgical procedure to remove all her emotions. Instead, she not only lost her china but also grieved the divorce deeply, even though she felt it necessary for her life. Through our work together, she recognized the layers of loss present within the divorce: the loss of the dream and the vision they had together, the future they believed in, and the years she lost by trying to make it work—as well as a loss of identity from being in a marriage that didn't feel right. The divorce also came with the loss of financial stability and the loss of friends who felt the need to choose between her and her husband, which complicated long-standing relationships.

Here is the paradox: This version of letting go is exactly why many hold tightly to their grief. Grief can feel like the last link to your person, so you cling to memories and connection. It's a defensive response to a cultural narrative of "moving on" and "getting over grief." When pushed to let go, the opposite may occur. The challenge here is that grief is often synonymously categorized with sadness or depression, and you can attach to the sorrow itself as a way of remembering. Cultural pressure to move on intensifies this attachment and increases suffering. When letting go is defined as forgetting, a complexity of figuring out how to move through grief can feel like moving through sludge. Forcing letting go in this way is a form of suppression.

When you try to avoid thoughts of your grief or push memories away, you may find that they return even stronger. This is known as ironic process theory.[8] The very act of stopping the thoughts has a rebound effect. In the early phases of loss, it's common to experience a flood of memories as your mind reviews the story of your life. Often, at the end, you find yourself thinking about the beginning. It's as if your spirit and brain are working in harmony, seeking to make sense of loss and impermanence. When you push the memories away, they come back stronger. This isn't a failure in your grieving process; it's how grief moves.

From an emotional perspective, memories are often woven into mementos such as objects, places, photos, trinkets, or letters. They might be journals or diaries. They might live in the walls of a home, a staircase, a familiar carpet, a kitchen window, or, in the case of Ana, her wedding china. They can be tied to events, trips, and vacations. Depending on the nature of the loss, they might even appear as artifacts from a past identity, such as old business cards, letterheads, work badges, certificates, or awards that no longer align with who you've become.

These reminders are invitations to meaning and not just obstacles to healing. When approached with compassion, they can help transform grief from something you fear into something you can relate to and learn from. Holding these memories gently allows the bond to remain while also allowing life to keep moving forward.

From the brain's point of view, this process is associated with what's known as autobiographical memories.[9] These are the types of memories that help you make sense of what has changed and maintain a consistent thread of identity during times of upheaval. It's important to remember that memories are not fixed snapshots. Each time you revisit a memory, your brain opens it for revision in a process called memory reconsolidation.[10] During times of loss, your brain engages in this natural process of updating. As memories of the past surface, your brain seeks to integrate them with your present reality, helping you adjust to what life now holds.

When this process is suppressed through forms of pseudo–letting go, where you take the approach of "mind over matter" or "tuck it under the rug," you interrupt your brain's capacity to heal. What you avoid emotionally remains unprocessed neurologically, which can keep you tethered to pain in subtle, lingering ways. Avoidance may bring temporary relief, but over time it interferes with your brain's natural process of memory reconsolidation. When grief is not given space to be processed and felt, these updates become incomplete and the emotional charge remains stored in the body and nervous system. The energy of grief then stays suspended, unresolved, and unintegrated, often surfacing as fatigue, irritability, or numbness.

When held in the presence of compassion and safety, even painful memories can be softened, updated, and integrated into your ongoing life story.[11] This is often why narrative practices are so helpful for grief. When you recall old memories, make sense of a story, and integrate the past into a continuing bond, you help your brain reorganize and regain clarity to restore a sense of direction.[12] Memories become sources of healing rather than pain you must avoid or forget. Healing begins when what was once avoided is met with gentle, compassionate attention. In that meeting, the brain can begin to reprocess and update the emotional imprint of the memory, allowing it to shift from something that haunts you to something that creates new meaning.

Gretchen, whose husband died suddenly years ago, found herself replaying their first date over and over. "I feel crazy," she said. "Why do I keep going back to the beginning?" I explained her brain was trying to make sense of the loss, returning to early memories of love as a way to integrate the ending into her story. That understanding eased her confusion. She realized her memories weren't traps or failures—they were part of her brain's natural healing process.

This is why ritual becomes such an important element within mourning and loss. Rituals provide structure and community, but they also serve a deeper neuro-emotional purpose. They create a safe space for meaning making and facilitate the natural process of reconsolidation that is unfolding within your brain and spirit.

Through ritual, memories are revisited in a context of safety and connection, allowing the brain to update emotional associations. Lighting a candle, speaking a name, or gathering with others in remembrance activates both neural pathways of attachment and networks of emotional regulation. In this way, ritual helps transform raw pain into integrated memory and becomes the bridge where love and loss can coexist, where the brain, heart, and community work together to help the grieving body remember differently.

Myth 3: Letting Go Means You've Made It Across the Finish Line

It's easy to imagine grief as a journey with a clear endpoint. Words such as *closure*, *completion*, and *acceptance* are often held up as goals to reach. Life itself can seem linear, so it's tempting to believe there's a final stage where the pain will simply end. When you haven't been taught how to be with big emotions, grief can leave you feeling helpless, powerless, and unsure of what to do with your pain. In that uncertainty, the idea of letting go often takes center stage, filling the vast and uncomfortable space of *I just want to get to the other side of this*. One of the most persistent myths about letting go is that there's a finish line.

Acceptance is an especially loaded word in the grief community. In our culture, acceptance is often portrayed as the summit, the peak, or the place where you finally find peace. But acceptance framed this way can create a false promise. We hear people say, "If I could just accept what happened . . ." Yet, as with letting go, acceptance is often oversimplified, diminishing the depth of love and the transformation that grief reveals.

Acceptance may offer the illusion that the past can be neatly placed behind you. For those who feel pressured to "accept" their loss, it can lead not to peace but to resignation, resentment, and a quiet sense of defeat that fuels anger or despair. For many it can feel like an injustice or even a punishment. When acceptance is treated as a destination, it can leave people feeling disempowered, believing they are supposed to reach some final state yet never arriving. Acceptance can lead to a form of arrival fallacy. Forcing grief into that shape is like trying to fit a living, breathing process into a mold that was never meant to contain it.

I remember sitting with Elena, whose teenage son died in a car accident. Months later, a friend asked her, "Have you reached acceptance yet?" Elena looked down and whispered, "I don't even know what that means. Accept what? That my son is gone? That he will never walk through the door again? How could I ever accept that?"

Acceptance is the fifth and final stage of the psychiatrist Elisabeth Kübler-Ross's well-known five stages of grief. While I honor her work, it is important to remember that these stages were originally developed for people facing a terminal diagnosis. Over time, perhaps because of society's desire for simple frameworks, these stages were misapplied to all grieving experiences. This has led many to mistakenly believe that grief unfolds in tidy sequential stages. It does not.

I don't think it's wise to say there are absolutes when it comes to grief. However, it is likely true that you will not grieve in stages. Each person grieves in their own way, shaped by their unique personality, culture, family systems, spirituality, and circumstance. There is no neat or uniform way to grieve. By allowing grief to be messy and imperfect, you also allow it to be authentic. In that authenticity, grief becomes a portal or a sacred threshold showing you who you are, what you love, how you love, and what matters most.

Undoubtedly, acceptance plays a role in grief. But in modern culture, it has been flattened into a word that fails to capture the rich texture of the grieving experience. Too often acceptance is heard as resignation or closure, as if grief should be completed and done. Instead, I prefer the word *embrace*. *Embrace* is a heart-centered word that emphasizes nurturing, allowing, and blossoming. It makes space for grief and grief emotions to rise and move like flowers: to bud, to bloom, and eventually to wilt. In this way, letting go is no longer about reaching an endpoint but participating in a living, organic unfolding.

Embracing allows your grief to breathe. It makes room for story, memory, poetry, and ritual to be part of your healing. It reframes emotions not as enemies to suppress but as companions to be welcomed. Just as a garden flourishes when many types of flowers grow together, your inner lives flourish when joy and sorrow, laughter and tears, love and longing are allowed to share the same soil.

The Dual Process Model of coping with bereavement, developed by the researchers Margaret Stroebe and Henk Schut, offers a more compassionate and realistic framework for understanding letting go.[13] Stroebe and Schut suggest that "loss-oriented coping" allows you to yearn, cry, reminisce, and engage with the emotional reality of your loss, whereas "restoration-oriented coping" helps you adapt to the practical changes in your life, such as new roles, routines, or responsibilities. This model recognizes that healthy grieving is not about choosing between feeling the pain or moving forward but "oscillating" between these two essential processes.[14] Just like the tide, it is normal to flow back and forth. One moment you may be immersed in the ache of loss, and the next moment you may be cooking dinner, paying bills, or even laughing with a friend. This rhythm is not a sign of brokenness. It is the process itself.

I think of Linda, who lost her husband after forty years of marriage. Through tears she once said, "I felt so guilty yesterday. I was sitting with my daughter, and we ended up laughing at a silly memory. For just a few minutes I forgot how sad I was. And then the guilt hit me. How could I laugh when he is gone?" When I shared the concept of oscillation with her, relief washed across her face. That moment of laughter was not a betrayal. It was her nervous system coming up for air, her heart reminding her that life continues alongside grief. It was permission to embrace the ebb and flow of grief's movement without judgment.

Think of it as the nervous system catching its breath. The oscillation between loss and restoration allows you to engage grief without being consumed by it, and to reengage life without leaving your grief behind. Over time, this rhythm helps integrate the loss into the ongoing story of your life. Instead of demanding that you move on, it affirms that your grief will naturally ebb, return, and evolve just as love itself does.

This is a practice of nonlinear grieving. It's a recognition of the winding path of highs and lows, ups and downs, moments of peace and times of challenge. Instead of seeing letting go as a linear process or thinking that "time heals all wounds," you can reframe it as a cyclical one. Like the seasons, letting go comes in cycles. Some seasons feel painful, sparse, and barren, like a long winter that is cold and unrelenting. Other seasons feel vibrant and full of vitality.

Our culture does not honor the emotional cycles of life. There is an expectation to live in summer or to be happy all the time. But just as in nature, it is the fall and winter that prepare the soil for new growth. Embracing the harder seasons of life gives greater depth and meaning to the springs and summers. Avoiding them only creates more complexity, often showing up as hypervigilance, anxiety, being on guard, and heightened sensitivity to emotional triggers.

Letting go doesn't happen all at once. Letting go unfolds in cycles and seasons. You may process a part of your grief for a time, then rest, and later return to it in a new form. This is natural. You do not "achieve" letting go. When a loss circles back, it is not a sign of failure. It is the normal rhythm of grief, inviting you to move through another layer with tenderness.

Letting Go Is Letting Flow

So, then, what is letting go? If you're not letting go of grief, what are you releasing? Here's the counterintuitive truth: When it comes to grief, letting go is about releasing the barriers that prevent you from grieving. Because big emotions, especially grief emotions, have such a bad reputation, and because modern society often teaches us to suppress or avoid difficult feelings, the real practice of release begins with allowing. It's about allowing the pain to move through you. Instead of pushing the pain down, you let it rise. Instead of burying emotions, you watch them surface. Instead of swallowing them back, you permit them to well up. Like a pressure cooker, the body and heart both need a release valve—a way for emotion to move and transform rather than build up and explode.

This is the opposite of what most of us have been taught about grief. Grief is not something to be released or conquered; it's a response that needs space to breathe. It asks to take up space, to be witnessed, to show you where love and tenderness still live within you. Letting go, in this sense, is not an act of detachment but deep surrender. It is the art of allowing love to flow and move by releasing the things that prevent your grief from flowing freely. The four most common obstacles to this natural flow are stigma, judgment, shame, and guilt. Letting go begins here—by loosening the hold these have on your heart.

1. **CONFRONT STIGMA BY BEING OPEN.** Stigma is the silent message that grief should be hidden, that it's too messy or uncomfortable to be seen. It's the social pressure to "get over it," to be strong, or to return to normal quickly. This creates isolation and internal conflict, making it harder to honor what you feel. Letting go of stigma means reclaiming your right to grieve openly, to be human in a culture that often fears emotion.

2. **REPLACE JUDGMENT WITH CURIOSITY.** Judgment is the inner critic that tells you your grief is wrong or that you are too much, too little, or taking too long. It measures your healing against imagined standards of progress. This voice keeps you trapped in comparison and competition. Judgment begins with *You are . . .* and fills in the blank of self-criticism. Letting go of judgment means meeting your experience with curiosity instead of evaluation, allowing grief to unfold in its own wise timing.

3. **MEET SHAME WITH WORTHINESS.** Shame says, *Something is wrong with me for feeling this way*. It's a deeply embodied emotion that makes you want to hide, to disappear from yourself and others. Shame can turn grief inward, distorting love into self-blame and furthering experiences of isolation and loneliness. Letting go of shame is about bringing the energy of deserving to the parts of you that feel unworthy or broken. When you meet your pain with kindness, compassion, and worthiness, shame loses its power.

4. **RELEASE GUILT BY FORGIVING YOURSELF.** Guilt often appears as *I should have done more* or *If only I had . . .* It binds you to an imagined responsibility for what was never in your control. While some guilt reflects genuine moral awareness, much of it in grief is misplaced—a sign of love searching for meaning. Letting go of guilt is not about denying care or accountability; it's about forgiving yourself for being human in circumstances beyond your reach.

When these four barriers soften, grief can finally move. Grief is not a heavy, solid object lodged in the chest; it is love seeking a way to flow. By its nature, grief wants movement, breath, and expression. But stigma, judgment, shame, and guilt constrict that movement. They tighten the chest, silence the voice, and imprison love inside where it cannot breathe.

It's easy to feel ashamed for having these very emotions—to judge yourself for judging or to feel guilty for feeling stuck. Yet doing so only deepens the imbalance. These barriers are not inherently bad; they serve a purpose. They are protectors, formed to keep you safe from pain too great to bear. Judgment tries to organize chaos. Shame seeks to guard belonging. Guilt desires to hold moral truths (maybe absolutes). Stigma wants to protect identity. Each one carries a fragment of care, though expressed through fear. When you can see them through this lens, you begin to understand they are not punishments but signals pointing toward healing.

Still, grief has a way of breaking through these constructs. It is stronger than the walls built around suppression. The dam that once protected and stifled you eventually begins to crack. This is why grief can feel like it's breaking you open. What feels like breaking down is often breaking through: the moment when the tears you've swallowed or the voice you've silenced finally demand to be felt. These inner barriers cannot withstand the force of love.

This is why tenderness and compassion are needed. The cracking open hurts. Resistance only makes the pain sharper. Letting grief breathe through softening, allowing, and trusting the body's rhythm is how release happens. It is not about fixing or forcing but remembering how to let love move again.

In letting go you release the resistance that keeps love from flowing. Letting go is not the end of grief; it is the beginning of freedom. It is the moment when feeling becomes safe again and love can move as it was always meant to—freely, fully, and alive within you. Here's a simple formula:

- **FACE:** Meet your fear with courage. Turn toward your grief instead of away.
- **EMBRACE:** Allow your grief instead of suppressing it. Give your grief permission to exist.
- **RELEASE:** Letting go happens as a natural result of feeling fully.

This is why embodiment is essential in grieving. When you include your body in this process, you drop these defenses. Your heart's innate intelligence and wisdom override the need to suppress your emotions, and it all begins to make sense. The ache in your chest is love speaking. A tight jaw may be a boundary asking for care. Shallow breath signals a nervous system seeking safe co-regulation. Tears are your body's ritual of release. And laughter, when it comes, is not betrayal but rather a natural expression of joy—a reminder that both sorrow and life can coexist.

When the body is a partner in your grief, it will give you the sense of "rightness." People often ask if there is a right time to let go. They wonder if they should pull off the Band-Aid to get rid of the "things" or wait until some distant future. They ask when or if they should let go of something. This often comes up when asking about a loved one's ashes. These questions arise from a longing to do it the right way, as if there is a manual for how to grieve and how to let go. You can often hear this longing in the word *should*, a quiet pressure that suggests there is a correct timeline or method. Grief has neither.

Instead, I invite the quiet unfolding, guided not by pressure but by the inner knowing that comes when the heart is ready. You do not have to force it. You do not have to rush. Letting go becomes possible when love has had time to speak its truth and when your body tells you that what you carry no longer needs to be held so tightly.

Ultimately letting go is what happens as a result of grieving. Just as your body digests food—absorbing and assimilating the nutrients, extracting and discerning nourishment, and eliminating what's not needed—your heart and mind are doing the same with loss. Grieving is an emotional digestion. When you face your pain, embrace your experience, and allow yourself to feel, release becomes a natural outcome.

Letting go is not detachment or forgetting but a quiet transformation of the bond that you carry. It's about allowing love to move and flow in new ways. Letting go is not a race to acceptance but a gentle rhythm—an ongoing oscillation that honors the ache of loss and the fullness of life. Release the resistance and allow love to flow.

Perhaps the real question is not *How do I let go?* but rather *How can I grieve in a way that letting go happens naturally?* As we'll discuss in the next chapter and dive into deeply in part two that follows, letting go begins in the body.

5

Embodiment as the Path to Peace

FRANCINE FOUGHT HER GRIEF, was ashamed of how she was grieving, and believed the platitudes she was told by her church community and friends. She felt pity for her sadness, beat herself up when she cried, and often put on a good face, saying, "I'm fine," when she knew she wasn't. She wasn't in denial about her grief; she was powerless to do anything about it and, it seemed to me, sought desperately to push it away. Yet she continued to grieve deeply—suffering amid the waves of grief attacks that came each holiday season, each Father's Day. Each time her husband's name came up or her social media memories served up an image of him smiling, the pang of pain hit her heart, and she criticized herself that she wasn't doing grief right.

Spiraling, she finally heeded a call from a dear friend and sought me out, hoping for tools to help her stop grieving and finally be done with the pain that had taken over her life for three years. What was apparent to me in our first few sessions was something that had been absent from her life long before her husband passed away: She was disconnected from her body. When emotions rose to the surface, her body tensed and became rigid. Her shoulders shot up to her ears and looked as if they were carrying a ton of weight. She was disconnected from the tender art of grieving and needed a way to release the powerful narratives that fought her grief.

Since we experience grief in the body, the body is where we need to meet it. I call this the embodied path of peace. With Francine, we began with shaking and movement practices to loosen her body to allow life-force energy to move. We then did some breathing exercises that focused on exhaling as a means of bringing in a fresh inhale for inspiration. Our work included mindfulness practices to help her learn how to observe her thoughts and emotions without judgment. I shared techniques she could do while walking her dog and writing exercises that taught her how to think differently about her grief. As she collected a toolbox of body-focused practices, she began experiencing spaciousness around the reactions that were causing her suffering. In a short time, she began relating to her grief in new ways. She stopped fighting her grief and met it on the playing field. Empowered with new skills, resources, and techniques, she was able to see her pain with new eyes and perspective.

Many of you may feel a bit like Francine did at the beginning: under-resourced, overwhelmed, and powerless to the tidal wave of feelings moving through you. When you have never been taught how to cope with the emotions of grief—fear, anger, sadness, overwhelm, anxiety, despair, numbness—it makes sense that you would fight them, flee from them, or try to shut them down. No one ever gave you the skills to be with them. No one ever showed you how to grieve. You walk through life in survival mode because survival is the only map you inherited. But grieving does not have to be a battle. It does not have to pull you into fight or flight. You are not meant to wrestle your grief into submission or force yourself to "move on." There is another way to be with grief—an embodied way that is grounded, compassionate, and empowering.

The truth is that grief draws you into your heart. Grief is an emotional experience, not an intellectual one. You cannot think your way through; you have to feel your way through. And as you probably know, feeling can be the hardest part, especially when you have spent years navigating life from the mind that's filled with thinking, planning, analyzing, staying busy, and holding everything together. When loss arrives, those familiar strategies suddenly feel thin. They cannot hold the weight of what your heart now carries.

Compassionate Grieving is a journey of eighteen inches, from your head to your heart. You already know this experience: the mind spinning, trying to make sense of what has happened, while the heart aches beneath it. You know what it is like to understand something logically yet feel unprepared to face the emotional truth of it. There's a gap between knowing and feeling, and it's this wilderness that grief asks you to cross. This wilderness is uncertain, unmapped, and often raw. The terrain is unfamiliar, and you may feel lost inside yourself, unsure of where to place your next step. Yet this inner landscape is also where healing happens. It is where emotion begins to move again and where you slowly rediscover what it means to be alive, tender, and true.

Embodiment is what helps you walk this path. It offers a way to listen to your heart through your body—gently, safely, and at your own pace. Bit by bit, the wilderness becomes walkable, and the journey from head to heart becomes less frightening and more familiar. Embodiment paves this path with gentleness and ease. It gives you orientation in the midst of disorientation. It anchors you when everything feels uprooted. It allows feeling to become safe again, so grief can move as it was always meant to: freely, fully, and alive within you.

What Is Embodiment?

Embodiment is the gentle practice of coming home to yourself. While the word *embodiment* literally means "to be in the body," the experience is much richer than that. It's the pause in a busy day, the quiet noticing of your breath, the awareness of your surroundings, and the subtle signals that arise from within.

Anything that brings you back to your body can be an act of embodiment—whether it's a curated movement such as tai chi, yoga, or qigong; a calming breath technique; or the free expression of dance. It might be a wail of grief, a shout of anger, or the softening that comes with forgiveness. It's the comfort of being held by a friend or the tension you feel in response to a platitude. It's the smell of aromatic flavors and the taste of your favorite meal. Embodiment is both the awareness of how your body expresses emotion and the practices that help you stay connected to yourself.

For those who are grieving, embodiment is often the first step toward feeling safe enough to experience emotion. It transforms numbness into awareness, overwhelm into grounding, and confusion into clarity. Through embodiment you learn to meet what arises within you with compassion rather than fear.

It is a bridge between your inner experience and conscious awareness, connecting what your body feels with what your heart knows and your mind seeks to understand. Embodiment offers a doorway to emotional safety, inviting you to meet your feelings in real time instead of shutting down or turning away. It softens resistance and helps you remain present as emotions move and change.

When suppression leads to separation, embodiment restores connection. It reminds you that you are not just a mind that thinks but also a body that feels. Rather than analyzing your experience, you learn to inhabit it. Through breath, movement, and mindful awareness, you quiet your mind and listen to what your body has been saying all along. As balance returns, your mind and body find a rhythm of calm, allowing your heart to open.

Embodiment teaches you to relate to your emotions as expressions of love rather than as enemies. Grief, after all, is love seeking a place to go. Embodied practices create a channel for that love, guiding you toward what needs care and release. When you are caught in stories of how you "should" grieve, emotional energy can become stuck. Embodiment frees it to move through you, restoring flow.

There are many pathways into embodiment. In part two of this book, you'll find over fifty practices—breathwork, movement, journaling, art, aromatherapy—each designed to help you return to yourself with compassion and trust.

Embodiment unfolds through awareness and presence. It begins as a return to your body but grows into a posture of tenderness toward your inner life. The more you engage with it, the more you discover that peace is not found by escaping emotion but by staying present with it.

Embodiment is the experience of peace within grief, not the search for peace from grief. It is the ground on which emotional safety is built—essential for those who are grieving. In Compassionate Grieving, I call this "mindfulness of emotions."

Before you move into the practices in part two, I want to share four key aspects of embodiment that support this journey: learning to feel what is present (interoception), naming what you feel (emotional literacy), allowing emotions to flow (emotional movement), and trusting your feelings (emotional safety). Together, these four components create a steady path toward peace within grief.

Interoception: Learning How to Feel

Feeling better begins with learning how to feel.

Sensations are the way your body expresses what you feel. They are the language of the body, a quiet vocabulary spoken through pulse, temperature, breath, and movement. The body speaks through sensation long before the mind finds words. A lump in the throat, a tightening in the chest, a warmth behind the eyes—these are messages; subtle vibratory cues of your heart speaking through your body.

This subtle communication is known as interoception.[1] Just as proprioception helps you understand where your body is in space, interoception helps you understand what is happening inside your body. It is your awareness of inner sensations. Interoception begins the moment you start listening to the signals rising within you. It opens the door to a new relationship with your inner life, one rooted in presence, curiosity, and compassion.

This listening is the beginning of peace. Peace does not come from controlling what you feel but from allowing what you feel to be heard. When you begin to notice the sensations of emotions moving through your body, you are no longer fighting yourself. You are not pushing away what hurts or bracing against what rises. You are learning to stay present with your own inner life.

As you learn to notice and stay with these sensations, something subtle begins to shift. Your body no longer needs to shout to get your attention. The tightness loosens. The heaviness lightens. The emotions that once felt overwhelming begin to move in gentler waves. Your system learns that it is safe to feel and that you are willing to listen.

In this way, sensations become the bridge between body and emotion. They are how the emotional body speaks. Each flutter, contraction, or sensation of warmth is an invitation to understand what is happening within you. By honoring these signals, you create a relationship with your inner world that is rooted in curiosity rather than fear. This is the foundation of embodiment and the beginning of peace within grief.

Yet many of us have inherited a culture that separates the mind from the body, treating any discomfort as a sign that something is broken. Like a machine, when the body aches or tightens, we assume it needs to be fixed. But not all discomfort is mechanical injury. Sometimes pain is the body's way of saying something needs care, not correction, and it's asking to be listened to.

When you strengthen interoception, you learn to listen to your body's signals without reacting to them. You neither get pulled into the mind's stories nor into the conclusions it tries to draw about what your emotions mean. You begin to recognize how each emotion expresses itself through the body.

For example, in the experience of anger, you might feel your jaw tighten or your face flush. Instead of storming off or escalating a conflict, you can learn to use these feelings as a signal. By noticing the sensations, you have a chance to reduce emotional reactivity. You become less impulsive. In that awareness, you create spaciousness.

That spaciousness is an expression of embodiment. Interoception offers this possibility.[2] It is an essential part of emotional fitness, strengthening your inner muscle to feel without reacting.

When interoception is weak, you feel disconnected from what is happening inside you.[3] The body's signals feel blurred or muted, and emotions gather pressure beneath the surface. Without awareness, they can build until they burst, suddenly flooding you with overwhelm. Anger feels like an eruption, sadness feels like collapse, and anxiety feels like a wave that comes out of nowhere. Without awareness of your body's cues, your mind fills in the gaps with stories, assumptions, or fears, often leading to more confusion or distress.

When interoception is weak, you might react before you realize you are reacting. You might shut down without knowing why. You might feel hijacked by your emotions or ashamed that you cannot control them. It is not because something is wrong with you. It is simply that the bridge between your body and your awareness has not yet been strengthened.

This is what makes grief feel so overwhelming for many people. It is not the emotion itself that is overwhelming. It's that you can feel ambushed by your emotions if you don't sense the early cues that can help you meet your emotions with compassion rather than panic or fear. Strengthening interoception changes this relationship. It helps you feel the first whisper rather than the full storm.

A woman once told me that every time she missed her mother, she felt tightness in her throat. At first she called it anxiety. But when she paused and simply noticed the sensation, she realized it was her body's way of holding back tears. When she allowed herself to breathe into that space, the tightness softened and she could finally cry. The sensation became her bridge to release.

This is the gift of interoception. By turning toward sensation rather than away, grief becomes something you can breathe with, move with, and hold with compassion. You begin to sense that your body isn't betraying you; it's guiding you.

Interoception in this way is medicine for the wounds caused by suppression and separation. It reconnects the heart and body as allies in healing. When you meet your emotions through sensation, you begin to trust that you can stay with them, that you can feel deeply and still be safe. Over time you develop an interoceptive literacy, understanding a vast language that is spoken between your heart, your nervous system, and your emotions.

When you listen to the language of your body, you are building a connection to an intelligence that knows how to hold grief. Relief comes not from pushing feelings away but from softening into them, trusting that each wave carries its own wisdom. This is what embodiment teaches: Peace is not something you find later, after you heal. Peace is what happens now, in the moment you stop fighting your experience. It arrives quietly, like the body's exhale after a long-held breath.

Emotional Literacy: Naming What You Feel

Once you begin to sense your emotions through the body, the next step is to give them names. This is the practice of emotional literacy—learning how to speak the language of what you feel.

Grief floods you with sensations and feelings that can seem tangled or contradictory. You might feel anger and tenderness in the same breath, or relief and guilt side by side. Without the ability to name what you feel, all of it can blur together into a single word: *bad*. Emotional literacy gives your inner life a vocabulary. It allows you to translate sensation into meaning and bring understanding where there was once confusion.

Emotional literacy is essential for clearing the fog that often settles in during grief. When emotional literacy is low, the mind quickly turns to analysis. You try to figure out why you feel this way, what caused it, or what it means. Instead of touching the emotion itself, you move into explanations. There is an important difference between naming an emotion and analyzing it. Naming the emotion brings you into your body. Analyzing it pulls you into your thoughts. It is common that when someone asks how you feel, you describe it with anything but an emotion. The story comes out, the justifications, the narrative of what happened, yet the actual feeling remains unspoken.

You do not drown in your emotions; you drown in your thoughts about emotions. Naming your emotions is not about making sense of them but rather meeting them. A simple word such as *sad*, *lonely*, *scared*, *overwhelmed*, *tender*, or *grateful* anchors you in the truth of your experience. Name them to claim them. Once named, your heart and body can begin to soften, settle, and breathe again.

When you can name something, you can acknowledge it. Like a friend who seeks to be seen and heard, emotions too seek recognition. When you acknowledge them, you can begin to care for them. Saying "This is sadness" or "This is loneliness" is like saying, *I see you. You belong here.*

It's common to think you have to fix or rise above your feelings, but literacy invites understanding instead of control. It's also common to label or judge emotions as good or bad, positive or negative. None of this is true. There are no "light emotions" or "dark emotions." Every emotion has a purpose. Anger can show you where your boundaries were crossed. Guilt can reveal your values. Longing points to love that still wants to be expressed. Each emotion becomes a messenger, not a mistake, failure, or weakness.

One man told me that when his father died, he kept saying, "I'm just tired." But as he paid attention, he realized that "tired" was hiding sadness, and sadness was hiding love. Once he could name what was really there, his exhaustion began to lift. His body was no longer carrying the weight of unnamed feeling.

Emotional literacy transforms confusion into clarity. It helps you recognize that grief isn't just one emotion but rather a landscape of many. Within a single day, you might move through anger, fear, relief, regret, gratitude, and love. Naming what is present keeps you oriented as you walk that terrain. There's a skill in being able to hold multiple things as true at the same time.

This practice also reduces the body's stress response. When you can name what you feel, your nervous system begins to settle. Research shows that naming emotions decreases activity in the brain's fear centers and increases regulation in areas associated with calm and understanding.[4] The body feels safer when the mind can say, *This is what's happening.*

You do not need perfect words. Start simply: "I feel sad." "I feel lonely." "I feel afraid." "I feel grateful."

Even if it changes from moment to moment, naming what is true in the present helps you stay connected to yourself. It becomes easier to notice when an emotion softens or shifts. You begin to trust that feelings move. They are not permanent states but waves of meaning passing through.

This is how you make grief smaller. By naming your emotions, you begin to untangle the knot of what feels overwhelming. Each word brings light to what was once tangled in shadow. Your body softens, your breath deepens, and you realize that what once felt enormous is made of many smaller threads you can now hold with care. Naming emotions becomes an embodied practice of relief and a way to feel safe and present with what once felt unbearable.

As you grow in emotional literacy, you begin to see that your feelings are signals of what matters most. They point you toward love, values, boundaries, and needs. They restore honesty between your inner and outer life. This clarity creates a bridge to emotional safety where feelings can be felt fully without fear.

Naming is the beginning of understanding. Understanding is the beginning of peace that bridges the heart with the mind.

The Movement of Emotion: Allowing What Needs to Move

Emotions are meant to move. The word itself, *e-motion*, carries *motion* in its name. When emotions move freely, they complete their natural rhythm. When they're held back, the body carries the weight of what's unfinished.

Embodiment helps you return to peace by reestablishing this natural flow of movement. When emotion moves, energy moves. When energy moves, your heart softens, your breath deepens, and your body begins to remember its own rhythm. Through sensing and naming what you feel, you begin to create space for emotions to move through rather than stay trapped within. The practice is trusting that your body already knows how to feel and release. Grief, in this way, becomes less of a burden to carry and more of a current to breathe with.

Emotions often move in waves—rising, cresting, and subsiding. You don't have to push them away or hold them still. The invitation is to let them move through you, not at you. The sensations that accompany emotion—such as tightness, trembling, warmth, or tears—are signs that something is seeking to sprout and blossom. Just like a flower, in an emotion's full expression, the sensations flower and then fade away.

Mindfulness of emotions is the art of allowing this organic and natural process without interference. You observe the movement with curiosity, staying close to the sensations as they shift and change. You don't need to understand or justify them. You simply let the body complete what it has been holding. Each time you allow emotion to move through, you strengthen trust in your body's innate intelligence. You begin to see that you are not the wave itself but the ocean that holds it. Emotions rise and fall, yet you remain.

This is the essence of embodiment as a path to peace. Peace is not the absence of emotions but rather the confidence to be with big emotions. Not stopping emotion but learning to surrender to its movement is a practice of peace. Not suppressing the feelings but letting love find its flow again helps to allow grief to move.

Emotional Safety: Trusting the Movement of Emotion

When you begin to use the three skills we've discussed so far—interoception, emotional literacy, and emotional movement—you can remain courageously present. You can stay connected. You can listen to yourself. As the sting of grief softens and the experience of grief transforms, you begin to experience something essential: the felt sense of emotional safety. Emotional safety is the confidence that you can feel what you feel without becoming lost, overwhelmed, or ashamed. It is the sense that your inner world is not dangerous and that you can remain with yourself through any emotion that arises. Emotional safety grows as you strengthen interoception, learn to name what you feel, and allow those feelings to move. Yet it is also its own essential skill. Emotional safety is the quiet trust that you will not abandon yourself when emotions come. It is the permission to be human, tender, messy, unsure, grieving, and still hold yourself with care.

Emotional safety is not an image of having it all together. It is not pretending you are "all good." It is real and authentic. At times it is raw. It is a presence you bring to yourself and a presence you allow from the sacred companions who walk with you. In this space, stigma, judgment, shame, and guilt lose their grip. The barriers that once protected you out of fear release their hold.

Through embodiment, you no longer resist emotion; you welcome it. In this welcoming something new emerges. Your body remembers its own wisdom. Your heart remembers its strength. You begin to experience emotional freedom, an inner resilience that meets your emotions without fear. It is not perfection or mastery. It is trust—trust that you can feel, trust that you can return to yourself, trust that you can soften and still be safe. This trust becomes a kind of emotional superpower, not because you conquer your emotions but because you no longer fear them.

What grows from this is compassion. Compassion is the fruit of emotional freedom. It is what naturally arises when you stay with yourself long enough to know your own humanity. Compassion for yourself. Compassion for others. Compassion for the tender places in the heart that grief exposes. Compassion becomes the way you carry your grief and your life.

Embodiment naturally gives rise to compassion. When you learn to feel your emotions, allow them to move, and trust your capacity to stay present, something softens inside. Compassion emerges as the gentle ability to meet yourself with tenderness instead of judgment. It is the quiet presence that says, *I can be with this, even when it hurts.* This compassion steadies you through grief and gives you the inner strength to move through life with greater ease.

The next part of this book offers the practices that help cultivate this compassion from the inside out. Through movement, breath, mindfulness, and expressive exercises, you will learn how to return to your body again and again with kindness. Embodiment is not something you finish. It is a way of being that continually deepens. Each time you come home to yourself, you strengthen your connection to life and build the emotional muscles that allow grief to move with greater freedom and peace.

PART TWO

Somatic Relief for Grief

THE NEXT SECTION OF THIS BOOK is an invitation to move from theory into practice. It is a call to create space for love to move and grief to flow. Grief is carried not only in your mind and heart but also in your breath, pulse, and rhythm. For healing to unfold, your body must be part of the journey, and that is where part two is grounded.

At the heart of this work is emotional fitness: the practice of strengthening your capacity to feel, endure, and carry emotions without being overwhelmed or broken by them. This isn't about perfection or control but cultivating a body and nervous system steady enough to hold grief with compassion. Through breath, rhythm, and movement, your body learns how to calm itself and return to balance, allowing emotions to flow and soften. Researchers refer to this as regulating the nervous system, increasing distress tolerance, or creating state change. You don't have to understand any of that to benefit; you can simply think of it as creating steadiness and safety inside yourself.

The exercises and practices in the following chapters will build your capacity for mindfulness and interoception—the skills that will help you notice and observe your inner world without judgment. As you begin to meet your grief in your body, I want to offer you some encouragement. I call these the three P's of the path to peace: permission, pause, and patience. I encourage you to give each of these to yourself, as often as you need, as you embark on this journey.

PERMISSION honors your humanness in a world that demands constant productivity. It allows you to rest, to feel, to set boundaries, to be messy, to be real. It is medicine against the push and pressure of endless doing.

PAUSE brings you into the present. It interrupts the racing mind that jumps to the past and future, and helps you return to this breath, this moment. The space between inhale and exhale is a sacred threshold where balance can return.

PATIENCE invites gentleness. It softens the demand to "get over it" and reminds you that grief unfolds in its own rhythm. Patience is less about waiting and more about flowing, like water carving its path over time.

Together, these practices soften the weight of the emotional obstacle course of life and the societal expectations to move on or let go. They are not about dismissing grief but carrying it with greater compassion.

The journey ahead is often described as a movement from head to heart. In grief, the mind may become fearful and distressed, spinning stories, judgments, and doubts. But the heart already knows how to grieve—through tears, trembling, sighs, and longing. The body speaks the language of love. As you enter into a conversation between body and mind through somatic practices, you'll learn to access the wisdom and brilliance of your physiology, regulate your nervous system, create emotional safety, and let your heart open to grieve with love.

Each chapter in part two meets you in the many ways grief expresses itself. The first chapters explore the physical ways loss shows up in the body, including brain fog, energy fluctuations, sleep disturbances, and digestive distress. The chapters that follow focus on emotions such as sadness, anger, fear, and numbness. The final chapters turn to joy, purpose, and aliveness—states you might not feel are available to you in grief but that will inevitably emerge if you allow emotion to flow through you.

Each chapter offers reflections, stories, and step-by-step practices to help you build a compassionate relationship with whatever arises. This approach is integrative and whole body, drawing from somatic and embodied practices, breath techniques, journaling prompts, sensory awareness, and creative expression. Many practices are rooted in mindfulness, psychology, neuroscience, and somatic awareness, and some are grounded in ancient traditions that honor the unity of body, mind, and spirit: Traditional Chinese Medicine, Ayurveda, and contemplative spirituality.

These tools are designed to meet grief from many angles, honoring the truth that different days require different kinds of support. They are here to help you lighten the weight of grief, not by bypassing it but by creating space within you to hold it. They offer practical ways to cultivate peace, tenderness, and resilience by honoring your body and quieting your mind. In that quiet, your heart can open and grief is revealed as both suffering and a profound journey into love.

These are not lessons to read once and set aside. They are resources you can approach in any order and return to whenever you need grounding, clarity, or comfort. When an emotion surfaces, come back to the chapter that speaks to what you're feeling. The practices will give you a way to be in conversation with your body and your grief, a way to soften fear into familiarity.

At the end of part two, you will find appendices that offer quick reference guides to the exercises, so you can easily find what you need when your heart is tender or your energy is low.

It's important to note that the practices in this upcoming part of the book are intended to support your emotional, physical, and spiritual well-being during grief. They are not a substitute for medical care, mental health treatment, or crisis support. If you have concerns about your health, trauma history, or emotional stability, please seek guidance from a qualified professional before beginning these exercises. Move slowly.

Listen to your body. Nothing here should cause strain, overwhelm, or distress. If any practice feels too intense, uncomfortable, or activating, it is completely appropriate to stop.

Every exercise in part two can and should be adapted to meet you exactly as you are. Grief changes from day to day, moment to moment, and your body will tell you what feels supportive. You may shorten a practice, take longer pauses, or simply imagine the movement rather than doing it physically. You can sit, lie down, stand, or move at the pace that feels right. There is no correct or perfect way to do these practices. What matters is staying connected to your breath, your body, and your own wise rhythm. Let the exercises meet you, not the other way around.

This is not about mastering grief. It is about softening into it, letting your body show you how to carry love in new ways.

Here is my wish for you as you begin to work with these practices:

May you remember the wisdom of your body.
May your breath guide you, steady and faithful, and remind you that every inhale carries life in and every exhale is an opportunity to let heaviness go.
May your heart find its rhythm again, beating not only with sorrow but also with the pulse of love.
When emotions rise like waves, may you have the steadiness to notice rather than judge, to breathe rather than resist, to feel rather than flee.
When grief blossoms like a garden, may you allow each flower of feeling to open in its time, showing you its color, its fragrance, and its truth.
May awe meet you in unexpected places: the quiet of a morning, the warmth of a touch, the stillness after tears.
May these practices open space in you, not to erase the ache but to weave it gently with tenderness, compassion, and peace.

Let's practice together.

6

Navigating Through Brain Fog

Sam found himself adrift in a way he had never known. Once sharp, decisive, and quick to solve problems, he now sat at his desk for hours, his eyes fixed on the screen, his mind blank. After his mother's death—his last surviving parent—he carried a strange new identity: orphan.

What surprised him most wasn't the tears or the longing but how grief had rearranged his mind. He thought loss lived in the heart, but it also lived in his head. Concentration slipped through his fingers. Deadlines came and went. Words he once commanded effortlessly now eluded him.

This is the quiet truth of what's known as "brain fog," "grief brain," or "grief fog." It's not laziness or lack of willpower—it's the cognitive toll of heartbreak. The brain, flooded by emotion and stress hormones, redirects energy from focus and planning toward sheer survival. The prefrontal cortex goes dim while the limbic system that facilitates and processes memory, fear, and attachment fires continuously, trying to reconcile the impossible fact that someone essential is gone.[1] In this haze, everything feels harder. Things such as finishing an email, remembering a meeting, responding to text messages, or remembering to eat are indications of this brain fog.

For Sam, the exhaustion compounded. Toggling between spreadsheets, funeral plans, and office deadlines, he was also the executor of his mother's estate. The pressure to perform like his old self became its own kind of torment.

Together we named the shame of comparison—between how he thought, felt, and produced before with how he feels now—and replaced it with something gentler: good enough. He began scheduling boundaries between work and estate duties, choosing lighter meals, asking friends to help with basic things, and taking short rhythm-and-breath breaks before meetings to steady himself.

Over time, the fog thinned. What returned wasn't the old clarity but a quieter kind—one that moved at the pace of his healing. He realized he didn't need balance, where every part of life competes for equal weight. Balance, for Sam, was what he was taught but never fulfilled. Work-life balance were words his corporate leadership used but a reality rarely accessible. When he tried to apply this work-life balance mindset with grief, managing tasks was difficult because everything was important. His executive functioning was operating slower than it used to and decision fatigue made him feel flat. He was falling behind on his tasks. What he needed was "harmony": a rhythm that allowed grief and work, love and fatigue, to coexist. *Harmony* as a word clicked for Sam. He recognized that estate planning wasn't an everyday job. It was often a hurry-up-and-wait situation. Some tasks required waiting for lawyers, bankers, and realtors to respond.

Harmony also provided a compassionate lens for his grief. As opposed to feeling like a fight for energy, he recognized that grief required attention each day. By making the time for his grief through reflecting, journaling, and giving attention to his feelings, he found his brain coming back online with greater ease.

Sam's story reflects what so many experience but rarely name: the mental disarray of grief. This chapter explores how loss reshapes the mind as much as the heart—how attention, memory, and motivation falter not because of weakness but because the brain is devoting itself to the enormous work of adaptation. Over time, clarity emerges as the mind's quiet proof that love and loss have both been integrated into who you are now.

You're Not Alone

If you've found yourself in a fog after loss, you're not alone. Forgetting appointments, struggling to follow conversations, or reading the same paragraph over and over without comprehension is very normal. You may find yourself unable to focus, asking people to repeat themselves, or staring blankly at your computer when trying to finish an email. This is grief's effect on the brain.

Mental fog, memory lapses, and difficulty focusing are some of the most common symptoms of grief.[2] They can be alarming, especially in a world that prizes productivity and performance. But these experiences are not a sign of decline or dysfunction. They are your brain adapting to overwhelming emotional pain.

Sandra, for example, kept losing her keys. At first she laughed it off. But after her husband's death, it became a daily struggle. She would walk from room to room retracing her steps, sometimes finding her keys in the refrigerator or on the bathroom counter. She felt embarrassed, even a little scared, wondering if she was developing memory problems.

When we spoke, I reminded her that this was grief. Her brain was overloaded, her nervous system was drained, and her working memory had less capacity. The simple act of setting down keys while her mind raced with memories, sadness, and plans for the future was enough to create blanks. Naming it as grief, not dementia or decline, helped her release the shame. She began leaving her keys in one basket by the door. Slowly she stopped panicking when the fog appeared and learned to meet it with kindness.

The Science of Brain Fog

Why does clarity disappear? The hippocampus, the brain's memory center, is highly sensitive to stress hormones such as cortisol. Under grief's stress, it works less effectively, which explains forgetfulness and memory lapses.[3] The prefrontal cortex, responsible for focus and decision-making, also struggles under emotional overload. With so much mental energy consumed by grief, there's less capacity for complex thinking.[4] The amygdala, which detects threats, becomes hyperactive and pulls energy away from higher-order thought.[5]

All of this is compounded by allostatic load, the cumulative wear and tear of chronic stress, which weighs down the nervous system and leaves mind and body fatigued.[6] Sleep disruption, poor appetite, and constant emotional swings make clarity even harder to maintain.

Research confirms these experiences. Studies show that bereavement impairs attention, memory, and executive function.[7] This executive dysfunction often looks like difficulty planning, organizing, shifting between tasks, or initiating new actions.[8] Neuroimaging has revealed heightened activity in brain regions linked to pain and attachment, which compete for resources otherwise used for cognitive clarity.[9]

One study described grievers staring at a page or screen without absorbing anything—a description echoed by Jordan, a graduate student who couldn't progress on his dissertation after his sister's death. His mind was too busy with grief. With gentler pacing and simple routines, his clarity slowly returned.

Other Ways to Understand Grief Fog

Western psychology calls it executive dysfunction. Traditional Chinese Medicine (TCM) describes it as disrupted qi flow through the lungs and spleen. Ayurveda explains it as tamas, heaviness that clouds the mind, and the buildup of emotional *ama*, or toxic residue. Each tradition recognizes that grief alters the way the mind organizes, initiates, and sustains focus.

Whether you call it scattered attention, clouded qi, or undigested emotion, the lived experience is the same: Grief makes it harder to think clearly. Seeing these perspectives side by side can soften self-blame as you realize it's a universal experience. Instead of assuming you're broken, you can recognize that your mind and body are working through grief in ways that are deeply human and acknowledged across healing traditions.

In TCM, grief is most closely tied to the lungs. The lungs govern breath and vitality, but they also govern clarity, since they direct the flow of qi upward to the head and brain. When grief burdens the lungs, qi becomes constricted, breath becomes shallow, and circulation to the mind is limited.

The spleen, considered the organ of thought and focus, is also involved in grief. When the spleen is taxed by worry or exhaustion, the mind loses its clarity. "Dampness" accumulates, clouding the clear yang qi that normally rises to the head, resulting in mental dullness and forgetfulness.[10]

For example, Lisa turned to energy drinks to power through her days after her father's death. They left her heavy and foggy. From a TCM perspective, stimulants fed dampness in a system already burdened by grief.

Ayurveda offers a parallel lens. Clarity of mind is governed by sattva, the quality of lightness and balance. Grief, however, increases tamas, the quality of heaviness, dullness, and inertia. When tamas predominates, the mind feels sluggish and foggy.

Ayurveda also emphasizes *agni*, the inner fire that digests food, experiences, and emotions. Grief weakens agni. Just as undigested food creates ama, undigested grief produces emotional ama that clouds the mind.[11]

Simply shared, the brain fog that arises from grief is a result of a kind of emotional inflammation. Recognizing this as a normal and natural grief response can build compassion, lessening the judgment and shame that further perpetuate cognitive load.

Shaping Everyday Focus

When grief fog sets in, many people reach for control. They drink more coffee, make longer lists, or fill their schedules to outrun the haze. Others retreat completely, ashamed of how slow or scattered they've become. All of these are natural impulses—attempts to feel normal again—but they tend to deepen the exhaustion instead of easing it.

A gentler path is to create conditions that let clarity find you. Keep routines simple. Write down what matters. Do one thing at a time. Let others know you may need reminders. Rest when you can and eat meals that stabilize rather than spike your energy. These small acts don't eliminate the fog overnight, but they give your mind and body the steady ground they need to recalibrate. They provide harmonizing with your grief as not something to fix, get over, or solve but something that asks for attention and tenderness.

When Lila's husband died, she was convinced she was losing her mind. Once a meticulous accountant, she suddenly couldn't remember passwords or balance her own checkbook. Instead of forcing herself to think harder, she began leaving notes to her future self—small kindnesses written on sticky pads around the house: "Breathe." "Eat something." "Call Susan before 3 p.m." "Drink water!" Over time, these gentle cues became scaffolding for her healing. One day she noticed she no longer needed the notes. The clarity had returned in a calm, unassuming way.

This is what grief invites: Clarity can't be forced, but it can be supported. The fog thins when you meet it with patience, tenderness, and compassion rather than punishment. It's counterintuitive to think that being kind to yourself will increase your clarity, but it does. It seems paradoxical that creating permission to rest and offering gentleness in your grief will lighten the load on your brain, but it's true. In this way, grief fog becomes its own quiet teacher, reminding you to move slowly, honor your limits, and trust that light will return—not all at once, but in its own time.

TECHNIQUES FOR WORKING WITH GRIEF FOG

Breath Practice: Walking Breath Meditation

Establish your walk. Find a safe place to walk where you can keep an even pace. Allow your steps to fall into a natural rhythm.

Coordinate breath and steps. Begin by inhaling smoothly for four steps, then exhaling smoothly for four steps. Once this feels natural, you can lengthen the cycle to six steps in and six steps out, or even eight steps in and eight steps out. Keep the breath gentle and steady, moving in harmony with your walk.

Try breathing in segments. For greater focus and vitality, practice segmented breathing while walking:

- Inhale with four short, sniffing breaths, one breath with each step, until the lungs are full.
- Hold the breath briefly at the top.
- Exhale in four short, segmented releases, one breath with each step.
- Continue this cycle for several minutes.

Return to natural rhythm. After practicing segmented breathing, return to a simple, steady cycle of four to six steps in and out. Walk for as long as feels nourishing, letting breath and movement bring you into presence.

WHY THIS HELPS

Walking breath meditation brings together movement, rhythm, and mindful breathing. It creates a bridge between body and mind, offering both calmness and vitality while reducing the weight of emotional stress. This practice has deep roots in ancient traditions, where rhythm—whether from drums, footsteps, or the heartbeat—helped people sustain long journeys and stay connected to body and spirit.[12]

Cyclic sigh breath, physiological sigh, or segmented breathing are all different names for a double, triple, or quadruple inhale that pauses between each one with a smooth exhale. It's shown to increase oxygen exchange in the alveoli of the lungs, improving mental clarity and helping to release internal stress.[13]

Exercise: Sensory Nerve Activation Practice

Arrive. Sit comfortably with your feet on the floor. Take one slow breath in and one long breath out.

Activate your hands. Start gentle clapping to activate your hands. Then with one hand, gently massage each finger from base to tip. Pause at the fingertip and begin softly squeezing against the tip and nailbed to activate the nerve endings. Move through all five fingers, then switch hands. Finish with opening and closing your hands to bring circulation into your fingers and knuckles.

Practice for one to two minutes.

Activate your feet. Bring one foot where you can reach it comfortably. Rotate your ankle to bring circulation. Massage each toe from base to tip, then gently squeeze the nailbeds and the tips of your toes. Massage around the arch, heel, ball of the foot, and ankle. Switch sides.

Practice for one to two minutes.

Integrate. Stand and shake. Move your body for fifteen to twenty seconds. Then rest. Place both hands at your sides and both feet on the ground. Take two steady breaths. Feel the sense of wakefulness and grounding in your body.

Even a few minutes of this practice can help clear mental fog and restore gentle clarity.

WHY THIS HELPS

This practice awakens the dense network of peripheral nerves in your hands and feet. These nerves communicate directly with the brain, helping to restore clarity, presence, and mental steadiness. By stimulating these sensory pathways through intentional touch, you support the nervous system in shifting out of fog and into focus. This practice is simple and soothing and can be done anytime your mind feels hazy, overwhelmed, or tired.[14]

Breath Practice: Alternate Nostril Breathing

1. **Sit comfortably.** Find a quiet space. Sit with your spine tall and your shoulders relaxed. Rest your left hand on your lap.
2. **Begin with your left nostril.** Bring your right hand toward your face. Use your thumb to gently close your right nostril. Keep the rest of your hand relaxed. Inhale slowly and smoothly through the left nostril.
3. **Switch sides.** At the top of the inhale, gently close your left nostril with the pinky finger of your right hand. Release your thumb and exhale through your right nostril.
4. **Inhale right.** With your left nostril still closed, inhale slowly through your right nostril.
5. **Switch again.** Close your right nostril with your thumb. Release your pinky finger and exhale through your left nostril. This completes one round.
6. **Continue the cycle.** Repeat for five to ten rounds, or practice for three to five minutes. Keep the breath smooth, steady, and gentle.
7. **Finish.** After your final round, return to normal breathing through both nostrils. Rest your hands in your lap and notice any shifts in your body and mind.

WHY THIS HELPS

Alternate nostril breathing is a yogic practice that balances the two sides of the nervous system, calming agitation while restoring focus and clarity. The gentle rhythm of switching nostrils slows the breath, which engages the parasympathetic nervous system and reduces stress. Research has shown that this practice can improve heart rate variability, lower blood pressure, and enhance cognitive performance. In grief, it offers a way to soothe the racing mind, quiet inner turbulence, and bring a steadying sense of balance between body and mind.[15]

Writing Practice: Expressing Yourself

Choose one or more of the following prompts (or more than one, if you would like) and write freely, without censoring yourself. Allow yourself to complete these sentences as many times as you like. Let them flow without judgment.

I am deserving of . . .
I am worthy of . . .

Sometimes clarity comes from desire and giving yourself permission to want. If there's permission to want, what would you say? Write down whatever arises as you ask yourself:

What do I want?
What brings me joy?

If you desire to have your person (or pet or job, etc.) back, honor the ache of that truth. Then gently ask:

How might I connect with this person beyond this life?
How might they be showing up for me through signs, memories, or quiet messages?
What kind of relationship can I build with them now, even if it looks different from before?

You can also honor grief through a practice called Love Notes. These are mini love letters that create space for love to flow even now. Try using prompts such as:

I think of you when . . .
I remember the time when . . .
These are the things I miss most about you . . .
This really annoyed me when you used to . . .
I apologize for . . .

I forgive you for . . .

I'm grateful for . . .

WHY THIS HELPS

Expressive writing activates neural and physiological processes that help regulate emotion and integrate memory.[16] Research indicates that expressive writing shifts neural processing and provides cognitive benefits.[17] This helps transform raw emotional energy—such as longing or regret—into coherent narrative memory, reducing physiological arousal and promoting psychological integration. In the context of grief, writing does more than document pain—it facilitates continuing bonds, a well-established therapeutic concept describing how relationships with the deceased evolve rather than end. Giving love a voice allows emotional energy to move from suppression to integration, transforming unexpressed or "frozen" attachment into an ongoing internal connection. Over time, this process restores coherence to both mind and body, reaffirming that while the form of the relationship has changed, its presence continues as an enduring part of one's emotional life.

Recipe: Ginger Pickle for Focus and Clarity

Ingredients

- 2–3 inches fresh ginger root, peeled and cut into thin slices or matchsticks
- Juice of half a lime or lemon
- A pinch of mineral salt (rock salt preferred)
- Optional: a drizzle of honey

Instructions

1. Place the ginger slices in a small dish.
2. Squeeze the lime or lemon juice over the ginger.
3. Sprinkle with a pinch of salt.

4. Add a touch of honey if desired to balance the flavors.
5. Let it sit for a few minutes to marinate.

WHY THIS HELPS

Eating one or two slices of ginger pickle before meals stimulates saliva, awakens digestive enzymes, and prepares the stomach for digestion. In Ayurveda, digestion is seen as the foundation of both physical and mental clarity. Ginger pickle is a simple, time-honored way to kindle agni, the digestive fire, before meals.[18] The warmth of ginger stimulates saliva and digestive enzymes, lime juice awakens the taste buds, and a touch of salt balances and grounds the flavors. Together, these ingredients prepare the stomach to process food more efficiently. Because digestion and mental clarity are closely linked in TCM and traditional Ayurvedic medicine, this small ritual not only supports smoother digestion but also enhances focus and alertness for the mind.

Summary

Allow your brain to rest from overfunctioning. Simplify, slow down, and let clarity come to you. Keep routines simple, write things down, and focus on one task at a time. Let reminders and structure hold what your mind cannot. Nourish the body to support the mind. Rest, hydration, balanced meals, and breath practices rebuild the nervous system's capacity for focus and calm. Practice gentleness over perfection. Give yourself permission to be good enough while your brain recalibrates.

Clarity does return—but it often comes softer, slower, and wiser than before. Let the fog be part of your healing—a way of giving yourself kindness in the midst of your pain.

7

Managing Energy

When Zach's wife died, his entire life seemed to collapse. In the weeks that followed, even the smallest actions felt impossible. He woke each morning already exhausted, as though he had run a marathon in his sleep. Making breakfast felt like moving mountains. Sorting the mail left him in tears. Friends encouraged him to rest, but no amount of sleep replenished the exhaustion in his body. His limbs felt heavy, his mind foggy, his heart like stone. One day he whispered, "I am so tired of being tired."

Grief had consumed his energy. What once seemed effortless—basic things, such as getting dressed, cooking dinner, replying to messages—were not basic to Zach. The simple tasks had become monumental.

Grieving requires energy. Most people underestimate just how much. They wonder why they feel so tired, why simple tasks take so much effort, why their body seems to move through molasses. The truth is simple and tender: Grief is labor. It draws energy from every part of you—body, mind, emotions, and spirit.

You need energy to manage the cognitive load of grief that includes the endless processing and reprocessing of what has happened, the mental effort of making sense of a world that no longer makes sense. You need energy to bear the emotional toll and to meet waves of sorrow, anger, guilt, or numbness that come without warning. You need energy to survive the disruption grief brings: to get out of bed, to face the day, to hold conversations while the world keeps spinning when your own has stopped.

Grief lives in the muscles, the breath, the nervous system. It can feel like your body has been rewired—like everything that once came easily now requires conscious effort. This chapter explores what that means; how grief changes energy, metabolism, and vitality; and how you can begin to restore your reserves.

I want to assure you that exhaustion is not failure. Exhaustion is evidence of profound inner work. Grief is the body's sacred labor of love that's metabolizing loss, repairing connection, and slowly and courageously finding the energy to live again.

The Energetic Burden of Grief

Grief is cognitively demanding. Psychologists describe grief as the burden of a high cognitive load.[1] The brain is constantly trying to reconcile an impossible reality: Someone, something, or some part of you that was central is now absent. Every reminder—an empty chair, a phone that will not ring, a plan that no longer exists—forces the mind to reprocess the loss. This repeated reorientation requires enormous mental energy.

The prefrontal cortex, the brain's executive center, is heavily taxed. It normally manages planning, working memory, and decision-making, but in grief it must juggle everyday tasks and the ongoing background work of digesting loss. This is why memory lapses, lack of concentration, and indecision are so common during grief.[2] The brain also shows heightened activity in the default mode network, which replays the past and imagines the future.[3] In grief, the mind oscillates between memories of "what was" and attempts to picture "what could have been." This looping drains mental energy, leaving you fatigued without even leaving your chair.

The emotional toll is just as consuming. Crying is an energetic release that involves rapid breathing, shifts in heart rate, and the release of neurochemicals.[4] Anger floods the body with increased blood flow and muscle tension.[5] Even numbness, which can often look like non-affect, is the nervous system shutting down into energy-conserving states of withdrawal.[6] All of these processes consume physical resources.

Suppression drains energy as well. Holding back tears, avoiding feelings, or putting on a mask of "being fine" requires continuous activation of the nervous system. Studies show that suppression increases heart rate and sympathetic nervous system activity, leaving the body tense and fatigued.[7] Both expression and suppression consume energy, but expression ultimately allows for release, while suppression prolongs depletion.

For those in caregiving and service roles, such as health-care workers, teachers, social activists, nurses, and doctors, grief often carries an added layer of energy cost from what is known as vicarious trauma or secondary grief.[8] Bearing witness to suffering, injustice, or loss in others can leave the nervous system carrying pain that isn't directly your own yet is still deeply felt. Research shows that repeated exposure to the trauma of others can cause symptoms that mirror post-traumatic stress, including exhaustion, irritability, and emotional numbing.[9] This type of grief is cumulative and the energy cost is enormous.

Brian, a middle-school teacher during the height of the pandemic, showed up every day for his students, many of whom had lost grandparents, parents, or neighbors. He could feel the heaviness of their fear and uncertainty every time he looked into their faces on the screen. They asked questions he could not answer—questions about safety, the future, whether life would ever feel normal again. By the end of each day, he was utterly drained. It was not only lesson plans and grading papers that consumed him. It was the grief of thirty children sitting in front of him, each carrying a story of loss he didn't know how to carry.

Collective and Invisible Grief

There's another layer of energy in grief that often goes unnoticed: collective grief. Even when you're not directly touched by personal loss, the sorrows of the wider world press on the nervous system.

Serena, who had been doing restorative justice work in her city for over a decade, began to notice this truth in her body. She spent her days listening to stories of violence, incarceration, fractured families, and broken trust. She believed deeply in the work, but her body felt heavy in ways she could not explain. She was exhausted before the day began, her sleep restless, her chest tight.

Every circle she held, every family she sat with, added to an invisible backpack she carried home at night. It was not her grief alone. It was the collective grief of a community that had suffered generations of loss. She had become both participant and vessel. Her fatigue was evidence of the human cost of holding collective pain.

Today, many people feel a similar onus. The grief extends beyond the personal and is intimately tied to what's happening in the world: global wars, climate disruption, political unrest, racial injustice, economic uncertainty. The news alone can leave you drained before the day has even begun. This is the grief of living in a world that feels fragile, unsettled, and sometimes apocalyptic. These invisible and collective sorrows are carried in the body, often unnamed yet still depleting.

Yet collective grief is also a measure of our aliveness. It's proof that we're still capable of feeling the world's pain rather than numbing to it. It means our empathy remains intact and our compassion present. The weight you carry for the suffering of others is an extension of your humanity. When acknowledged and tended, collective grief can become a source of solidarity and connection rather than despair. It reminds us that we aren't alone in our heartbreak and that healing, too, must be communal.

Learning to Work with Energy

Because grief consumes so much of our energy, it's a good idea to learn how to manage and work with energy in self-nourishing ways.

One way to understand energy in grief is through the metaphor of gears. Sometimes you're driving in sixth gear, racing down the freeway, when your body and mind can only handle first gear, the slow rhythm of making tea or folding laundry. At other times, you feel like the gas tank is nearly empty and you're sputtering down the road with no reserve. Learning to shift gears is learning to pace yourself. First gear may mean making one phone call. Third gear may mean working a few hours. Fifth gear may mean attending a social gathering. When you recognize which gear you're in, you can stop judging yourself against the old pace and instead move with compassion for the vehicle you've been given.

Traditional Chinese Medicine (TCM) provides another perspective.

Grief is tied to the lungs, the seat of qi. The lungs govern breath, vitality, and circulation of energy. When burdened by grief, qi becomes depleted or stagnant, showing up as shallow breathing, fatigue, or heaviness in the chest.[10] The lungs are paired with the large intestine, which helps us release what no longer serves us. If grief is not expressed, energy becomes stuck, showing up as tension, digestive sluggishness, or emotional flatness. Practices that move qi—such as walking, breathwork, qigong, or even weeping—restore energy by releasing stagnation.

Grief also asks us to redefine what "normal" looks like. Many wonder, *Will I ever be myself again?* Energy is tied to identity, so when it changes, it can feel like losing who you are. Yet grieving means recalibrating expectations. Doing one load of laundry may be an accomplishment. Cooking a simple meal may count as success. A shower and a walk may be a full day's labor of love. Energy in grief is measured not against the old standard but against what the heart and body carry now.

Practical tools can also help. The spoon theory is a simple metaphor for managing limited daily energy.[11] Imagine waking up with a set number of spoons. Each task costs you one or more spoons. When they're gone, they are gone. Grief reduces the number of spoons available because energy is already being spent on the invisible labor of sorrow. The practice is to spend spoons wisely, allow yourself to stop when they run out, and recognize that this is wise stewardship of your energy.

Energy mapping is another helpful practice. Track your energy for a week. Notice when you feel most capable and when you feel most depleted. Align tasks with your natural rhythms. If mornings bring clarity, use them for important calls or errands. If afternoons bring a slump, reserve them for rest or quiet. Instead of pushing against cycles, cooperate with them.

But first and foremost, exhaustion is a sign that your body deeply needs rest. Honor it. Pushing will only deplete your reserves and make you more tired, for longer. Rest with great reverence.

Lastly, remember that energy is both individual and shared. Sitting with someone who listens without judgment, being part of a grief group, or simply walking in nature allows you to borrow energy from outside yourself. This is how human beings have survived loss throughout history.

TECHNIQUES FOR WORKING WITH ENERGY

Breath Practice: Breathing Life into the Body

Stand with feet hip-width apart.

1. Close your hands into fists and place your knuckles on either side of your lower spine, in the soft, fleshy area between your ribs and your pelvis.
2. Rotate your hips in a slow, wide circle, pressing your knuckles gently into these points as you move forward. Continue for about one minute, then reverse direction.
3. Stand upright and use your palms or knuckles to massage the lower back on either side of the spine.
4. Rub your palms together briskly until they feel warm, then place them over your lower back.
5. Breathe deeply into this area, imagining your breath moving directly into your palms and into your lower back.
6. Visualize a deep blue ocean behind you, filling your lower back with calm, steady life force.
7. Rest for a few moments, noticing sensations of warmth, grounding, and quiet renewal.

WHY THIS HELPS

In TCM, the lower back is linked to the kidney energy system—the root of vitality and resilience. Grief often drains this reservoir, leading to fatigue, fear, and adrenal depletion. Gentle circular motion and warmth stimulate circulation and support the kidneys' energetic flow, helping restore balance to the nervous system. The act of visualization further engages the parasympathetic response, calming the body while replenishing deep reserves of energy. This simple daily practice helps rebuild energy, vitality, and resilience from the inside out.[12]

Exercise: Spine Flex and Flow

VARIATION 1: SEATED

Sit at the edge of a chair with your feet flat. Place your hands on your knees.

1. Inhale as you flex the spine forward, lifting the chest.
2. Exhale as you round the spine back, drawing the chest inward.
3. Continue in a steady rhythm for several breaths.

VARIATION 2: STANDING

Stand with your feet shoulder-width apart, legs steady and grounded.

1. Bend your arms with elbows slightly out to the sides.
2. Inhale as you flex the spine forward and open the chest.
3. Exhale as you round the spine back, pressing the breath out.
4. Repeat several times, moving smoothly with the breath.

Note: In either variation, make this practice rhythmic and fluid. Start with small flexion and extension with reduced range of motion as you begin the practice each time, then slowly increase as you warm up. Reduce any strain or jerky motions, emphasizing fluidity. Practice for two to three minutes.

WHY THIS HELPS

The spine is central to the flow of life energy. It houses and protects the nervous system. Key acupressure points that run along the spine are stimulated, each linked with different organ systems and emotions.[13] When big feelings build up and are not fully processed, these points can become wells of stagnant energy, creating inflexibility for the body as well as the emotions. Moving the spine helps release that stagnation, restoring energy not only for daily tasks but also for holding and working through grief.

Breath Practice: Mindfulness of Breath

Find a comfortable position, sitting or lying down. Take a few natural breaths.

1. Notice the sensations of breathing: coolness at your nostrils, the rise and fall of your chest, or the expansion of your belly.
2. When thoughts arise, notice them without judgment. Imagine them as waves passing across the surface of the ocean. Gently return to the breath.
3. Continue for a few minutes. When ready, deepen the breath, open your eyes, and notice how you feel.

WHY THIS HELPS

Mindfulness is well known for reducing stress and fostering inner peace, yet it also helps sustain energy, sharpen attention, and improve efficiency.[14] The practice is not about stopping the mind or silencing thoughts but letting them move naturally, like waves rising and falling in the ocean. The breath serves as an anchor, a steady rhythm you can return to whenever your focus drifts. Each time you notice your mind wandering and gently return to the breath, it strengthens your brain's capacity for regulation and calm. Over time, this repeated mental bicep curl supports greater emotional buoyancy, clarity, and renewed energy.

Exercise: Sorting What Belongs to You

Here's a simple practice for telling personal grief apart from collective grief. Collective grief from the world can blend with your own and drain your energy without you noticing. This practice helps you separate the two so you can care for yourself with more clarity and strength.

1. **Settle your body.** Sit comfortably. Place one hand on your chest and one on your belly. Take a slow breath and say inwardly, *I am here.*
2. **Name your personal grief.** Take a blank page and write at the top "This is my grief." Allow a few words or phrases to surface. These may be connected to a:

    - loss
    - change
    - relationship
    - memory
    - part of you that is hurting

    Write only what feels essential. You are not creating a list. You are identifying the place within you that is tender and personal.

    Pause and breathe.
3. **Name the collective grief you carry.** On a new page, write at the top "This is the world's grief." Without overthinking, jot down the sorrow you absorb from outside:

    - wars
    - violence
    - humanitarian crises
    - injustice
    - environmental destruction
    - suffering in the news
    - pain in your community
    - fear in the culture

    Notice how much space these take up in your mind and body. You do not have to fix or solve any of it. You are simply acknowledging what enters your system.
4. **Draw a boundary that protects your energy.** On the page labeled "This is the world's grief," draw a simple boundary symbol:

    - circle
    - box

- line
- frame
- gentle container

This symbol represents your energetic limit. It does not reject the world's suffering. It simply honors your capacity. Internally communicate with yourself: *I care, but I cannot carry everything.* Let the boundary be an act of compassion, not detachment.

5. **Return to what belongs to you.** Place your hands over your heart and belly again. Look at the page labeled "This is my grief."

   Say inwardly, *This is what I am responsible for. This is where my energy must go first. This is where I can create healing.* Let your breath deepen. Let your energy come home.

6. **Close with a small ritual of release.** Fold the page with collective grief in half or place it under a stone or book. Let this action symbolize putting it down for now. You can return to it when you choose.

   Say inwardly, *I release what is not mine to carry. I tend to what belongs to me. My energy is sacred.* Sit in stillness for one final breath

WHY THIS HELPS

Collective grief can blur your emotional boundaries and drain your energy without you realizing it. Naming the difference between personal grief and the grief of the world helps your nervous system discern what requires inner work and what requires compassionate witnessing from a healthy distance. This distinction brings your energy back into your own body and strengthens your capacity to respond to the world without becoming overwhelmed by it. By recognizing what is yours and what is not, you reclaim the possibility of healing, presence, and grounded engagement.

Writing Practice: Reflection on What Gives Life

Grab your journal or a few pieces of paper. Take a few minutes to reflect on the following:

What activities help me feel lighter, more present, or more renewed?
What people and/or places give me more than they take?
What activities drain me and feel like constant withdrawals without return?
What people and/or places take from me more than they give?

WHY THIS HELPS

An energy inventory shines a light on what truly nourishes you and what quietly drains you. By pausing to notice where your energy goes, you create space to make choices with more compassion for yourself. Sometimes the things that deplete you are not actually required and simply naming them opens the possibility of release. This practice helps you align your time and attention with what gives back to you, fostering balance, clarity, and greater resilience.[15]

Sensory Experience: Adaptogen Teas

Common adaptogens include:

- **Ashwagandha:** Calms the nervous system and supports rest and recovery.[16]
- **Tulsi (Holy Basil):** Uplifts mood and balances energy.[17]
- **Licorice Root:** Nourishes and harmonizes the body's stress response.[18]
- **Ginseng:** Gently increases vitality, energy, and stamina.[19]
- **Reishi Mushroom:** Supports immunity and relaxation.[20]

SAVORING MOMENTS THROUGH TEA RITUAL:

1. Boil water and choose your preferred adaptogenic herb(s) or a preblended mix.
2. Add 1–2 teaspoons of herbs per cup of hot water.
3. Steep for 5–10 minutes, covered, to preserve the aromatic compounds.
4. Strain the tea and pour it into your favorite mug.
5. Sit somewhere comfortable and hold the cup with both hands, feeling its warmth.
6. Inhale the aroma before sipping. Let each sip be slow and mindful.
7. As you drink, imagine the herbs replenishing your energy and calming your system.
8. Repeat this ritual daily, adjusting herbs to your body's needs or the season.

WHY THIS HELPS

Adaptogen teas support the body's stress circuitry, helping smooth cortisol spikes and rebuild steadier energy during grief. The warm, unhurried brewing-and-sipping ritual also engages the parasympathetic nervous system via breath, scent, and heat—quieting vigilance, easing muscle tension, and restoring a felt sense of safety. Over time, the plants and the practice work together to soften stress, stabilize mood, and replenish resilience without the crash of caffeine or sugar.[21]

Summary

Grief consumes energy. Your fatigue is a reflection of love's effort. It's emotional labor. Offer yourself compassion, as it's normal to feel tired and exhausted while grieving. Energy in grief is meant to be witnessed and tended, not conquered or forced. Pushing and pressure will activate the stress response, leading to further energy peaks and valleys. Notice how energy moves through stillness, tears, rest, and breath.

Cultivate energy with compassion: Rest when you are tired, pace yourself as you need, nourish your body, and let community hold you when your strength fades. Recognize the layers of collective grief that are present. Discern what is yours to carry in this moment. Energy will return in new rhythms, just as dawn follows night. For now, honor the dark as part of the natural cycle of renewal.

Grief reshapes your relationship with vitality. When you meet your exhaustion with kindness instead of judgment, with tenderness instead of pressure, with compassion instead of productivity, you invite harmony and balance to slowly reemerge—and with it, the quiet return of life's seasons and cycles.

8

Getting Better Sleep

Shelley's story began not with a death but with depletion. Her losses were quieter—threaded through constant change and the invisible labor of adapting. Her partner's new executive role had meant several moves within a few years, each one taking her farther from the family she loved. Making new friends was difficult, her work was demanding, and the pandemic had added another layer of strain. She worked remotely while he traveled often. At night, loneliness settled in beside her, keeping her awake.

They had not been married for very long and were still learning the rhythms of partnership and homelife. Shelley didn't come to talk about sleep. She came because she felt low—ungrounded and adrift, uncertain as to why. No one close to her had recently died, but as we talked, it became clear that something in her system had stopped recovering from constant change. Her grief was a response to many small losses, none of them witnessed, all of them stored in her body.

She fell asleep easily but awoke most nights between 1:30 and 2 a.m., mind spinning. At first, she lay still, bargaining with her thoughts. Eventually she began getting up—folding laundry, reading, checking emails—trying to outpace the restlessness. Some nights it worked; mostly, it didn't. Fatigue set in like fog.

Her sleeplessness wasn't just about anxiety or hormones or blue light from her phone. It was her body saying, *I can't metabolize this pace anymore.* In the silence of night, every unprocessed emotion rose for attention, and her body was shouting from the disconnection, the loneliness, the relentless doing. Beneath her overthinking was exhaustion. Beneath the exhaustion was her unnamed grief.

We began to slow everything down. Together we named the transitions she'd sped through, the identities she'd shed, the parts of herself she left behind. I offered simple evening rituals such as gentle breathwork, grounding touch, and quiet reflection to create signals of safety for her nervous system. Over time, her sleep deepened. Her dreams returned. And with rest came the recognition that her body had been grieving all along and that sleep was not an escape from grief but one of its essential medicines.

Sleep is one of the most essential yet fragile forms of healing in grief. When the world feels uncertain and the heart is heavy, rest becomes both refuge and repair. In sleep, the body quietly restores what waking life consumes. Sleep allows the nervous system to recalibrate, for the heart rate to slow, for the immune system to steady, and for the mind to begin the work of integration that talking alone cannot do.

Grief interrupts these rhythms, yet it also depends on them. Deep rest allows what feels unbearable to settle, to soften at the edges, and to be held by something larger than willpower. Sleep is the body's way of remembering how to trust life again—one breath, one night at a time.

Here are some of the ways your body's capacity to rest can be compromised by grief:

DIFFICULTY FALLING ASLEEP: The mind will not quiet, thoughts replay, and worries spill into the silence of night. While some may relegate this to overthinking, it's actually the body's stress response, with cortisol sometimes surging at the wrong time of day and keeping the nervous system on alert when it should be settling into rest.[1]

MIDDLE-OF-THE-NIGHT WAKING: You may fall asleep easily, then wake in the wee hours of the morning and struggle to return to slumber. These hours can fill with racing thoughts or loneliness that grows louder in the dark. Your body can't find balance, so your mind spins and your heart remains restless.[2]

EARLY-MORNING WAKING: You may rise at 4 a.m. or 5 a.m., heavy with sadness or regret, your energy drained before the day begins. This often reflects how grief can dysregulate mood and circadian rhythms, disrupting the chemistry that helps you feel restored.[3]

EXCESSIVE SLEEPING: Some turn to sleep for refuge, sleeping for many hours yet still waking unrefreshed. This can be a shut-down response to overwhelming emotional fatigue, the body's attempt to retreat from a world that feels too heavy.[4]

RESTLESS, FRAGMENTED NIGHTS: Tossing and turning, vivid or unsettling dreams, and light sleep that never drops into the deeper rhythms where the body heals can mark the grief period. Even if the clock shows enough hours, your heart knows otherwise.[5]

These patterns remind us that in grief, quality sleep can be elusive. Our body longs for rest, yet the compounded sorrow, stress, and transition into a new way of life can disturb the delicate rhythms that sustain it.

Understanding Sleep and Energy Regulation

Jonathan worked in a memory-care facility and was beloved by both staff and patients. Yet the repeated sadness of loss after loss began to take its toll. At night he dreamed so vividly it felt as though he had been awake the whole time. Although he always tried to go to sleep and wake up at the same time every day, he always arose each morning even more exhausted, carrying the weight of both his waking and sleeping hours.

Sleep is governed by rhythms larger than willpower. Deep in the brain, the hypothalamus holds a master clock called the suprachiasmatic nucleus (SCN) that organizes circadian rhythms.[6] This clock resets each day primarily by light. Morning sunlight signals through the optic nerve that it is time to be awake. Evening darkness allows melatonin to rise and the body to prepare for rest.[7] Spending twenty to thirty minutes outdoors within the first hour of waking helps regulate circadian rhythms and stabilize energy.[8] Just as important is dimming lights in the evening, especially blue light from screens that suppresses melatonin.[9]

We also need to recognize the ways that stress, a natural bodily response, can be amped up in times of grief and impact our sleep. Cortisol, the body's stress hormone, naturally peaks in the morning to help us wake and tapers at night to allow rest.[10] In grief, this rhythm often falters. Elevated cortisol at night can keep the body on alert and make it harder to fall or stay asleep.[11] It's not just the mind that races; so does the physiology of the body.

Before his divorce, James loved to sleep in on weekends. After the separation, sleep felt broken. He fell asleep easily, then woke at 4:30 a.m. with a heavy chest and a mind that just wouldn't settle. "Divorce is hard," he said. "Someone told me once that divorce is death without a body. I feel that." In the quiet before dawn, he replayed arguments, worried about the future, and carried the ache of what could not be undone. By sunrise, he already felt drained. "I wake up tired of being tired. I also wake up activated, almost anxious. That's not usually me." His mornings show how grief can steal the energy you need to heal.

Coffee can also play a role in sleeplessness. Caffeine blocks adenosine, the neurotransmitter that builds sleep pressure. Because caffeine can linger for up to twelve hours, an afternoon cup may echo as restlessness at midnight.[12] Yet for many grieving people, fatigue drives the impulse to reach for coffee in the first place. The temporary lift masks depletion but does not repair it. Over time, the cycle compounds—poor sleep leads to exhaustion, exhaustion leads to caffeine, and caffeine leads to more disrupted rest. What begins as a way to cope with weariness can quietly keep the nervous system on alert, preventing the deep restoration that grief so desperately needs. Gentle awareness of this cycle can help the body relearn its natural rhythm of rise and release.

The invitation is compassionate rhythm, not rigid control. Notice how you greet the morning, move through the day, and prepare for night. Sleep is not an isolated act. It is the culmination of how you lived the day.

Traditional Wisdom for Sleep

In Traditional Chinese Medicine, sleep is a dance between yin, which is rest and stillness, and yang, which is activity and movement. Grief often depletes yin and leaves yang unchecked. Elementally, this is like fire without water. It can look like trouble falling asleep, waking in the early hours, or feeling restless despite fatigue.[13] Recognizing this imbalance invites more nourishing evening practices that include warmth, quiet, and rhythms that settle the heart.

Ayurveda offers a similar concept: *dinacharya*, daily rhythm. Lifestyle medicine echoes this wisdom. Rising near sunrise, eating meals in daylight, and winding down with calming rituals align life with natural cycles and support longevity and vitality. Modern chronobiology affirms that timing is medicine.

Grief asks for compassion more than correction. Rather than forcing sleep, create conditions that invite it—an approach reflected in both Ayurveda and TCM, where harmony with natural rhythms restores balance to body and mind. Morning light helps regulate the body's inner clock and awaken vital energy within an hour of rising.[14] Steady rhythms of regular meals, gentle movement, and consistent sleep times stabilize qi and support dinacharya. Evening wind-down rituals—dimming lights, taking a warm bath, or engaging in gratitude journaling or guided imagery—help transition the nervous system from stimulation to rest. Soothing inputs such as a weighted blanket, calming tea, or breathwork with long exhales invite the parasympathetic response that calms *vata* and grounds the spirit. A cool, dark, quiet space protects the sanctity of the sleep environment and supports the yin quality essential for deep restoration.

These are small acts of love for the grieving body that help restore the natural rhythms both traditions view as the foundation of healing.

TECHNIQUES FOR WORKING WITH SLEEP

Exercise: Sleep Meditation in Bed

1. Rub your palms together until they feel warm, building gentle circulation and preparing your hands for the practice.
2. Interlace your fingers and place them at the base of your skull on the bony ridge called the occiput. Let your elbows fall out to the sides and relax. Breathe comfortably for about one minute.
3. Then bring your palms over your closed eyes with your fingers resting lightly at your hairline. Rest here for about one minute.
4. Next place one hand over the other at the center of your chest. Breathe comfortably into your heart space for as long as it feels comfortable.
5. Finally rest your hands over your belly button, one on top of the other. Breathe slowly into your belly for as long as you wish.

WHY THIS HELPS

This in-bed sequence releases tension and prepares body and mind for rest. It connects with acupressure points that calm the nervous system, settle the spirit, and replenish yin energy. The sequence traces energy downward from the head into the body. It helps release rumination, quiet active thoughts, and ease the transition into sleep. As a yin-nourishing practice, it cultivates restoration, balance, and calm for the night ahead. By placing your hands in these specific spots, you activate key acupressure points to help you relax.

Exercise: Releasing Jaw Tension

1. Rub your palms together until they feel warm.
2. Place your palms gently over your eyes for a few breaths and let the warmth soothe your face.

3. Use your fingertips to make small circles along the jawline, especially near the back of your jaw.
4. Using your fingertips, gently and rhythmically tap on your cheeks and jaw.
5. Cup the sides of your neck under your ears, so that your fingers reach your cervical vertebrae. Using your fingers, gently massage the muscles lateral to the spine.
6. Finally, place your hands beneath your chin, palms supporting the jaw. Keep your mouth slightly open and breathe slowly.
7. Relax fully. Let your shoulders and neck soften. Stay for a minute or two, breathing calmly until you feel release.

WHY THIS HELPS

This quick practice calms facial tension, settles the nervous system, and prepares the body for sleep.[15] When you carry tension in your jaw, you are often holding more than muscular strain. You may be holding emotional stress, nervous system activation, and unspoken grief. The jaw is a key site for clenching and bracing, especially in grief, sadness, guilt, or anxiety. By gently releasing that tension, you signal to your nervous system that your body is no longer in a protected state. The warmth of your palms, the gentle circles, the soft taps, and the opening of your mouth all invite the parasympathetic branch of your nervous system to engage. This helps support deeper, more restful sleep. When the head, neck, and jaw soften, it becomes easier for the body to let go of vigilance, drop into safety, and move into sleep readiness.

Exercise: Simple Acupressure to Soothe the Heart

1. Turn your palm upward and measure about three finger-widths down from the wrist crease. The point lies between the two central tendons in the lower arm, about two inches from the base of the palm.

2. Use the thumb of the opposite hand to press gently, applying steady, comfortable pressure. Hold for one to two minutes while breathing slowly.
3. Inhale through your nose and exhale slowly through your mouth, imagining tension in your chest or stomach softening and leaving with each exhale.
4. Switch arms and repeat. Continue for three to five minutes, or until you feel more settled.

WHY THIS HELPS

Pericardium 6, or Nei Guan, is a calming point on the inside of the forearm. It can soothe the heart, settle anxiety, ease nausea, and open the gate between heart and mind.[16] Activating this calming point is helpful when emotions feel overwhelming or when you need grounding, and this simple practice helps regulate the nervous system, calm emotional intensity, and create an embodied sense of peace. You can do it discreetly any time of day or in bed if you're having trouble sleeping.

Exercise: Positive Appreciation Reflection Before Bed

1. Lie comfortably and place one hand on your heart and one on your belly. Take three slow breaths, softening with each exhale.
2. Think of three moments from your day that you appreciate—small things, such as a kind glance, a warm cup of tea, or finishing a task.
3. For each moment, pause and notice how it feels in your body. Let the warmth of appreciation spread through your chest or face.
4. Stay with that feeling for a few breaths, letting it be the final note of your day.
5. Optionally, repeat quietly, *I am grateful. I am enough. I can rest now.*

WHY THIS HELPS

In grief, gratitude can sometimes feel like too much to ask. The pressure to be grateful can turn into a subtle demand that makes you suppress or bypass your pain. This practice shifts the focus from forced gratitude to gentle appreciation. It creates space to hold both grief and gratitude together, without one canceling the other. By noticing the smallest moments—a kind glance, a stranger's kindness, a warm cup of tea—you nurture a quiet balance. These little reflections soften the heart, reminding you that even in sorrow, small lights of care and connection are still present. This gentle nightly ritual also signals to the nervous system that it's safe to rest, creating a bridge between wakefulness and sleep.[17]

Exercise: Yoga Nidra at Home

Yoga Nidra is a guided meditation practice meant to encourage a state of deep relaxation. Choose a Yoga Nidra recording through a meditation app or video streaming service (sessions usually last twenty to forty minutes).

1. Find a quiet place to lie down—a mat, blanket, or bed works well. Add a pillow under your knees or head if needed. Dim the lights and make the space comfortable.
2. Lie on your back with your arms by your sides, palms up. Close your eyes, take a few slow breaths, and let your body soften into the surface beneath you.
3. Allow yourself to drift. You may fall asleep or stay in a dreamlike state—either is fine. Let the guidance carry you.
4. When the session ends, take a few deep breaths. Wiggle your fingers and toes, roll to one side, and slowly sit up. Notice how you feel.

WHY THIS HELPS

Yoga Nidra, or yogic sleep, is a guided meditation that invites deep physical, mental, and emotional rest while keeping a trace of awareness. It works by shifting brain waves from active beta states toward slower alpha and theta states—those associated with calm and repair. This practice balances the nervous system, reduces cortisol, and supports healing from fatigue, anxiety, and insomnia.[18] In grief, Yoga Nidra offers a way to rest without effort, helping the body recover energy and the heart find ease. Even twenty minutes can feel as restorative as hours of rest.

Summary

Let sleep be tender. When it feels far away, remind yourself that your body is carrying grief and doing its best to protect you through the night. Welcome gentleness into your evenings—dim the lights, slow your breath, and treat rest as an offering, not an obligation. Begin each morning with light and movement, small gestures that remind your body that rhythm and safety still exist. Trust the pace of your healing. Even brief moments of ease are signs that rest is returning.

Sleep is not something to master but something to be met with kindness. Your body remembers how to rest; it only asks for patience as it relearns the way.

9

Tending Digestion

During one of my busy inpatient shifts as a hospital chaplain, I stepped into the room of a young woman admitted after a devastating car accident. Her mother, Janelle, was at her bedside, waiting for her daughter to wake. Janelle had barely left the room except for a quick trip to the cafeteria. Quiet signs of vigil sat around her, such as a half-eaten bag of chips, candy wrappers, a cafeteria tray. The choices were limited. Her energy was limited too. She didn't want to miss a single update that might hint at what the next days would bring.

For the first few visits, we mostly sat in silence. In time, stories began to surface. She reflected on her daughter's light, the way she showed up for friends, her generous spirit, and the growing dream of becoming a nurse after watching nurses care for her grandfather through metastatic lung cancer. Beneath the stories were layers of grief and the shock of sudden change, an uncertain future, and milestones that might never arrive.

Janelle's daughter had suffered a serious brain injury. It wasn't expected to take her life, but it would significantly change its course. The road ahead would be long and uncertain, asking for patience, resilience, and courage. It would also bring unexpected expenses and lost income. Hopes and plans shifted hour by hour.

By day five, the staff could see the strain on Janelle's body. She slept in a chair. Meals were whatever she could quickly grab, such as fries, burgers, and chips. Someone wondered if another family member could bring food or sit with her daughter so Janelle could tend to herself. That wasn't possible. The accident happened an hour from home. Money for gas was tight. There was no nearby support to lean on. Staying put was the best she could do.

That afternoon Janelle developed severe abdominal pain and cramping. The nurses urged her to visit the ER. After a night of tests, she was discharged. The pain was deemed "stress-related," not an acute emergency. But her body was speaking. The gut, which is sensitive to nourishment and emotion alike, had become a portal for her grief and exhaustion. She could not eat well. She could not rest. Her health began to echo the sorrow she was holding.

As a clinician trained in Traditional Chinese Medicine (TCM), I often lamented the choices available in hospitals, especially when it comes to food. The place we turn to as a beacon of health only seems to offer food that inflames a body already under strain. I noticed how Janelle sat with her arms crossed, palms pressing lightly into her abdomen, an unconscious attempt to soothe a stomach in knots.

During her child's long hospital stay, Janelle ate fries and quick burgers most days. *At least I'm eating something,* she told herself. The salt and grease dulled her nerves for a moment. Over time she noticed more cramping, restless sleep, and a heaviness she could not shake. The food filled her stomach but left her more depleted.

Two weeks later, a neighbor drove up with a thermos of homemade chicken soup and a loaf of bread. Janelle told me later that the first spoonful brought her to tears because it reminded her that she wasn't alone. That night she slept a little more deeply, and her stomach pain eased.

Moments like these reveal a deeper truth about grief and digestion: Nourishment is about more than food. After loss, the body struggles to take in and metabolize life—food, emotion, even kindness. Digestion becomes a mirror for how we receive the world. When care and connection return, something inside begins to soften. The body remembers that being fed is also a way of being held.

As a side note, it was stories like Janelle's that led a team of nurses, physicians, and our chaplaincy team to build a fund that supports families displaced from their homes by major, life-altering experiences. By providing financial and material support, we hoped to offer dignity and compassionate care for those who were holding vigil for their loved one.

How the Gut Speaks Grief

Grief lives in the body as much as in the heart. Even when the loss is invisible, it can settle deep in the gut—the body's emotional center. Many people find themselves unable to eat or eating too much; feeling nauseated, tight, or hollow. This is the body trying to metabolize what the mind can't yet name. How we speak about this is revealing. We speak of being gut-wrenched, punched in the gut, tied in knots, hollow inside. These phrases are evidence of how grief moves through the same systems that digest our food and feelings.

Clinical research links grief and chronic stress with nausea, appetite changes, bloating, diarrhea, and constipation.[1] Stress physiology activated through the sympathetic fight-or-flight system can alter gut motility, secretion, sensitivity, microbial balance, and intestinal permeability.[2] In simple terms, your body may literally struggle to "digest life" when grief is present. Hunger cues may vanish or you may eat compulsively. Comfort foods may soothe for a moment but ultimately leave you feeling heavier. Further research is needed to explore "grief gut" and the ways grieving impacts digestive and microbial function.

There's a two-way street between food and mood. Highly processed foods and refined sugars can spike and crash blood sugar, stressing the stress-hormone system and worsening irritability, fatigue, and mood swings.[3] Diets that disrupt the gut microbiome can fuel inflammation that maps onto depressive symptoms and grief fog, while fiber-rich, anti-inflammatory patterns support steadier emotions.[4]

As a person who loves to eat his feelings, I understand how quickly sugar calls my name. The impulse is immediate. When the emotional waves rise, my mind knows it wants comfort and my body reaches for the fastest source it knows. Sugar is quick. Sugar is predictable. Sugar gives that brief sense of relief that feels like a soft landing in the middle of emotional turbulence. Even when I know it will not feel good in the long term, the pull still makes sense. It is not a failure. It is a coping mechanism. We're often taught to eat our feelings and to swallow back emotions. It is my body trying to soothe itself the only way it learned in moments of overwhelm.

And do not get me started on pizza. As soon as my wife says the "*p* word," it is as if something in me decides immediately that this hunger must be satisfied. Besides sugar, pizza is my go-to. The salt, the cheese, the warm bread, the first bite that feels like a hug from the inside. Sometimes I genuinely wonder why pizza is not considered to be its own food group and why something that tastes so comforting can make me feel so miserable afterward. These cravings are not about weakness or lack of will. They are about the body trying to find a quick path out of emotional intensity. Food becomes a bridge when emotions feel too heavy to bear.

When you are already carrying sadness, overwhelm, or exhaustion, food choices can either steady you or quietly intensify the burden. Reaching for something quick and comforting is completely understandable, especially when you feel too drained to cook and when cravings hit hard. This is one of the catch-22s of grief. The foods that feel amazing going down, that offer a brief moment of pleasure or relief, often end up amplifying the very fatigue, irritability, or emotional heaviness you are trying to escape. It is not about blame or perfection. It is simply recognizing that grief is sensitive, and the way we eat can either soothe the system or make the emotional burden a little heavier. Awareness gives you more choice, more gentleness, and more care for the body that is already carrying so much.

The conversation about grief and the gut is really a conversation about nourishment—not only the nourishment of food but life itself. The sweetness of cozy connections. The warmth of a listening ear. The freshness of friendships that remind you who you are. Grief often aches for this kind of nourishment. And the body, in its own way, seeks it too.

Food can become part of that care when the choices are small, gentle, and supportive. A warm soup that settles the stomach. Fresh fruit that brings a quiet brightness. Whole grains that steady the system and give the nervous system a little more room to breathe. These simple offerings help restore balance at a time when your inner world feels unsteady.

Instead of reaching for chips, you might try roasted sweet potatoes with olive oil and a touch of sea salt. Swap soda for warm ginger tea with honey. Replace a fast-food meal with rotisserie chicken, frozen vegetables, and rice. None of this is about perfection. It is about kindness and recognizing your body as an ally in your grieving journey. These small, loving swaps help the gut feel steadier and remind your body that nourishment can be both comforting and gentle, even in the midst of grief.

The Body as Witness

When Anne received the phone call about her brother's sudden death, her first response was a wave of nausea so strong she had to sit on the floor, hands at her belly. Her gut reacted before her mind could make sense of the words. The body often knows first.

Long before modern physiology gave us language for the connection between the brain and the gut, the gut was viewed as a seat of intuition and emotion—a measure of what you literally can or cannot stomach. In Ayurveda and TCM, digestion includes not only food but experience. Unassimilated grief might show up as bloating, fullness, or constipation, or as loose stools and acid.[5] In Ayurveda, the digestive fire, agni, metabolizes both nutrients and impressions. Supporting agni during grief can help the body digest what the heart cannot yet name.

Modern research continues to map these intuitions. Your gut contains hundreds of millions of neurons—more than the spinal cord. It is often called your "second brain."[6] This system sends signals that shape mood, immunity, and emotional life.[7]

The gut-brain axis is an ongoing conversation between the central nervous system, the enteric nervous system (i.e., the gastrointestinal tract), the immune system, and the microbiome that lives within you.[8] When stress or grief strikes, the hypothalamic-pituitary-adrenal (HPA) axis releases hormones such as cortisol and adrenaline. These chemical messengers can speed up or slow down digestion, shift the balance of gut microbes, and weaken the protective lining of the intestines.[9] In seasons of bereavement, these same pathways are stirred, and the result can be an undercurrent of inflammation that mirrors the inner fire of sorrow.[10]

In TCM, the lungs and large intestine are paired organ systems.[11] The lungs hold grief; the large intestine lets go. When your grief is suppressed, you may see constipation or diarrhea. If the large intestine is weak, the lungs may struggle, and sadness deepens. Modern science echoes this. Researchers describe a "gut-lung axis," showing how intestinal health affects breathing and immunity.[12]

What this means for your grieving body is that sorrow reverberates through the gut, shaping how you digest food and even how you digest experience. The very system that nourishes life becomes a mirror for how we experience loss.

Even when grief is held quietly, its energy migrates into the body. Prolonged sympathetic arousal and reduced vagal tone can impair digestive regulation.[13] Symptoms may follow, such as discomfort in your bowels, skin issues, weight changes, or sleep disruption. The gut becomes an expression of feelings that are hard to put into words.

When you "swallow your emotions," your body has to carry what your heart never had the chance to express. This is not just a metaphor. The gut is intimately connected to the emotional centers of the brain. When feelings are held in, braced against, or pushed down, the digestive system absorbs the overflow. The stomach tightens, the intestines slow, the diaphragm constricts, and the whole system begins working overtime. It becomes a kind of indigestion or an emotional constipation.

Swallowing emotions often comes from necessity. You may have learned to be strong, to keep peace, to put on a brave face, or to hold yourself together for others. In grief especially, you may swallow tears, grief responses, anger, or words you are not ready to speak. But the body does not ignore what is held back. The gut will store, carry, and become one of the first places to bear that weight. The result is heaviness, lethargy, indigestion, emotional fog, and a sense of fatigue that feels deeper than tiredness.

Allowing yourself to feel, express, and release emotions invites the gut to rest. When you let your body be an ally rather than a container for unspoken feelings, your digestion settles. Your breath deepens. Your nervous system shifts out of vigilance. And your emotional landscape becomes easier to navigate.

Supporting the gut through nourishment is part of this healing. Warm and simple foods, gentle herbs, hydration, and small acts of care help your system digest not only what you eat but also what you feel. Nourishing the gut provides steadiness for your body, clarity for your mind, and a softer place for your emotions to land as you move through grief.

TECHNIQUES FOR WORKING WITH DIGESTION

Breath Practice: Kapalabhati Breathing (Skull-Shining Breath)

1. Sit comfortably with your spine tall. Rest your hands on your knees or belly.
2. Take a deep inhale through your nose.
3. Exhale sharply through your nose by sharply contracting your belly inward. Allow the inhale to happen passively as your belly relaxes.
4. Begin slowly with a round of twenty to thirty exhales, then pause and breathe normally.
5. Rest for a few breaths before starting another round. Beginners may do two or three rounds.

WHY THIS HELPS

Kapalabhati is a yogic breathing practice made up of short, forceful exhalations followed by passive inhalations. It initially activates the system but is followed by a relaxation response. The practice is known for clearing the mind, energizing the body, and awakening the digestive fire, or agni. The rhythmic pumping of the belly massages the stomach, intestines, and abdominal organs, stimulating circulation and motility. It strengthens the diaphragm and abdominal wall, improving tone in the digestive tract. It also helps release tension in the solar plexus region, where stress often blocks digestion. The cleansing quality of sharp exhalations helps expel stagnant air and toxins, creating more space for fresh energy and vitality.[14]

Kapalabhati is energizing and best practiced in the morning on an empty stomach. Avoid it if you are pregnant, have uncontrolled high blood pressure, or experience dizziness.

Exercise: Abdominal Massage for Digestive Regulation

1. **Warm your belly.** Begin by making loose fists and gently massaging around your belly button. Circle above, below, and to the sides. Then expand the massage to cover your whole belly, following the path of the large intestine: up the right side toward your ribs, across the bottom of your rib cage, and down the left side into your lower abdomen.

   Repeat this spiral or circle a few times, breathing deeply as you move.
2. **Apply acupressure with your fingertips.** Curl your hands slightly and use your fingertips to gently press and hold the following points. Breathe slowly and evenly at each point for thirty to sixty seconds:

   - Stomach 25 (ST-25): About two finger-widths to either side of your belly button. These points regulate digestion and relieve abdominal tension.
   - Ren 6 (Sea of Qi): About one and a half inches below your belly button, on the midline. Supports energy, vitality, and elimination.
   - Ren 10: About two inches above your belly button, on the midline. Helps stimulate stomach function and relieve bloating.
   - Spleen 15 (SP-15): About three to four finger-widths to either side of your belly button. Supports the intestines and helps release stagnation.
   - Ren 4 (Gate of Origin): About three inches below your belly button, on the midline. Nourishes your body's reserves and supports emotional release.

- Ren 12 (Middle of the Stomach): About four inches above your belly button, on the midline. A key point for harmonizing the stomach and calming digestion.

3. **Integrate.** After pressing each point, rest your hands gently on your belly. Take several slow breaths, imagining warmth and light filling the abdomen. Feel both physical digestion and emotional letting go being supported with each exhale.

WHY THIS HELPS

This meditation supports both physical digestion and the emotional digestion needed in grief. By gently massaging and stimulating key acupressure points around your belly, you help regulate energy flow, ease tension, and encourage the release of what no longer serves you.[15] Physically, this practice can ease discomfort and improve circulation in the belly. Emotionally, it supports the release of grief, shame, or heaviness that often collects in the gut, making space for renewal.

Exercise: Digesting Grief—Naming and Telling Your Losses

1. **Name your losses.** Take a piece of paper or open your journal. At the top, write "Losses I've carried but never named." Let your words flow freely. Write down whatever comes, whether big or small, recent or long ago, from childhood or adulthood. There is no need to explain or justify. Simply let the page hold what you have carried.
2. **Craft your grief story.** Once you've named your losses, begin shaping them into a story. Write your grief story as you have lived it, focusing on the experiences of loss, not just on the positives that may have come later. Allow the story to be raw and real, acknowledging the heartbreaks that have shaped your journey.

Your grief story can take many forms: poetry, personal narrative, memoir, or simple journaling. Whatever feels natural, allow it to carry meaning and purpose.

3. **Share and witness.** If possible, share your story with a trusted friend, companion, or listener who can hold sacred space, anyone can who listens without interruption or judgment. Speaking your grief aloud transforms silent suffering into witnessed truth.
4. **Integration.** As you tell and shape your story, notice how it feels to move from silence into expression. This process allows you to release through naming and to cultivate a new relationship with yourself, your losses, and the meaning they now hold in your life.

WHY THIS HELPS

This practice invites you to digest grief through naming your losses and shaping them into a narrative (see page 38 for a list of losses). Digesting grief is not about forgetting or fixing but rather making space for what has been carried silently. Naming losses validates their reality, while storytelling integrates them into the larger arc of your life. Research on narrative therapy shows that giving voice to grief helps people process emotions, reconstruct identity, and create meaning in the face of change.[16] This practice transforms grief from a hidden burden into a recognized part of your story, one that can be honored and digested with compassion.

Recipe: Kitchari to Ease Digestion

Serves 4

Ingredients

- 1 cup split yellow mung dal, washed and soaked for 1–2 hours if possible
- ½ cup basmati rice, washed
- 2 tablespoons ghee (or coconut oil for vegan option)
- 1 teaspoon cumin seeds

- 1 teaspoon mustard seeds
- 1 teaspoon ground turmeric
- 1 teaspoon ground coriander
- 1 teaspoon ground cumin
- ½ teaspoon ground or fresh grated ginger
- ½ teaspoon ground cinnamon (optional for warmth)
- 6 cups water or vegetable broth
- 1 teaspoon salt, or to taste
- 2–3 cups seasonal vegetables, chopped (carrots, zucchini, spinach, green beans, sweet potato, or whatever is available)
- Fresh cilantro, for garnish
- Lemon or lime wedges, to serve

Instructions

1. **Rinse the grains.** Wash the mung dal and rice until the water runs clear. If soaked, drain before cooking.
2. **Toast the spices.** In a large pot, warm the ghee over medium heat. Add the cumin seeds and the mustard seeds until they pop. Stir in the turmeric, coriander, cumin, ginger, and cinnamon. Let the spices bloom for 30 seconds.
3. **Add the grains.** Stir in the mung dal and rice, coating them in the spices.
4. **Add the liquid.** Pour in the water or broth, add the salt, and bring to a boil. Reduce to a gentle simmer, partially cover, and cook for 20 minutes.
5. **Add the vegetables.** Stir in the chopped vegetables and continue cooking until everything is soft, about another 15–20 minutes. Add more water if you want a soupier consistency.
6. **Finish.** Adjust the seasoning, then remove from heat. Garnish with fresh cilantro and serve with lemon or lime wedges.

WHY THIS HELPS

In Ayurveda, kitchari is considered a healing food because it's simple, nourishing, and easy to digest. It balances the body by giving the digestive system a rest while providing complete nutrition.[17] The combination of mung dal and rice is gentle on the stomach and helps soothe digestive discomfort while providing essential proteins, carbohydrates, and fats in a light, easily assimilated form. It supports the body's natural cleansing processes without depletion and can be made light and soupy for cleansing or thicker and heartier for comfort and grounding. Warm, soft foods such as kitchari also help regulate the nervous system, offering calm and comfort during stress or grief. For this reason, it's often prepared during times of transition, recovery, or emotional intensity—giving the body what it needs most: nourishment, simplicity, and balance.

Summary

Eat in ways that support your healing. Choose warm, simple meals that are easy to digest and remind your body that nourishment can be an act of care. Notice how grief expresses in your gut. Sensations such as cramping, nausea, bloating, or loss of appetite can signal that your body is processing what may be hard to feel. The gut responds to loss as well. Listen to your body. Pay attention to cravings and notice how your emotional state may mirror your digestion. Choose foods and rhythms that steady rather than deplete.

Remember that nourishment includes connection: Being fed by love, presence, and small kindnesses restores more than energy—it restores belonging.

Your body is already working to digest what your heart might not yet have named. Meet it with tenderness; part of healing is remembering that to be fed is also to be held, and gut nourishment is one way you can let love move through you.

10

Working Through Anger

RACHEL CAME IN TIRED, but not the kind of tired that sleep could fix.

"They keep saying we're burnt out. I don't think I'm burned out," she said. "I think I'm angry." She reflected on a leadership meeting titled "Managing Physician Burnout for Better Outcomes." Her voice was steady, but her hands told a different story, fingers tightening and releasing as if something inside of her were trying to find its way out.

A physician in a large hospital system, she was brilliant, devoted, the kind of doctor who stayed a few extra minutes because she knew those minutes mattered. But over time, those minutes had been taken from her. Appointments shortened. Documentation expanded. Decisions filtered through layers of policy. Days ended with charting long past her shift. "I know what my patients need," she asserted, "and I can't give it to them." Her jaw tightened.

Outside of work, her life was unraveling. A recent divorce had reshaped everything she thought her life would be. "I feel like I'm failing everywhere," she admitted. We sat with that.

As she spoke, her breath became shallow. Her words came quicker, sharper: "This isn't why I became a doctor." Her hands clenched. I invited her to notice what was happening in her body: the tightness in her chest, the pressure behind her eyes. She closed her eyes. "It feels like something is building," she said, "like it wants to break through."

We stayed there, gently. Not pushing it away, just listening. After a few moments, her voice softened. "It's not just anger," she voiced. "It's . . .

something else." There was a long silence. Then, almost in a whisper, "It's grief."

She began to name it: grief for the kind of medicine she thought she would practice; grief for her patients, who deserved more than the system allowed; grief for the life she had imagined, now changed in ways she did not choose. "I've been sitting with my anger," she said, "but I didn't realize what it was holding." I shared with her the words of C. S. Lewis: "I sat with my anger long enough until she told me her name was grief." Her breath deepened. The anger did not disappear, but it changed. It became less sharp, less isolating. It began to feel like something protecting what mattered.

Recognizing this, she began to shift. Instead of abandoning her anger, she let it inform her. She started having more honest conversations at work and advocating in small, steady ways. And with herself, she softened. "I think I've been expecting myself to just move on," she said. But grief does not move on like that; it asks to be felt. She took a deeper breath, her shoulders lowering. "I care," she said. "That's what this is." Yes. That's what this is.

Like every emotion, anger is a normal and natural response. Yet it often carries a heavy stigma—it is often seen as dangerous, shameful, or unspiritual. From the perspective of your mind and body, anger is an ancient survival signal. It is your system's way of declaring, *Something essential has been blocked. Something is not right.*[1] Anger can arise in several ways: as a response to bodily distress, as protection in the face of threat, or as protest when desires are blocked and frustration builds. In grief, these pathways converge. Your body feels the ache of loss, your heart registers the threat of separation, and your mind collides with the impossibility of reaching for what is gone. Anger reflects activation of ancient circuits designed to preserve life when confronted with inescapable change.[2]

Paradoxically, in grief, the "enemy" is not external. You cannot fight the inevitability of death or loss, so anger often feels confusing and subtle. It can shift into irritability, blame, resentment, or even self-punishment.

From a somatic perspective, your experience of anger is not just metaphorical. You might notice it as heat or pressure in your body, as interoceptive circuits translate heightened arousal into alarm.[3] When anger arises, your heart rate variability—a marker of nervous system flexibility—often shifts, leaving you less resilient.[4]

In Traditional Chinese Medicine (TCM), anger belongs to the liver system. When your liver qi flows freely, emotions move smoothly through your body. When you suppress anger, qi becomes stagnant and you may notice increased irritability, frustration, or explosive outbursts.[5] In Ayurveda, anger is linked to excess pitta, the fire element, which can burn hot in both mind and body.[6] If you ignore this, the fire can scorch you from within and drain your energy.

In this chapter we'll explore four common forms of anger that can accompany grief:

1. anger from internal pressure (liver qi stagnation)
2. anger from exhaustion (liver yin deficiency)
3. hot anger that is rage (excess fire)
4. cold anger that turns inward (suppressed anger)

Each has its own physiology, its own way of showing up in your body, and its own invitation toward healing.

Anger from Internal Pressure: Liver Qi Stagnation

Anger is one of the few emotions that's openly displayed in our Western culture. From sports to media, explosive anger often seems normal, while the subtler feelings beneath it are overlooked. In reality, anger frequently functions as a mask for deeper emotions—such as sadness, fear, or shame—that may feel unsafe to express. Our emotions are layered, and when we ignore those layers, anger can build up like steam in a pressure cooker without a vent.

From a TCM perspective, this pattern reflects liver qi stagnation. The liver keeps your qi—your vital energy—moving smoothly throughout the body, and it plays a role in emotional regulation. When you suppress your emotions, qi can get stuck. Over time, this stagnation can look a lot like the stress response: muscle tension, shallow breathing, headaches, digestive upset, and a feeling of being trapped.[7] Your body becomes a pressure cooker for unexpressed feelings.

This kind of anger often looks like irritability, frustration, or a quick temper. Sometimes it is directed at people closest to you; other times, it turns inward as harsh self-talk or perfectionism. You might feel immense pressure to handle everything yourself and carry the burdens of life alone. The effort it takes to hold back other emotions can generate internal heat that further fuels your anger.

A father who lost his job after thirty years once told me, "I don't know why I snap at my kids so much. I love them, but I yell over the smallest things." His anger was not about his children. It was the grief of losing his job, his identity, his financial security, and his sense of purpose. When he finally allowed himself to cry over the job loss, the eruptions happened less frequently.

The invitation here is to practice emotional honesty. If your anger is agitation covering up sadness or shame, "anger release" techniques may not work. What you really need is a safe space to name your losses, express the hidden emotions, and let your body release what it's been holding. In TCM, this is unblocking the liver qi—restoring flow so you're no longer suppressing your stuck emotions.[8]

Anger from Exhaustion: Liver Yin Deficiency

This kind of anger often shows up when your inner reserves are depleted. It might feel like annoyance, edginess, or restlessness. Suddenly little things seem huge. You're exhausted, but sleep becomes difficult. Your body is tired, yet your mind won't settle. You may find yourself doomscrolling, binge-watching shows, or staying busy because slowing down feels intolerable. Beneath the surface is a nervous system stretched thin and begging for rest.

In TCM, this state reflects liver yin deficiency. Yin comprises the cooling, nourishing, restorative forces in your body. Chronic stress, sleeplessness, caregiving, or overwork can deplete yin energy, causing the liver to lose its ability to anchor the body's natural heat. Without that cooling balance, yang rises unchecked, leading to agitation, irritability, and reactivity.

You might also notice insomnia, dry mouth, dizziness, or tension headaches.[9] This anger doesn't come from too much energy. It's your body's way of signaling that reserves are running dangerously low.

A mother caring for her terminally ill son once confided to me, "I get mad so easily. My sister is helping, but I blow up about how she loads the dishwasher." This was not rage—it was exhaustion. Months of hospital life had left her hypervigilant. Her anger was her body's cry for restoration. As a chaplain, I recognized the pattern and worked with the care team to give her breaks. Even small steps such as these resulted in large changes. Her agitation softened, and she was able to be more present with her son in such a sad time.

Patterns of angry exhaustion are fueled by staying busy. We set unrealistic expectations for ourselves, hope others will read our minds, and snap at those closest to us. We keep working or caring because stopping feels like falling apart. Headaches, migraines, or digestive upset often accompany this form of anger. Sometimes people turn to alcohol or other depressants to take the edge off and dull the fire, but the underlying depletion remains.

What is needed is rest—deep rest and a reset. Hydration, quiet, and restorative practices such as gentle yoga, craniosacral therapy, or energy work can help rebuild your reserves. The paradox is that slowing down can make your grief more visible, and staying busy can feel safer than facing helplessness. That's completely normal. Awareness is the first step. Support groups, grief coaching, and grief resources can help you feel less alone and create the safety you need to rest. In TCM, restoring liver yin replenishes your cooling, stabilizing energy so the heat of irritability can be anchored again.[10]

Hot Anger: Excess Fire

Sometimes anger is just anger—pure heat. When grief corners you, you might not freeze or flee. You might fight. This kind of hot anger can feel like raw protest against injustice or loss. It might be directed at God, fate, or the sheer unfairness of life. Sometimes it's a cry for truth and safety.

In TCM, this reflects excess fire in the liver system. If qi stagnation or yin deficiency are not resolved, heat builds up and transforms into fire. This fire can blaze upward, showing up as a flushed face, red eyes, a pounding headache, high blood pressure, or sudden and explosive outbursts.[11] Unlike the simmering irritability of stagnation or the edgy depletion of yin deficiency, excess fire erupts with force and immediacy. It is rage that is raw, consuming, and hard to contain.

A widow once screamed in session, "Why did God take him and not me? How could life be so cruel?" She did not need to be calmed—she needed validation that her fury was sacred, that it was an expression of love as much as sorrow. In time, she channeled that fire into advocacy for widows instead of suppressing the anger she felt.

An activist told me, "Every time I see another headline about racial injustice, I feel my chest explode." Her grief fueled organizing protests, community vigils, and advocacy. In her case, rage became fuel for justice. This is the paradox of fire: It can destroy but it can also purify.

At the same time, it's important to find safe and constructive ways to release this fire. Surges of anger can raise your cardiovascular risk in the short term, especially in the two hours after an outburst.[12] Studies show that even recalling anger can temporarily impair vascular function, which is one way unchecked rage can affect your heart.[13]

If your grief shows up as hot anger, safe expression is essential. Break-it rooms, martial arts, boxing, or vigorous exercise can help move this energy through your body. Practices such as exhale-focused breathwork and heart rate variability biofeedback can calm an aroused nervous system and help the body recover more quickly after anger spikes.[14] When you acknowledge and channel this energy wisely, it can become a catalyst for justice and transformation. When denied or suppressed, it can consume your body from within.

Cold Anger: Suppressed Anger Turning Inward

Not all anger erupts outward. Sometimes it turns inward and becomes cold. This is the kind of anger that's been buried or denied for so long it transforms into resentment and bitterness. Instead of exploding, it constricts.

Many of us learned early on that anger was unsafe. If you grew up with an alcoholic parent or in a violent home, anger may have felt terrifying. To survive, you pushed it down. Over time, that suppression can calcify into cold anger. On the surface, it may look like detachment or indifference, but underneath is a quiet corrosion that isolates you and hardens your heart.

In TCM, long-term suppression and unresolved heat can damage your yin and qi and lead to stagnation. Your energy no longer flows freely. Residual heat from old anger can burn out your reserves and leave you feeling constricted.[15] Instead of erupting outward, the anger freezes inside and may show up as digestive issues, chronic fatigue, cold hands and feet, or emotional numbness.

One client told me quietly, "I don't really get angry. I just shut people out." She had grown up in a violent household and buried her feelings so deeply that her anger resurfaced as withdrawal and bitterness. What she needed most was gentleness, warmth, and the reminder that she was not her parent—and that her feelings didn't make her dangerous.

Another woman, after a devastating divorce, insisted, "I'm fine, really. I just don't care anymore." On the surface, she seemed composed, but her jaw tightened and her lip quivered. Her body told the truth—she was holding everything in. This was cold anger, and it needed a different kind of support.

Working with cold anger is different from working with rage. It can't be forced open. It needs compassion, patience, and someone who can simply listen. People caught in this pattern often use their intellect to override their emotions. They might be therapists, lawyers, or physicians—skilled at analysis but with feelings locked away. Healing requires warmth, safety, and validation. In TCM, this is the slow work of thawing stagnation and restoring flow.[16]

Cold anger often manifests as grudges, withdrawal, or trouble receiving love. It can create defensive walls or codependent cycles and also weaken your immune system under chronic stress.[17] The work here isn't to unleash fire but to bring gentle warmth. Safety, compassion, and a nonjudgmental listener can create the conditions for thawing what has been frozen.

Every form of anger in grief is asking for relationship. Whether hot or cold, anger isn't here to destroy you—it's here to be heard. Even cold anger, once thawed, points you back to the truth that beneath resentment and hardness are love, longing, and the desire for connection.

TECHNIQUES FOR WORKING WITH ANGER

Any of the practices listed here can support you when anger arises, though some will be especially helpful for specific expressions of anger. I will note which practices best serve each type so you can choose what feels right for your experience.

Exercise: Deep Release to Discharge Anger

For any type of anger. Most effective for hot anger and anger from internal pressure.

1. Stand with your feet straight and shoulder-width apart. Relax and prepare yourself for the exercise.
2. Initiate the movement. Using the power of your legs to generate movement in your arms, raise your arms up over your head.
3. Release the energy. Powerfully swing your arms down toward the ground as if throwing the excess energy into the earth. Let your arms fly behind you naturally and use the power in your legs to bring your arms back up. Continue swinging your arms rhythmically. Inhale as you raise your arms, and exhale as you swing them down.
4. Maintain the rhythm. Bounce slightly with your legs and swing your arms up and down. Use your breath to release tension with each downward swing.
5. Keep movements controlled and safe. Remember that anger is natural and this practice might release stored energy.
6. Practice for several repetitions or for up to one minute. Aim for a deep sense of release.
7. Relaxation and integration: Afterward, lie down on a soft couch or the ground. Take deep breaths and allow your body to integrate the discharge.

WHY THIS HELPS

A deep release helps discharge the intense energy of anger so that it does not stay trapped in your body. By giving anger safe expression, your nervous system completes its stress cycle, softening any tension in the body and opening the space for clarity and healing.[18]

Exercise: Standing Twists for Releasing Stagnant Energy

For any type of anger. Most effective for anger from internal pressure.

1. Stand with your feet shoulder-width apart. Soften your knees and relax your shoulders.
2. Twist from the waist and hips. Rotate to one side, letting one hand extend behind you while the other swings forward.
3. Return to center on an inhale.
4. Exhale and twist in the opposite direction.
5. Continue a relaxed, rhythmic flow without forcing, allowing your arms to swing gently around you.

WHY THIS HELPS

Standing twists coordinate breath and movement, helping your body discharge the heat and muscular tension of anger. In TCM, anger is often linked to liver qi stagnation, and twisting movements support the liver channel by encouraging the smooth flow of qi through the torso. Research shows that yoga-based somatic practices such as this one can help improve emotional regulation, including managing anger, which supports the idea that mindful movement helps alleviate tension and restore balance.[19]

Breath Practice: Cooling Breath for Anger (Sitali Pranayama)

Effective for hot anger.

1. Sit or stand comfortably with a straight spine. Relax your shoulders and jaw.
2. Curl the sides of your tongue into a tube if possible. If not, purse your lips as if sipping through a straw.
3. Inhale slowly through the curled tongue or pursed lips, feeling the coolness of your breath reach your lower ribs and belly.
4. Close your mouth at the top of the inhale.
5. Exhale through your nose.
6. Repeat for ten slow breaths.

WHY THIS HELPS

Sitali Pranayama helps cool the body and mind, reducing the inner heat often stirred up by anger or emotional intensity. By drawing air across the curled tongue, you naturally lower agitation and soothe your nervous system. This breath supports both physical cooling and emotional balance, offering you a path to calm presence in moments of overwhelm.[20]

Writing Practice: Releasing Resentments

For any type of anger.

1. Prepare a safe, quiet space and set aside fifteen to twenty minutes for this exercise.
2. In a journal or on a piece of paper, write "I feel resentment toward . . ." and write freely, whatever comes to mind.

3. Give the resentment a voice: "I resent you because . . ."
4. Acknowledge the cost: "This resentment has cost me . . ."
5. Invite release: "What I long for instead is . . ."
6. As a closing ritual, read aloud what you wrote, then place the pages in water, bury them in the ground, or burn them in a safe fire. As you do, whisper, *I choose freedom.*

WHY THIS HELPS

Resentment is a heavy emotion that keeps us tied to the past and drains our energy in the present. Writing can help give form and voice to what you've been holding inside, allowing it to be seen instead of suppressed. By naming your resentment, acknowledging its impact, recognizing its cost, and creating a ritual of release around it, you begin to release its hold on you, transforming it into freedom and renewed vitality.[21]

Sensory Practice: Gaze upon Beauty

For any type of anger.

Find a place of natural beauty—a quiet park, a garden, a peaceful shore, or a woodland. Find something beautiful to rest your gaze on. Notice the colors, textures, and shapes. If there is a fragrance, breathe it in. Allow the beauty to soften you. In Ayurveda, anger is connected to the fire element and the sense of sight. Let what you see be an anchor that cools and steadies you.

WHY THIS HELPS

In Ayurveda, the eyes are the gateway to the pitta dosha, which governs metabolism, transformation, and the fire element in the body and mind. When anger or irritability builds, this inner fire can overheat the system, creating inflammation, tension, and restlessness. Softening your gaze on something beautiful redirects that fiery energy outward in a cooling, harmonizing way. It soothes the nervous system, steadies the emotions, and restores balance between inner fire and outer peace.[22]

Exercise: Channeling Anger into Service

For any type of anger.

When you channel your anger into meaningful action—whether by volunteering, raising awareness, or supporting a cause—you give intense emotion a new direction. Instead of letting anger simmer inside you or explode all over others, you turn it into compassionate effort. Many people who volunteer find that their empathy and sense of purpose grow stronger, particularly when their actions are tied to something that matters deeply to them. Consider choosing one small action this week—write a letter, plant a tree, cook for a neighbor, or join a local effort—that channels your conviction into service and reminds you of your capacity to create change.

WHY THIS HELPS

Brain imaging studies show that when you support others, your brain's stress centers—areas that light up with pain and distress—quiet down.[23] Your body's stress response eases, and you return to a more balanced state.[24] In other words, turning anger into service doesn't just ease feelings of helplessness; it also activates the parts of your brain and body that foster resilience, connection, and calm. By taking action, you can transform your anger into something that not only helps others but also heals you.

Summary

If your anger is pressure, look underneath. What sadness, fear, or shame is asking to be felt? If your anger is exhaustion, rest, restore, and replenish. If your anger is hot, channel it safely through movement, sound, and advocacy. If your anger is cold, surround it with compassion, warmth, and a listening ear.

Like every emotion, anger is not your enemy. It is a messenger of grief, pointing you back toward love.

11

Connecting with Sadness

"SADNESS" AND "A HEAVY ACHE IN MY CHEST" were the first words my client Meena used to describe her experience in our initial session. "It feels like a cord has been cut. There is a deep pain in my chest that makes it hard to breathe," she shared. That pain began after the death of her identical twin sister nearly five months earlier. In her words and presence, the sadness was palpable. The grief she carried was not only emotional but embodied, visceral, and undeniable.

Recognizing the intensity of her experience, we began with body-based practices as a foundation for her healing. Meena's doctor had already ruled out heart-related conditions, which allowed us to focus safely on the emotional and energetic layers of her grief.

Over the next several months, we met weekly, using breath and movement to ease the tension in her chest and create space for release. As Meena softened into the practice, she further opened up about her sister, the closeness they'd shared living near each other, and a circle of mutual friends that shaped their lives.

As grief unfolded, another layer emerged. The loss of Meena's sister stirred unresolved grief from earlier life, especially around family dynamics and her mother. From a young age, Meena had stepped into the role of the responsible one, often prioritizing others' needs over her own. This pattern shaped her relationships with both her mother and her sister. Her grief was not only about losing her twin. It was also about a life in which her own needs had not taken center stage.

In grieving her sister, Meena was also grieving the life she'd never had the chance to live.

The movement and breath practices offered a container to release this long-held sorrow. Her body began to shed the weight of years of emotional suppression, unlocking grief that had been quietly present for far longer than this recent loss.

As the first anniversary approached, we designed a healing ritual. Meena planned an international trip and joined a women's retreat, something out of character for her yet deeply aligned with what she needed. It was a bold act of self-honoring.

She returned with a profound insight: Sadness and grief would always be part of her life. Rather than a burden, this realization felt liberating. There was no need to rush toward resolution or wait for the pain to end. Without the pressure of a finish line, she could be present with her feelings, and presence allowed compassion instead of resistance.

In time, the sharpness in Meena's chest faded. The deep void softened. Through body-based grief work, she released the edginess and tightness that surrounded her grief, creating space to mourn and connect with her honest, raw feelings. She also felt a deeper relationship with her sister and her mother. Though both had died, those connections felt more available now than when they were alive. She came to see that letting go of pain was never about forgetting. It was about making room for love, memory, presence, and—most importantly—herself.

The Taboo of Tears

How often do you hear, "Don't cry," "Don't feel bad," "Everything's going to be all right," "Just take a deep breath"? Sadness and tears largely remain taboo in modern culture. The iconic line from the film *A League of Their Own*, "There's no crying in baseball," still echoes a broader cultural truth. Many spaces do not allow emotional expression. Even now, public displays of emotion are met with discomfort and stigma.

When you cry, you may instinctively cover your face, hide your tears, or feel ashamed to be seen. The tendency is to retreat and sob in solitude. You might isolate in a bedroom, hide in a bathroom, or hold your tears until late at night when no one will witness your undoing. Unlike other emotions, sadness shows on the outside. Sometimes we even call it the "ugly cry." Tears reveal sadness. They show the outward wounds of love.

There is pressure to suppress sadness, to keep up the appearance of composure, to stay strong. "I'm fine" becomes a reflex. Crying is often misjudged as a lack of willpower or proof that you've lost control or even dignity. You apologize, saying, "I'm sorry," as if your tears ruined the moment or lowered the energy in the room. You may even call yourself a Debbie Downer, a buzzkill, a killjoy, or a party pooper. Playful or not, words shape beliefs. These labels quietly shame sadness and train you to tuck grief out of sight to protect others' comfort.

After her mother died, Sarah cried only behind closed doors. One evening her eight-year-old asked, "Do you miss Nana?" Sarah nodded and, for the first time, allowed a few tears at the kitchen table. Her daughter reached for her hand and said, "I miss her too." That brief, honest moment became a family ritual of naming feelings before dinner. No one broke. Everyone softened. And it brought them together.

Parents sometimes hide tears to protect children. Yet children read nonverbal cues and are sensitive to caregivers' emotional states. Not witnessing healthy crying when grief is present can stunt emotional growth and create a taboo around feelings. Showing your grief helps normalize children's experience so that they grow into adults who welcome the movement of grief rather than perpetuating its suppression.

A Good Cry Shifts Your Energy

Tears are one of the body's most natural and intelligent ways of releasing sadness. Emotional tears have a distinctive biochemical profile compared to basal tears that lubricate the eye or reflex tears that respond to irritants.[1] Emotional tears, the kind that are shed when you're sad or moved, contain different patterns of substances such as prolactin, manganese, potassium, and serotonin.[2] In plain language, emotional tears help the body clear stress-related by-products while they moisten and protect the eye.

Even so, crying can feel hard. There is a surge of energy that feels uncomfortable. You may try to hold back tears and end up feeling more stressed. This pressure is not only emotional. Before and during crying, the body often shifts into sympathetic activation, the fight-or-flight response,[3] which brings a spike of emotional and physical arousal. As crying resolves, the parasympathetic system, the rest-and-recover mode, steps in to rebalance.[4] There is a built-in recovery that follows a good cry.

Crying out loud and voicing your cry can also activate the body's natural pain-relief chemistry. Vocal crying helps engage endogenous opioid pathways that ease part of the sting of sadness.[5] Crying is a self-soothing behavior supported by physiology, not a failure of willpower.[6] Suppressing tears disrupts this natural rebalancing.

Research shows the chronic inhibition of suppressing emotions is linked to greater risk for self-harm and suicidality,[7] weakening of immune function,[8] and decreased activity in brain networks involved in empathy and emotional intimacy.[9] Suppression contributes to disconnection, stress-related illness, and long-term isolation.

On her drives home, Heather, a nurse, shared with me that she plays the same three sad songs when ending a shift. She sings off-key, lets her throat open, and sobs in waves. She arrives home quieter. Her headaches are less frequent on those days, and she describes it as "emptying the cup before it spills." This is a powerful example of how the release of our emotions gives us space for clarity and compassion toward ourselves.

Sadness in the Chest: Heartache and Lung-ache

In addition to crying, sadness often shows up in the chest and throat. You may notice aching, heaviness, vague pressure, or a hollow sensation. Sometimes it feels sharp and precise. When grief is strong, breathing can feel difficult. In fact, it can be so powerful it can induce a physical condition known as "broken heart syndrome," or Takotsubo cardiomyopathy, which can mimic a heart attack. If you experience chest pain or unusual shortness of breath, seek medical care to rule out urgent conditions but know it might also be an energetic broken heart.[10]

What many call heartache can sometimes arise from the lungs as a kind of lung-ache. In Traditional Chinese Medicine (TCM), the lungs are the organ system most intimately affected by sadness and grief. Prolonged sorrow is said to disperse and deplete lung qi, leading to tightness or fullness in the chest.[11] Classical sources describe how emotional disruption can impair visceral lung function,[12] noting that "grief and sorrow disperse the qi of the lungs."[13]

With sadness, breath can become shallow or constricted. Some people hold their breath without noticing. Tension builds in the ribs, diaphragm, and chest. Because of this tightness, you might feel stuck, breathless, or numb. Although the lungs exchange gases, breathing is powered by the diaphragm, abdominal wall, and rib cage. The rib cage must expand for full respiration, yet under the weight of grief, it can become rigid—more like a cage than a flexible protector. That tightness restricts breath and reinforces the feeling of distress.

When you suppress your breath and your diaphragm can't expand, you impair the generation and distribution of qi. In TCM, qi governs processes such as circulation, digestion, immunity, and emotional balance.[14] When qi is depleted or blocked, you may notice chest emptiness or pressure, exhaustion, poor focus, memory slips, grief fog, emotional dullness, and low motivation. The patterns become clearer once you know where to look, which is something I often help clients recognize.

After her partner died, Tessa caught herself sighing all day. She worried it meant she was getting worse. I shared that many people sigh more frequently when they're sad; it's the body's way of trying to move lung qi and reset breathing depth. That simple reframe brought her relief. She began practicing slower exhales, and the tight band around her ribs softened within a week.

From this perspective, grief disrupts rhythm and flow. Breath-based practices are not only about oxygen. They reopen channels of life force, restore circulation, and invite presence and aliveness back into the body. Sadness is not a personal failure. It is a natural result of grief's impact on breath and body. When qi becomes blocked, vitality decreases. When qi flows, vitality increases.

Strengthening the lungs and regulating the breath helps restore heart coherence—the natural rhythm between breath, heartbeat, and emotion. From this steadiness you can meet grief without being overwhelmed, shifting from feeling small and powerless to feeling larger, steadier, and less ashamed when sadness arises. Letting go becomes letting flow.

The practices below ease the physiological impact of grief and support sadness in all its forms. They are not about fixing, bypassing, or erasing. They help grief breathe. If you experience chest pain, new shortness of breath, or symptoms that feel unusual, seek medical care promptly to rule out urgent conditions. Return to these practices when you are medically cleared.

TECHNIQUES FOR WORKING WITH SADNESS

Breath Practice: Pulse Breathing to Reestablish Qi Flow and Heart Coherence

1. **Open and round the chest.** Stand comfortably. Interlace your fingers with your palms facing you. Inhale and draw your hands toward your chest, expanding the ribs and gently opening the elbows. Exhale as you rotate your palms forward and extend your arms, rounding your back and softening your chest inward.

   Continue this flow. Inhale as your hands come in. Exhale as your hands press out. Keep the breath smooth and even for one to three minutes.
2. **Stretch skyward and close your elbows.** From standing, keep your fingers interlaced and turn your palms upward as you extend your arms toward the sky. Inhale, lengthen through your spine, and feel the expansion around the ribs. Exhale, bring your elbows toward each other, rotate your palms toward you, draw your hands toward your chest, round your back, and release your breath.

   Repeat the rhythm, inhaling to expand upward, exhaling to round inward. Continue for one to three minutes with smooth, fluid motion.

WHY THIS HELPS

These pulsed breathing movements support breath, rhythm, and movement, a foundational practice of qigong and mindful movement.[15] Expanding the chest on the inhale and softening it on the exhale helps the body's vital energy (qi) to circulate freely through the heart and lung meridians. The squeeze on the exhale forces the breath out, creating an opportunity for a fresh inhale to follow.

From a TCM perspective, this gentle opening and release balances emotional weight held around the chest and supports harmonious flow through the heart and lung channels. In modern physiology, paced breathing of this kind enhances heart rate variability, the marker of autonomic stability and emotional resilience, by strengthening vagal activity and promoting coherent heart rhythms.

Together, these exercises help release stored emotional tension held around the lungs. They increase flexibility through the chest and ribs, balance inhalation with exhalation, and support smoother breathing. Over time, this helps reestablish harmony between lungs and heart, supports heart coherence and vagal tone, and deepens the relaxation response.[16]

Exercise: Self-Hug When You're Feeling Overwhelmed by Sadness

1. Sit comfortably with a naturally upright spine.
2. Place each hand underneath the opposite armpit, forearms facing outward. Keep your thumbs separate from your fingers and rest them on your upper chest. This will put them near the lung meridian.
3. Squeeze your hands lightly and press your arms against them. You'll feel gentle tension beneath the armpits. This area corresponds with the beginning of the heart meridian and working with it can bring relief for the heart and emotions.
4. Lean slightly forward. Find a relaxed, steady breath. Notice any sense of containment or safety.

5. Remain in this position for a few minutes. Release and shake out your hands when complete.

WHY THIS HELPS

Sometimes a hug is exactly what we need when emotions feel overwhelming, and sometimes that hug can come from our own selves. Sometimes you feel tired and exhausted from crying and need a little reprieve, a pause from the immense tears or sadness. This simple act of self-soothing provides a form of self-care that helps release oxytocin, the body's natural "calm and connect" hormone. The hand position also activates both the heart and lung meridians. The thumbs rest near Lung 1, while the fingers press beneath the armpits at Heart 1. Engaging these points with a gentle self-hug calms the chest, supports circulation in the meridians, and offers relief when the heart feels heavy. This posture creates both physical spaciousness and emotional reprieve, reminding the body it is safe to soften, breathe, and rest.[17]

Breath Practice: Diaphragmatic Breathing

1. Place one hand over your belly button and the other hand on top of the first hand. Inhale into your belly as if inflating a balloon into your hands. Exhale gently. Repeat several rounds.
2. Slide your hands to the sides of your waist, placing your thumbs around the back and your fingers around the front. (This position is sometimes described as "putting your hands on your hips," even though that's not anatomically accurate.) Inhale and feel the sides of your torso expand into your hands. Exhale and gently squeeze inward. Repeat several times.
3. Lean forward slightly and relax your shoulders. Inhale toward your lower back and sense expansion there. There will be less movement than in the front or sides. Match the number of breaths you used earlier.

4. Place one hand on your belly and the other on your chest. Inhale into your belly, then ribs, then chest. Exhale from your chest, then ribs, then belly. Continue in a slow, gentle wave.
5. Let your arms and hands relax. Inhale to expand your belly, ribs, and chest. Pause briefly at the top. Exhale fully—chest, ribs, then belly. Repeat several times, emphasizing a complete exhale.

WHY THIS HELPS

Just as grief and letting go are life skills we are rarely taught, so too is learning how to breathe well. Many people inhale by pulling the belly in, which tightens the chest and limits the lungs. Over time, this pattern reduces breath capacity and can even intensify sadness and stress. True diaphragmatic breathing allows the belly to gently expand like a balloon on the inhale and relax on the exhale. The diaphragm is the key muscle that separates the abdominal and chest cavities, and when it's restricted, the chest can feel tight and the breath shallow. Practicing diaphragmatic breathing restores flexibility to this muscle, expands breath capacity, and helps the body shift out of survival mode. In grief, this deeper breathing reduces biological stress factors, creating calm and spaciousness for emotions to move.[18]

Writing Practice: Listening to Grief

1. Write to the prompt "What is right with my grief?" rather than "What is wrong with it?" Explore how grief shows your capacity to love, your humanity, and your courage to feel.
2. Write from grief's perspective. Use the prompt "If my grief could talk, it would say . . ." Let grief express its wisdom, longing, and tenderness.
3. When you are complete, read what you wrote. Notice any feelings of comfort, clarity, or perhaps even a surprising sense of companionship.

WHY THIS HELPS

Sadness can carry the thought that there is something wrong with you for feeling so deeply. This practice honors grief as a sign of love and connection rather than a flaw to fix. By giving grief a voice, you allow it to teach you. You open space for it to share its wisdom. As you attune to yourself, new meanings can emerge from difficult emotions that come from turning toward grief rather than resisting it. This technique honors grief and sadness as part of your humanity, allowing clarity, comfort, and even companionship to emerge, instead of the challenges that come from suppressing or pathologizing grief.[19]

Exercise: Grief Altar for Self-Compassion

This is a living invitation to reclaim your humanness by granting permission to rest, feel, and set healthy boundaries. You will need:

- a small table, shelf, or quiet corner
- a photograph or memento
- candle(s) to symbolize sacredness and light
- symbols of boundaries, such as a smooth stone or small shield
- self-care reminders, such as a note, a fabric swatch, a crystal, or any token of comfort
- personal items that hold meaning

1. **Set your intention.** Sit quietly, breathe, and dedicate the altar to love, remembrance, and self-compassion. Name the permissions you want to honor by offering yourself words of encouragement that affirm your worth and your permission to rest, feel, and say no.
2. **Arrange the core elements.** Place the photo or memento at the center of the altar. Surround it with symbols or written encouragement and self-care reminders. Place and light candle(s) where they feel appropriate.

3. **Add symbols of permission.** Include boundary objects and tokens that remind you to relax and receive care.
4. **Engage in the ritual.** As you place each item, speak simple affirmations: "I grant myself permission to rest," "I allow every emotion," "I can set boundaries that protect my well-being."
5. **Give thanks and gratitude to your process.** To close your ritual, blow out any candles and offer a simple bow of gratitude to your body, its process, and any influences of compassion that may have entered your space.
6. **Visit daily for reflection.** After your ritual is complete, be sure to visit your altar on a regular basis. Light a candle. Read your encouragement. Sit for a few minutes in quiet attention.

WHY THIS HELPS

Grief from deep loss often brings a new relationship with absence that can feel challenging and even unwanted. When grief is suppressed or stigmatized, that weight only grows, demanding attention. Creating an altar acknowledges grief's presence and reframes it as love rather than something to hide.[20] The act of elevating grief into a place of reverence offers radical permission to honor your experience. This altar is not only a memorial for the person who is no longer in your life—it is also a sacred space to honor your grieving self.

Summary

If your sadness feels heavy in your chest, breathe into it—expand your ribs, soften your diaphragm, and let your body make room for grief to move. If your tears feel embarrassing, remember they are your body's wisdom releasing what words cannot. If you feel overwhelmed by your emotions, gently sit with a soft hug or a dear friend or animal to nestle close to. Allow oxytocin to nourish you. If the world tells you to stay composed, give yourself permission to slow down, to be seen, to let feeling take its rightful place. If you fear that sadness is a loss of dignity, remember that expressing your emotions freely releases stuck energy and gives others, especially young people, permission to feel and free their own emotions.

Sadness is a natural experience that attunes us to the body's wisdom. It is love made visible through your body—each tear, each breath, a reminder that you are still alive to what matters.

12

Facing Anxiety

JENNIFER WAS IN IT. She was reeling from the loss of her dear pup of twelve years, her soulmate, the love of her life. She could hardly remember the thirty-five years of her life before Wally arrived. Wally, a Border collie–Aussie mix with the most soulful brown eyes and tricolor fur, had just died of natural causes.

Jennifer had anticipated the loss, but she hadn't anticipated how overwhelming his absence would be. He had been with her through formative years, relationship changes, career transitions, and countless moves. Wally was her steady force. Friends and family supported her with a sweet memorial and made sure he was well cared for at the end, but none of that could quiet the emptiness she felt in his absence.

Then something new began to take shape. Jennifer noticed more anxiety rising in her life. She had always known stress, driven by her hard work and high performance at her job, but now her mind raced constantly. She spoke quickly, rushed through meals, reached for her phone, and rarely paused. Her friends noticed too. She seemed fully activated, unable to slow down.

When I first sat with her, I could hardly get a word in, which I welcome in grief work; sometimes the flood of words is its own form of release. But here it felt different. There was a restless urgency in her speech, as though the ground had disappeared beneath her. Instead of trying to match her pace, I steadied my own. I let my breath deepen, softened my posture, and offered her quiet presence.

It took a little while, but she began to notice. She took a fuller breath. Then she exhaled with a deep sigh. Her shoulders lowered. She started to naturally mirror the calm around her. What she carried was still immense, but for a few moments the storm slowed.

When an anchor like Wally is lost, the body can become unsettled, the nervous system reaching for ground that is no longer there. Jennifer's anxiety was grief in motion, a natural response to the new void in her life. What she needed most was not quick answers but steadiness, grounding, and loving companionship. Sometimes sitting together, breathing together, and not turning away becomes the medicine that allows a grieving heart to rest, if only for a moment.

From my experience, it's perfectly normal to get anxious just thinking about anxiety. Who doesn't feel anxiety these days? What was once a situational experience—something you felt before a big test, an important meeting, or an unexpected life event—now feels almost like the background hum of modern life. From global conflict to societal division, from feeling helpless about injustice to the ever-present existential stress of being human, anxiety has become an undercurrent woven into daily existence.

When grief enters the picture, anxiety often intensifies. The rupture of loss makes the world feel less stable, less safe. What you once relied upon may now feel uncertain. Anxiety becomes grief's companion.

How Anxiety Shows Up amid Grief

In grief, anxiety can look like:

- racing thoughts at night when the world is quiet
- fear of the future or of breaking down in public
- worry about letting go of memories or not grieving properly
- irritability or withdrawal from relationships
- restlessness and the inability to focus

Naming these expressions helps soften shame. Anxiety is not a sign that you are broken. It is a sign that your nervous system is overwhelmed.

What Is Grief-Anxiety?

Grief-related anxiety is different from generalized anxiety disorder. It is not necessarily a clinical condition, though it can feel just as overwhelming. It's the body and mind responding to loss, the unknowns of the future, and the fear of not being able to hold it all together. Grief-anxiety often shows up as waves of worry about forgetting, dread of more loss, restlessness about how to move forward, or panic in moments that unexpectedly trigger memories. Rather than a pathology, it is better understood as the body's instinctive attempt to protect you during a time of profound vulnerability.

In grief, anxiety becomes a kind of umbrella for many emotions that stir up overthinking: overwhelm, insecurity, dread, fear, even guilt or shame. These emotions feed into the mind's spirals, and anxiety becomes the name we give to all of them swirled together.

Physiologically, anxiety reinforces itself. Breathing becomes shallow, your shoulders tighten, your body tenses. Your survival system is activated through the autonomic nervous system, preparing you to fight, flee, or freeze. The body may sweat, tremble, or feel restless. This state, once meant for short-term danger, becomes chronic when grief and stress linger.[1]

Many people fear that anxiety means they're doing grief wrong. It's important to know that anxiety is one of the most common experiences within grief. Research on autonomic dysregulation and emotional disorders helps explain why anxiety frequently accompanies bereavement and non-death losses by way of reduced heart rate variability and heightened hyperarousal.[2] You are not alone if you find your mind spinning, your body restless, or your heart racing long after the immediate shock of loss. This is love colliding with uncertainty, expressed through the body's attempt to keep you safe.

The Nervous System Response

The autonomic nervous system has two branches. The sympathetic nervous system (SNS) drives the fight-or-flight response. The parasympathetic nervous system (PNS) governs rest, digestion, and repair. Both are essential, and we feel our best when they operate in balance. The SNS is supposed to surge when danger arises and then recede. Today, however, many live with the SNS stuck in a permanent "on" state, the body trapped in a loop of hyperarousal. This chronic survival state contributes not only to anxiety but also to broader dysregulation across cardiovascular, metabolic, inflammatory, and emotional domains.

Anxiety emerges here as both a psychological and physiological response. The perceived threat keeps the stress system active, and the stress system keeps the mind searching for threats. It is a feedback loop, and grief intensifies it.

What often gets undervalued is the physiological foundation beneath emotional experience. The body informs the mind more than the other way around. Before you even recognize a thought as anxious, your body has already changed your breathing, quickened your pulse, and shifted your chemistry. This recognition is essential for emotional regulation.[3] To change the story the mind is telling, you must first change the state of the body.

The Vata Lens

Ayurveda has long described this anxious pattern as an imbalance of vata dosha. Vata, composed of the elements of air and space (or ether), governs movement, circulation, breath, nerve impulses, and thought. Its natural gifts are creativity, adaptability, and inspiration. But when disturbed, vata becomes scattered, cold, light, and unstable. Your mind races. Your body trembles. Sleep fragments. Your nervous system feels unmoored.[4]

Ayurveda describes this specifically as a disturbance of prana vata, the subtype of vata in the head and nervous system that regulates mental activity and breath.[5] The image is of wind without anchor: quick, irregular, and impossible to pin down. This mirrors modern science's picture of chronic sympathetic activation, low vagal tone, and hypothalamic-pituitary-adrenal (HPA) axis stress.[6] Both languages describe the same storm: anxiety as vata in excess, or movement without ground.

I worked with Sophia, who loved her yoga classes. They gave her a sense of calm and balance, a pocket of stillness in her otherwise full life. She was also a dedicated runner and a caretaker for those around her. I often wondered aloud how she managed to fit so much into one day.

When her sister was diagnosed with cancer, Sophia's life shifted. She began traveling back and forth between cities in the Bay Area to be by her sister's side. The constant movement, the emotional weight, and the sleepless nights began to take their toll. Sophia noticed her moods changing. She felt anxious and tired at the same time, but she kept pushing through, determined to do it all.

This is how vata imbalance often shows itself. Too much movement, irregular routines, and constant giving can leave the body and mind depleted. The air and space qualities of vata that are classically defined as light, quick, mobile, and ungrounded were magnified in Sophia's life, leaving her restless and anxious, even as her energy ran thin.

I've seen other expressions of similar energy across different people. Whitney described her mind as feeling like a hummingbird, darting in every direction without rest. Josh shared that he often felt spacey, forgetting things such as appointments or where he had placed his keys. Sally admitted that she once forgot an important doctor's appointment. These, too, are expressions of vata imbalance in the form of being unanchored.

When grief leaves you feeling vacuous and empty, the mind can become light, scattered, and unable to land, mirroring the air and space qualities of vata that leave the body ungrounded. It can feel like wind blowing erratically along the shore or swirling at the top of a mountain—it feels chaotic and unsettling, as if you might be swept away. This restless wind, the overactive air element of vata, often shows up in the mind as racing thoughts, distraction, or forgetfulness. Ayurveda helps us see these not as personal failings but as elemental expressions of how energy moves through the mind-body continuum, another way that anxiety can take shape in grief.

The Relational Impact

Anxiety caused by grief often ripples into our relationships. You may notice yourself becoming more irritable, quick to anger, or hesitant to trust.

Or you may find yourself leaning more heavily on others, seeking reassurance that never quite feels like enough. Both are natural responses. Naming this with loved ones by saying, "I know I'm not in danger, but my body feels like I am," can create compassion and connection rather than misunderstanding.

I grew up with panic attacks. It was part of how my body tried to cope with all the grief I had pressed down inside. Eventually my body could no longer contain it, and the intensity would break through in the form of a full-blown panic attack. This went on for years, and it was incredibly hard for those closest to me, especially my parents. In my dysregulated state, I often made everyone feel as though they were walking on eggshells, not knowing what might set me off or how to help.

One family member did something I will never forget. In the middle of one of those overwhelming moments, she simply held me. Despite the warmth of South Asian culture, tender touch can be something many of us feel timid about. The warmth of her touch, the care in her embrace, the love she poured into that moment felt like an energy transfer. Slowly I came back to calm. That experience taught me something I carry to this day: The body holds the key. In that touch I began to realize that healing my anxiety was not only about calming my mind but also about letting my body feel safe again.

Grounding Back into Safety

Here's a reframe that may surprise you: Your anxiety is trying to love you. In fact, it's your body's misdirected way of keeping you safe. The mind spins, the heart races, and the breath shortens, not because you are weak but because your biology is devoted to protecting you from further pain. The paradox is that this protection often increases the suffering it tries to prevent. Recognizing anxiety as misguided care rather than failure helps soften your relationship with it.

Before the mind registers safety, the body must feel it. This is why practices that slow, warm, and ground are so essential. Ayurveda teaches that regular routine, warm and nourishing food, touch through self-massage, and breath practices pacify vata.[7] Modern research echoes these outcomes through increased vagal tone, lowered cortisol, and parasympathetic activation.[8] These traditions converge on one truth: The body needs rhythm and safety to quiet the storm of anxiety.

Anxiety as Teacher

Anxiety in grief can feel like a curse, yet it can also become a teacher. It teaches the importance of slowing down, creating rhythm, and anchoring in the body. It reminds you that safety is not just an idea; it is a physiological experience that can be cultivated. Whether you see it as calming vata or strengthening your parasympathetic nervous system, the practices are the same: warmth, steadiness, breath, touch, and presence.

Grief-anxiety is not forever. It is the nervous system's temporary way of navigating the immensity of loss. With practice, patience, and compassion, you can learn to regulate the body and soften the mind. Anxiety may still visit, but it doesn't have to stay. Over time, your body remembers its rhythm, your mind learns steadiness, and love—not fear—becomes the ground you stand on.

Grief often arrives like the wind, carrying change that feels chaotic, unpredictable, and disorienting. It can sweep through your life suddenly, leaving you unsettled, unanchored, and unsure of where to stand. It reminds you to seek ground, to return to what steadies you, or to create a container where the winds can move without becoming overwhelming. To ground, to root, to set a container—all of these are practices of calm. The very chaos of grief can become the invitation to discover your inner anchor, the place within you that no storm can take away.

To find your inner anchor, reflect on questions like these:

- When does my anxiety feel strongest: morning, night, or after social contact?
- What do my racing thoughts usually circle around?
- What helps my body remember safety?

Such questions are not meant to solve the anxiety, as if it were a problem, but to give you language and awareness, which is the first step in choosing how to respond.

TECHNIQUES FOR WORKING WITH GRIEF-ANXIETY

Qigong Practice: Grounding the Winds of the Mind

1. **Begin standing.** Place your feet shoulder-width apart, knees soft and spine relaxed but upright. Take a few deep breaths to center yourself.
2. **Inhale and gather.** Slowly raise your arms out to the sides and then upward, as if gathering energy from the sky or the tops of the trees. Feel yourself expanding with the breath.
3. **Exhale and ground.** Turn your palms downward and lower your arms slowly in front of your body, as though washing yourself with this energy of life. Imagine it flowing down your head, chest, belly, and legs into the ground.
4. **Repeat the cycle.** Inhale again, lifting the arms out and up in a wide circle to gather energy from above and beyond. Exhale as you lower your arms in front of you, palms down, smoothing the energy over your body and releasing it into the earth.
5. **Continue as a meditation.** Move in this slow, flowing rhythm for several minutes, breathing deeply and evenly. Allow the repetition to calm the winds of your mind, quieting restlessness and restoring balance.

WHY THIS HELPS

This classic qigong practice helps regulate the nervous system, settle anxious energy, and create a grounded sense of containment and calm. From a Traditional Chinese Medicine perspective, many of the body's largest meridians begin in the head and descend toward the ground. When anxiety shortens the breath and tightens the chest, stress rises upward, creating too much ascending energy that fuels an overactive mind and racing thoughts. This practice helps reestablish the natural descending flow of the stomach, gallbladder, and bladder meridians, which together contain more than 150 acupuncture points and connect with much of the body. By guiding energy downward, the exercise quiets your mind, opens your chest, and restores balance between ascending and descending energy. This gentle practice helps calm anxiety, ground vata energy, and create a container of steadiness for the nervous system.[9] It can also be practiced before bed to settle an overactive mind.

Exercise: Rhythmic Shaking to Release Overwhelm

1. Begin with your lower body. Stand with your feet hip-width apart. Gently start bouncing through your ankles, letting the movement rise into your knees and hips. Keep the rhythm light and natural.
2. Add your arms. Allow your wrists, elbows, and shoulders to loosen. Let them feel soft, almost like noodles, moving with the rhythm.
3. Include your torso. Let your chest, spine, and belly join the flow, following the natural pulse of your legs and arms. Feel your whole body moving in a gentle wave of shaking.
4. Release tension. As you shake, imagine stress, discomfort, or emotional intensity moving out of your body. Exhale deeply through your mouth from time to time, letting the breath carry anxiety and stagnant energy away.
5. Pause in stillness. After one to two minutes, come to a gentle stop. Stand quietly with your feet grounded. Notice the sensations in your palms, fingers, chest, and anywhere else in your body. Feel the circulation and energy settling.
6. Integrate and repeat. Rest for ten to twenty seconds, then begin another round if you wish. Alternate between rhythmic shaking and short moments of stillness for several cycles.

WHY THIS HELPS

Rhythmic shaking helps the body release stored tension from overwhelming experiences. Suppressed emotions often lodge in the body, showing up as pain, discomfort, or a sense of being overwhelmed. This practice provides a safe outlet to discharge that internal pressure, creating relief and spaciousness. It creates a smooth flow of qi by releasing emotional stagnation. When practiced regularly, it conditions the nervous system to move from agitation back into calm presence with greater ease.[10]

Breath Practice: 4-7-8 Breath for Calming Intensity

1. Sit or lie down in a comfortable position. Soften your shoulders and jaw.
2. Inhale gently through your nose for a count of four.
3. Hold your breath lightly for a count of seven.
4. Exhale slowly and fully through your mouth for a count of eight.
5. Repeat this cycle for four to six rounds, or until you notice a shift toward calm.

WHY THIS HELPS

The 4-7-8 breathing pattern calms the body by extending the exhale, which activates the parasympathetic nervous system. When emotions feel overwhelming, the body often shifts into sympathetic activation, the fight-or-flight state. The breath becomes shallow and rapid, often around fifteen or more breaths per minute. By consciously slowing and lengthening the exhale, you can activate a parasympathetic response that brings relaxation and safety to the body. Practices that emphasize longer exhales, such as this one, are associated with beneficial shifts in autonomic function.[11]

Holding the breath briefly between inhale and exhale also allows oxygen and carbon dioxide levels to rebalance, helping reduce physiological arousal. By slowing the breath to fewer cycles per minute, this practice shifts the nervous system out of a stress response and into relaxation, creating calm in both body and mind.[12] By practicing regularly, you retrain your body to move from shallow, rapid breathing toward a slower rhythm.

This practice not only calms your body but also helps shift the emotional story attached to overwhelming feelings. By changing your physiological state, you create space for your mind and heart to find new perspectives.

Writing Practice: Listening to Anxiety

1. **Find a quiet space with your journal.** Sit comfortably and take three slow breaths. As you exhale, imagine tension leaving your body. Place one hand on your heart or belly to remind yourself that you are safe in this moment.
2. **Invite the voice of anxiety.** On a fresh page, write the prompt: "If my anxiety could speak, what would it say it is trying to protect me from?" Let your pen move freely. Write in the voice of your anxiety, allowing it to express its fears, worries, and protective concerns. Do not edit or judge.
3. **Respond with compassion.** After you have given anxiety a voice, pause. Take another breath, then write the second prompt: "How might I reassure this part of me that I am held, supported, and safe enough to move forward with trust?" Write as though you're speaking directly to the anxious part of yourself, offering comfort, kindness, and grounding words.
4. **Close with integration.** Reread what you have written, noticing any shifts in your body or heart. Place your hand on your chest again and take a final breath, whispering quietly, "I am safe. I am supported. I can trust this moment."

You can return to this practice whenever anxiety feels overwhelming. Over time, it teaches you to meet fear not with judgment but with gentleness and reassurance. You can also add the following affirmations to your journaling:

I am safe and secure at this moment.
I trust in my ability to handle whatever comes my way.
I release the need to control everything and allow life to flow.
I am grounded, calm, and at peace.
I am in control of my breath, and my breath calms me.

WHY THIS HELPS

Anxiety is often the nervous system's way of trying to keep us safe, even when it feels overwhelming. By giving anxiety a voice on the page, you shift from battling the feeling to understanding its protective message. Responding with compassion helps integrate this part of yourself, reducing fear and building inner reassurance. Over time, this practice retrains the mind and body to meet anxiety with gentleness rather than resistance, creating greater calm and resilience.[13]

Exercise: The 5-4-3-2-1 Technique

The 5-4-3-2-1 technique is a simple grounding exercise designed to reconnect you with the present moment by focusing on your senses. It can reduce anxiety and overwhelming emotions by anchoring you in the here and now.

1. **Set the stage.** Choose your environment. You can practice this technique whether you are sitting in a quiet space, walking outside, or in a stressful moment. Get comfortable, either sitting or standing with a relaxed posture.

2. **Engage your senses.**
   - **Five things you can see.** Look around and name five things. Add details about colors, shapes, textures, and patterns.
   - **Four things you can feel.** Notice four physical sensations, such as your feet on the ground or the texture of your clothes. Describe them specifically.
   - **Three things you can hear.** Identify three sounds, near or distant. Name their qualities, such as hum, buzz, or rustle.
   - **Two things you can smell.** Notice two scents in your environment. If none are obvious, recall a smell you love or attend to subtle ambient scents.
   - **One thing you can taste.** Notice a taste that is present or imagine a familiar flavor you enjoy.
3. **Deepen the practice.** Extend the duration for several minutes if helpful. Use descriptive language, as if writing a short poem about your senses. Practice regularly, alone, or with a friend.
4. **Reflect.** After completing the exercise, notice any changes. You may feel more centered, calm, and present. Repeat as needed.

WHY THIS HELPS

The 5-4-3-2-1 technique helps you return to the safety of the present moment by noticing the simple gifts around you based on what you see, hear, touch, smell, and taste. When your mind is racing or heavy with worry, this practice steadies you by bringing your attention back to your body and your surroundings. By leaning into your senses with kindness, you remind yourself that you are here, you are safe, and you can rest in this moment.[14]

Summary

If your anxiety feels like chaos, ground yourself through breath, warmth, and rhythm. If your anxiety speeds your thoughts, slow the body first—safety begins below the neck. If your anxiety isolates you, let another's calm presence steady your nervous system. If your anxiety feels endless, remember it is grief in motion, not a permanent state.

Anxiety is not your enemy. It is love searching for ground—an invitation to return to your breath, your body, and your essential belonging.

13

Honoring When You Feel Numb

Amanda sat with glazed eyes in the hospital room, curled in the uncomfortable recliner of the neuro ICU. She was frozen. Sleep would not come. Food had no taste. She was there, but not. Just days earlier, she had learned that her husband, Brad, had been in a golf cart accident with his friends. The cart had toppled over, and he'd suffered a traumatic brain injury. At first there was hope. He was alive on his way to the hospital. But the swelling in Brad's brain quickly exceeded its capacity. Before surgery could even be attempted, the doctors declared him brain-dead.

Overwhelmed by the devastation, Amanda chose to give the gift of life through organ and tissue donation, believing it was something Brad would have wanted. The donation and family advocates were kind, and together we tag-teamed grief support as the logistics unfolded.

Amanda was numb. Her whole life had changed in an instant. More often than not, we simply sat in silence together. Then, without warning, she would share a story about Brad, her voice catching, before drifting again into quiet. Sometimes tears came, and she wiped them with the sleeve of the lemon-yellow sweater she had worn since the day she heard the news.

Amanda was in a state of overwhelming disbelief. She stared at Brad's body in the ICU bed, ventilated and lifeless, trying to reorient herself to this new reality. There was no forcing her feelings, only patience and tenderness. What she was experiencing was not just emotional; it was also deeply physiological. Her body was slowly processing in the ways it knew how.

The hospital is not an easy place to grieve, though warm blankets and endless soup can offer small comforts. When she needed to meet staff or face more logistics, I encouraged Amanda to wash her hands, wrists, and forearms in cold water and to splash her face. These were simple acts that gave her body a way to keep moving through what was being asked of her without succumbing completely to numbness.

We can often feel numb in the face of grief. But the truth is, even that numbness gives us hints that grief isn't just one emotion. It's many emotions, often at the same time. It's a whirlwind of feelings such as love, sadness, anger, longing, fear, confusion, emptiness, loneliness, relief, and so many others bundled into a powerful knot inside you. It can be like a tidal wave knocking you over or an experience of drowning and panicking for breath. It can be expressed as a deep ache in your chest or uncontrollable crying.

But sometimes, instead of feeling everything, you feel nothing. You go into a state of detachment, a fleeting and momentary experience of pseudo-peace, where you forget, disconnect, or even dissociate from the intensity all around. That nothingness is numbness, but it's not a lack of emotion. It's a physiological shutdown and the body's way of saying, *Whoa, whoa, whoa—this is too much!*

Numbness is a normal response to emotional overload. When too many feelings rise simultaneously and it becomes more than the nervous system can handle, the body shifts into a kind of emotional shutdown. It's not uncommon to feel this after a significant loss. People might interpret this as doing well because on the outside you seem calm, going about your day—even as you feel like a ghost in your own life and know that something isn't quite right.

You might be saying to yourself, *What's wrong with me? Why can't I cry?* In your lack of tears, you might wonder if you're broken inside or just plain heartless. It can be scary, confusing, and disorienting to have a powerful grieving experience and not feel anything. The mind may claim there's something fundamentally wrong with you or that you didn't really love them or that you're a bad person. None of this is true.

The Layered Experience of Numbness

Numbness is a very real response to grief. It usually takes shape as disbelief, as an unreal "I cannot believe this is happening" kind of experience. You might move between incredibly intense emotions in one minute and then feel numb in the next. Just like all layers of grief, your whole being is affected—physically, emotionally, cognitively, spiritually, and relationally.[1] Let's look at each of these.

Somatic and Physiological Effects

Somatically and physiologically, numbness can manifest as fatigue or exhaustion without a physical cause. It can feel like bodily heaviness, as if you're dragging weight around or wearing heavy, wet clothes. You may see yourself in the mirror and notice an absence of facial expressions, which others might mistake for calm. Your appetite may fade. Your hands and feet may feel cold. Your body language may reflect a sense of languishing.[2]

After her divorce, Priya told me she wore the same oversized gray sweater every day for a month. "It's the only thing I can feel," she said. Food had no taste. Music sounded flat. She was not depressed in the way she had known before. She was paused. Her body had fully engaged the brakes.

Emotional Effects

Emotionally you may feel a sense of *meh* or blankness, as well as apathy about things that used to matter. You may have an inability to cry, which some people interpret as doing well or, unfairly, as being cold or heartless. As you learned in chapter 3, people have opinions about how you should or should not feel.

Leslie came to see me months after her father's passing. She spoke softly, almost apologetically. "I haven't cried," she admitted. "I don't know what's wrong with me. I feel so ashamed." She continued, "He was my favorite person, but I feel nothing. It's like my heart shut down."

Friends told her she needed to "let it out," but she couldn't. Grief felt distant, as though behind a wall she couldn't reach through. As we talked, I invited her to notice what her body felt rather than what it didn't. She closed her eyes and said, "My chest feels like glass. Brittle. If I breathe too deeply, I'll shatter." That image told us everything. Her body was protecting her from the grief, not denying it. The numbness was an expression of her body's intelligence and not an absence. Her nervous system had found a way to keep her safe until she could bear more.

When you go numb, you may not feel joy, but you also don't feel sadness, anger, or relief. You may feel shame or guilt about what you're supposed to feel or fear that you're doing grief wrong.[3] For many, feelings of numbness happen in the initial or acute stage of grief and subside relatively soon.[4] But there is no timeline for this, so don't be hard on yourself. Your grieving will take the time it takes.

Cognitive Effects

It is not unusual with grief for motivation to vanish. Eating, showering, doing the dishes, or performing everyday tasks can feel impossible. There may be persistent dullness or grief fog. Your thoughts might drift in a detached, dreamlike way. Your memory might be affected, and it might be difficult to focus or hold your attention on anything.[5]

Marcus returned to work two weeks after his dad's death, but it was two weeks of hustle and bustle, including cleaning out his dad's home, organizing his papers, getting rid of his clothes, and managing details such as the death certificate and bank accounts. Dealing with someone's estate can be a huge logistical challenge at the worst possible time. He shared that when he returned to work, he opened his laptop at 9 a.m. and blinked, and it was 3 p.m.—with the same spreadsheet still open.

"I'm here," he told his manager, "but I'm not here." Thankfully, his boss was supportive and moved his meeting load, giving Marcus space to take a walk outside each afternoon. We began working together to normalize his experience. Initially he shared that he didn't feel a whole lot on those walks. He just paid attention to his steps and listened to the birds, knowing that feelings would come later.

Relational Effects

Feeling numb can impact close relationships as others around you can misunderstand your numbness as distraction or emotional withdrawal.[6] Intimacy can feel far away. When we're in overload, the usual things we do to feel close to others—touch, closeness, and even hugs—can feel overwhelming. Although it isn't personal, others might feel it as rejection. It's as if all the energy in your body has moved deep inside to protect you, and touch on the skin feels like your soul is being touched. For anyone grieving, this can feel raw and exposing, as though there isn't enough of a buffer. Because so much communication is nonverbal, especially through facial expression and eye contact, numbness can create miscommunication. If numbness is judged or shamed, confrontation can lead to further withdrawal.

Jim and Steve had just lost their beloved dog, Tasha, to a disease they didn't even know she had. One day she was fine, and the next she began having seizures. Within a week, she was gone. They were devastated.

Steve shared with me that Jim was struggling. He spent entire days under the covers, Netflix playing in the background. Steve, on the other hand, wanted to connect with friends, bring people over, and grieve openly. Their different styles of grieving began to create tension.

Because Steve was a longtime client, we spoke about the reality of numbness. I explained that Jim's withdrawal wasn't a lack of love for Tasha, nor was it weakness. It was numbness—his body's way of shutting down after being overwhelmed by grief. Naming it helped Steve soften. Instead of judging, he began to meet Jim with compassion, recognizing that while his own way of grieving was outward and social, Jim's way was inward and quiet.

It's important to remember that numbness is not the absence of love. It's the nervous system's way of surviving too much love, too much loss, too much pain all at once.

Spiritual Effects

Numbness can also appear in your spiritual life as a loss of purpose or meaning.[7] You may feel a deep disconnection from God, Source, Spirit, or the Divine as you define it. Prayer and meditation might lose their spark, and rituals can feel mechanical and uninspired. Awe can become harder to access. Art, creativity, and nature can feel dull and uninteresting. A favorite song no longer brings the same feeling.

When I walked into the waiting room of the hospital, Ruth had her rosary in her hand. She had requested it from another chaplain a few days before as she waited for her husband to wake up from his coma. For years, she'd said the rosary faithfully. But thinking about what life would be like without Martin after fifty-five years floored her. She sat still and unmoving, almost mimicking his quiet, frail body.

"I'm not angry at God," she said, "I just can't reach God right now." We sat together in silence. The silence didn't "fix" anything, but it made ample room to contain her current experience. It was in that silence she started to share about her husband, telling stories about their first date and then how he proposed and how her father didn't like him at first. It was in these stories that she started to call out to God, almost wailing. Tears flowed. Her body softened. After several moments and many stories, she looked at me with gratitude. The connection was coming back.

While there might be a sense of emotional flatness with numbness, the mind may be very active with questions about fairness, injustice, order, or the goodness of life.[8] These questions may feel out of sync with your spiritual or religious community's beliefs and create a feeling of isolation, which compounds grief. Uninformed spiritual leaders may minimize grief with phrases such as "God won't give you more than you can handle" or "God has a plan." Platitudes such as these can be painful in the face of the heavy existential load you're carrying.

It's important to know that numbness can also be associated with what is called "the dark night of the soul."[9] This is a time of life when you feel challenged and adrift—familiar sources of faith no longer console you. Prayer feels hollow. The sacred feels absent. In this space, your soul can feel as though it's been stripped bare. Although deeply unsettling, many mystical traditions recognize this space as a sacred threshold. That's because this is the place where old views might fall away and new insight takes root. What feels like abandonment is often a process of purification that prepares the heart for deeper union.

Within this journey is an awakening to paradox and uncertainty, to what the psychiatrist and Holocaust survivor Viktor Frankl referred to as "creating meaning within the chaos."[10] These times can be humbling. They can bend us low and bring us closer to a larger love, if we allow it.

Numbness: The Body's Attempt to Protect Us

Numbness is the body's wise attempt to protect us when emotion exceeds our capacity. Polyvagal theory describes how our autonomic nervous system responds to threat.[11] We have already talked about the fight-or-flight response, where the sympathetic nervous system activates, preparing us to act. But when the threat is too great, too fast, or too prolonged, and we perceive no escape, the system can shift into freeze.[12] The body can experience the strong emotions of grief as threatening. The same neurological circuits that respond to lions in the jungle will respond to unfamiliar and overwhelming inner states. This can cause you to freeze, a state of shutdown known as the dorsal vagal response.[13]

On the ladder of the autonomic nervous system, the body moves down from fight or flight into a parasympathetic state. But unlike the rejuvenating rest-and-digest parasympathetic state, called ventral vagal, the dorsal vagal state is characterized by a physiological, emotional, and cognitive shutdown. Think of your body like a smart circuit breaker: When emotions overload the system, the breaker flips to protect the house.

I ran into Jerry at the grocery store one afternoon. He had bumped into a display of cereal boxes and froze as they scattered onto the floor. I began picking them up when he blurted out, almost without thinking, "My wife was just diagnosed with stage 4 terminal breast cancer."

Shocked, I stopped gathering boxes and simply looked at him. "Yeah," he said quietly, "she's the one who normally does the grocery shopping. When did there get to be so many cereal options?"

We both chuckled for a second, but then his eyes grew distant. He stood there, unfocused, while shoppers moved around us. A store clerk asked if he was okay. He nodded, but his presence seemed far away.

I met his gaze and said gently, "I appreciate you sharing with me." At that, tears welled and fell down his cheeks. It was only a two-minute exchange, but in that ordinary aisle, the depth of grief and numbness was unmistakable.

Each of us has an emotional range where we feel safe and connected. Because grief education is rare and emotions are often labeled good or bad, the onslaught of grief can push us outside that range. The psychiatrist Daniel J. Siegel calls this the "window of tolerance."[14] When we fall below the window, hypoarousal—marked by numbness, collapse, exhaustion, and disconnection—can occur.[15] In grief, this often looks like you are emotionally numb.

It is not uncommon to cycle between the sympathetic nervous system's fight or flight and the parasympathetic nervous system's dorsal freeze repeatedly. It can feel like a yo-yo, which is one reason grief can feel exhausting and disorienting. Developing an understanding of how your autonomic nervous system works can help. When you can notice the body's small cues and respond with care, the waves feel less like a crash and more like a sway. Recognizing your rhythm doesn't erase the pain, but it can create companionship with your body.

Numbing and Avoiding as Coping

Numbness is not only a physiological response. It's also something you might do to cope. In the early phases of grief, numbing out can be a necessary resource.[16] Doomscrolling, staying endlessly busy, excessive workouts, or binge-watching can create a buffer. There is no shame in coping. We all do it. Some strategies are quirky and harmless. Others can become costly over time.

Many avoidant behaviors are so normalized in our culture that we don't recognize them as avoidance. Productivity is a common one: staying busy to escape silence, working long hours when it's not needed, taking on extra projects to avoid being alone with your emotions. Eventually this approach overactivates the sympathetic nervous system and can add physiological strain on top of grief.

In the modern era, dissociation often shows up as digital distraction. Doomscrolling can help us both avoid feelings and provoke intense ones. The renowned psychotherapist Miriam Greenspan calls this "emotional pornography."[17] Once we start avoiding our own inner life, we may chase intensity elsewhere to feel alive.

Food- and body-based coping mechanisms are also common: emotional eating or not eating, overexercising to control sensation, strict dieting or detoxing to feel in charge. These may be praised culturally, but they can become ways to avoid rather than ways to heal.

Avoidance can also show up in spiritual life through spiritual bypassing,[18] which in this case involves using positivity or transcendent language to leap over the darker realities of grief. This can slide into toxic positivity,[19] which fragments the spirit into light versus dark rather than allowing wholeness.

From an Ayurvedic perspective, numbing behaviors increase tamas,[20] the heavy, dulling quality that blocks perception and slows the digestion of life experience. From a Traditional Chinese Medicine perspective, patterns of avoidance can dampen the Shen (spirit), disrupting the movement of qi and the digestion of experience. Over time, this can look like cognitive fog, lethargy, and disconnection.[21] In their book *The Grief Recovery Handbook*, the bereavement experts John W. James and Russell Friedman call these STERBs, or short-term energy-relieving behaviors.[22]

If you are engaging in any of these behaviors, the essential question to ask yourself: *What is my motivation?* Are you eating to nourish your body or to avoid a feeling? Exercising to care for yourself or to silence your emotions? Reaching for a drink to push away grief? These behaviors are not moral failings. They're protective adaptations. With practice and support, this self-protection can evolve into presence, and you can develop the capacity to be with the difficult feelings of grief.

There is a powerful invitation here: Turn toward your grief rather than away from it. Create spaciousness for memories to arrive. Welcome feelings as guests. Facing and embracing allows for releasing.

Numbness itself is not bad. It's just the protective mechanism that naturally kicks in when emotion exceeds capacity. Over time, though, what protected you can also imprison you. As you grow emotional fitness and widen your window of tolerance, capacity returns. You can learn to sit with sorrow, to witness pain, and to feel again.

TECHNIQUES FOR WORKING WITH NUMBNESS

Exercise: Progressive Muscle Relaxation

1. **Settle in.** Find a comfortable position. Let your hands rest softly by your sides or in your lap. Take a slow breath in through your nose and a long breath out through your mouth.
2. **Begin to focus on your hands and arms.** Gently make fists. Hold the tension for three to five seconds. Then release and let your hands soften completely. Notice the difference between tightness and ease. Repeat once if needed.
3. **Now focus on your shoulders.** Lift your shoulders toward your ears. Hold for a few seconds. Release with an exhale, allowing your shoulders to fall.
4. **And now bring attention to your face and jaw.** Scrunch your face or gently clench your jaw. Hold briefly, then release and soften your expression. Feel the space around your eyes, mouth, and jaw relax.
5. **Draw your awareness now to the chest and belly.** Take a gentle inhalation and subtly tighten your chest and belly. Hold just long enough to notice the effort. Exhale fully and allow your torso to soften and expand.
6. **And focus on your legs and feet.** Press your heels into the ground or point your toes upward. Hold for a few seconds. Release and let the tension drain down through your legs.
7. **Finish with integration.** Take a final slow breath. Feel your whole body as softer, steadier, and more grounded. Allow yourself to rest in this sensation of ease.

WHY THIS HELPS

Grief often creates chronic tension in the muscles. Progressive muscle relaxation helps break that cycle, signaling to your body that it is safe to soften. As the muscles release, your breath deepens, your heart rate steadies, and your mind becomes clearer. This practice gently supports the nervous system in finding balance again.[23]

Qigong Practice: Qi Massage to Release Emotional Congestion

1. Stand with your feet about shoulder-width apart.
2. Using loose fists, begin to rhythmically massage or tap over the length of your chest on either side of the sternum. Take three slow breaths as you rhythmically tap.
3. Using your right hand, massage along the ridge of your left collarbone. Extend your left hand with the palm up and sweep your right hand down the inner side of your left arm to your left palm and fingers. Turn your left palm down and sweep your right hand along the outside of your left arm up to the shoulder. Repeat this three times on each arm.
4. Rhythmically tap your lower back with cupped hands. Take three slow breaths.
5. Using the cupped hands, vigorously tap down the backs of your legs to your ankles and then up your inner legs to your hips. Repeat three times.
6. End with a gentle full-body shake. Notice any spark of sensation.

WHY THIS HELPS

Numbness often arises when grief or overwhelm blocks the natural circulation of energy in the body. Qi massage uses touch, pressure, and gentle movement to stimulate the flow of qi and blood, awakening areas that feel disconnected or shut down. By bringing warmth, circulation, and awareness back into the body, this practice helps soften protective numbness and restores a sense of presence and aliveness. It offers both comfort and reconnection, reminding the body it's safe to feel again.[24]

Exercise: Sound and Vibration Practice (Humming or Chanting)

1. Sit or lie comfortably. Place a hand over your throat or chest to feel the vibration and movement.
2. Take a deep breath in through your nose and exhale with a low hum. If you like, you can also use a key or instrument to harmonize with.
3. Feel the vibration in your chest, throat, and lips. Continue humming slowly for several breaths.
4. Experiment with tones, using lower tones for grounding, higher tones for lifting.
5. Let the sound move through your body like a wave, dissolving tension or heaviness.
6. End in silence, noticing the subtle resonance that remains in your body.

WHY THIS HELPS

Vibrational humming or toning practice stimulates the vagus nerve, improves heart rate variability, and can restore emotional fluidity.[25] Sound penetrates the layers where numbness lives and awakens embodied presence without forcing emotion. Sacred songs and chanting are part of a long history of moving grief emotions and developing regulation. If your tradition uses mantras, sacred sounds, hymns, prayers, or chanting, allow this to be part of your practice.[26]

Exercise: Permission Slips

Write small notes that begin with "You have permission to . . ." Place them where you can see them, such as on a microwave, a mirror in the bathroom, on a computer or TV screen, and so forth. Add notes such as:

- You have permission to feel what you feel.
- You have permission to rest.
- You have permission to grieve at your own pace.
- You have permission to not have all the answers right now.
- You have permission to smile and feel moments of joy.
- You have permission to be angry, sad, or numb.
- You have permission to soften and receive care.
- You have permission to release what no longer serves you.
- You have permission to honor both your grief and your love.
- You have permission to simply be as you are in this moment.

Add any others that offer you the kind of support you need.

WHY THIS HELPS

Radical permission is an act of self-compassion. It softens the judgment and shame that so often arise from believing grief must follow certain rules or timelines. This practice loosens the weight of "shoulds" and "supposed to's," and instead recognizes that you're allowed to grieve in the ways that work for you. By granting yourself this freedom, you create space for authentic healing that's also gentle and true for your heart's process.[27]

Drum Practice: Returning to Rhythm

When numbness settles in, the body often feels silent and far away. Drumming offers a gentle way to awaken sensation through vibration and rhythm. Across Indigenous, African, Asian, and diasporic traditions, drumming has long been used to reconnect with the earth, community, and the heartbeat of life. This practice invites you into that lineage of rhythmic healing. The goal is not to feel something dramatic but simply to notice the quiet pulse beneath the numbness.

1. **Choose your drum or create one.** You can use a hand drum, frame drum, djembe, or even a Taiko practice pad. If you do not have a drum, create one with a thick pillow, a folded blanket over a table, your thighs, your chest with gentle tapping, or a book with padding beneath your hands. The vibration matters more than the instrument.
2. **Sit comfortably and begin with stillness.** Let your feet rest on the ground. Let your shoulders soften. Allow the breath to settle into something gentle. You do not need to feel ready. You simply need to be here.
3. **Begin with the heartbeat rhythm.** Start with a slow, steady beat: *dum . . . dum . . . dum . . . dum. . . .* A little slower than your resting heart. This rhythm is universal. It is the rhythm of the womb, the rhythm of many Indigenous ceremonies, the rhythm that reminds your body it still belongs. Let the vibration travel through your hands into your arms, chest, and spine.
4. **Let your rhythm evolve.** After a minute or two, allow the pattern to shift naturally. It may quicken. It may soften. It may pause. There is no right or wrong. You are simply listening to what your hands choose. If numbness remains, that is all right. Rhythm often works below awareness.
5. **Let your body join if it wants.** You might notice a tapping foot, a swaying shoulder, or a deeper breath. These tiny movements are signs of thawing. Do not force anything. Let your body respond in its own time.
6. **Close gently.** Gradually return to the heartbeat rhythm. Slow the beat. Soften your hands. Allow silence to return. Sit for a moment and feel whatever is present, even if it is still numbness.

Finding Rhythm Beyond Your Home

If you feel drawn to explore drumming in community or through cultural traditions, there are gentle ways to engage with respect and curiosity.

One way is to attend a local drum circle. Many communities host open drumming gatherings where all levels are welcome. You might look for community drum circles, African drumming groups, Taiko drumming classes, West African djembe circles, or local cultural centers offering traditional drumming sessions. These spaces offer shared rhythm, which can be deeply grounding and connective.

You can also explore drumming traditions by joining community classes or attending performances. Examples include Taiko drumming from Japan, West African djembe and dunun traditions, Brazilian samba or batucada rhythms, Afro-Caribbean and Yoruba-inspired drumming, and Indian styles such as tabla, jori, or dhol. Remember, these are not simply musical styles—they are cultural lineages. Approach them with respect, curiosity, and a willingness to learn.

If you prefer to begin privately, try listening to traditional drum tracks. Options include Native American powwow drum songs, Indigenous heartbeat drumming for grounding, shamanic frame-drum rhythms for journeying, or slow ceremonial drumming from various traditions. Let the rhythm wash through you. Even listening can awaken sensation.

WHY THIS HELPS

Rhythm reaches parts of the brain and nervous system that go quiet during numbness. Drumming can stimulate somatic awareness through vibration, bring gentle activation to the nervous system without overwhelm, create grounding through predictable patterning, reconnect you to the pulse of life and community, and offer a sense of belonging when you feel disconnected. In many Indigenous teachings, the drum is a reminder that the earth is alive and that we are held within a larger rhythm. When numbness takes over, this remembrance can become a quiet path back into connection.[28]

Exercise: Cold Plunge or Cold Shower

Brief cold exposure can be a way to reawaken sensation. Start with fifteen to thirty seconds of cool water at the end of a warm shower. Breathe with long exhales. Warm yourself gently afterward. Over time, increase the level of coldness or the duration of the shower if you're called to do so, perhaps even working yourself up to immersive cold plunges.

WHY THIS HELPS

Studies show that brief cold-water immersion can boost dopamine levels, which enhances focus and mood, and reduce cortisol, the stress hormone, supporting recovery from emotional strain.[29] Even short immersions have been found to increase positive affect and shift brain network activity toward greater flexibility.[30] Longer-term cold immersion has been linked to better vascular health and reduced inflammation, which is tremendously helpful for circulation of blood and qi.[31]

Cold exposure can feel like a shock to the system, but that very jolt is what helps pierce the fog of grief and numbness. The cold awakens circulation, sharpens awareness, and brings you back into your body. By leaning into the challenge of the cold, you practice meeting intensity in a safe and contained way. Over time, this can help you build internal resilience and the ability to hold strong emotions without being overtaken by them.

Cold can become a teacher: What feels sharp and uncomfortable at first can, with practice, become a doorway into clarity, strength, and renewed aliveness.

Summary

Numbness is not wrong; nor is it weakness or failure. It's the body's wise attempt to protect us when emotions exceed our capacity. Over time, what protected us can become what imprisons us. Then the gentle thaw begins. It's possible to slowly build the skills we were never taught—by sitting with sorrow, witnessing pain, and learning to feel again. Healing does not require feeling everything at once. It asks that we stay, breath by breath, with what is true.

When numbness begins to soften, you may notice flickers of emotion returning—grief, tenderness, even small joys. Welcome them gently. Emotions that arise out of times of numbness are indications of healing, not failure. Allow gentleness, softness, and kindness to be part of your practice as your body shifts between varying states of autonomic regulation.

14

Navigating the Abyss of Fear

"We never thought this would happen to us": These are words I've heard repeatedly in the quiet room of the emergency department, as families absorb the unbearable news delivered by police or physicians.

One night, Miranda arrived after her husband had been flown in from a car accident. They were moving states. She had gone ahead with the children while he drove the U-Haul, determined to push through the night so they could start unpacking and begin their new life in Arizona the next day. Just hours from their new home, a driver on the wrong side of the road hit him head-on.

When the physician delivered the news, Miranda collapsed onto the floor. We all went down with her: police officers, residents, nurses. In that moment, it was our role to remain by her side. I sat with her on the cold tile, gently guarding her head as she wailed and flailed, her cries echoing through the room. Then came silence, numbness, a feeling of utter exhaustion. We leaned together against the chairs, under the harsh fluorescent light, staring at the muted pastel wall as her body tried to absorb the unabsorbable.

Between long pauses, Miranda spoke about what she and her husband had hoped for. She reflected on the house they bought, the plans they made, the life waiting for them. Shock and disbelief pulsed through every word; this new reality was physical as much as emotional.

Later, she walked into the room where her husband lay. Once more, Miranda collapsed—holding his hand, wailing, then whispering stories about him. She spoke of the loving father he had been and how they had first met. Although it didn't seem as though she was talking to anyone in particular, I recognized her fervent need to tell it all, almost as if she were trying to speak back into the room his presence and impact on her.

The tragedy of Miranda's story reveals a part of grief that emerges when trauma is present, when loss is sudden. If you have experienced this, you may recognize what follows. The world may no longer feel trustworthy. Fear can arise quickly, even in ordinary moments. Hours later, after sitting, crying, and laughing with Miranda, something softened. Nothing about the loss had changed, but she was no longer alone inside it. As her family took her home, she moved slowly, her body still shaken but gently steadied by this awareness of how fragile and precious life can be.

When Fear Takes Hold

When fear takes hold, your body often knows it before your mind does. If you're paying attention, you might feel your stomach clench or your jaw tighten. Your chest may grow heavy, your breath short. But given your state, you probably won't notice these signs.

Fear is often the shadow companion of grief. When something overwhelming and unimaginable happens, you learn—sometimes for the first time—that life isn't as safe, predictable, or controllable as you once believed. The unthinkable has already happened. What you once whispered to yourself—*That could never happen to me*—suddenly becomes real. With that realization, the ground of normalcy dissolves, fracturing into a landscape of deep crevices and yawning canyons.

When the reality of your worst fears arrives, it's a profound jolt to your system. Once your precious bubble of safety bursts, life is never the same. Mortality confronts you and it won't be denied. For some of us, the arrival of grief itself is the realization of our deepest fear: a devastating diagnosis, the loss of a child, the sudden death of a spouse. We're pulled out of the familiar and dropped into a reality that feels foreign, chaotic, unlivable. We're automatically enrolled in the membership (widow, widower, orphan, surviving parent, etc.) no one ever wanted.

The body understands this membership too. The shoulders rise as if bracing for impact. The hips grip tight, especially through the psoas, a deep muscle of protection. Fear sets the body in a posture of guarding, as if waiting for the next blow.

When your worst fear is actualized, a dark cloud of uncertainty dawns. Nothing feels stable and everything can feel like an empty void. This is the menacing presence of fear in grief. Your mind tries to grasp the experience of normalcy but feels utterly lost. As you experience the loss, everything feels fragile. Nothing feels permanent. It all exists under the shadow of loss. Such uncertainty can be unbearable.

This fear is not the same as ordinary anxieties about work, money, or failure; it's existential. It shakes the very roots of identity and belonging. Fear after loss can say, *If this can happen, then anything can happen. If they can die, I can lose anyone. I can lose myself.* This is why you may feel unsafe in your own life—why you feel a sense of mistrust toward the world.

Fear lives in the body, which is here in present time, but it also lives out of time. It pulls you into futures that have not yet happened while keeping you tethered to what you've already lost. Your mind will ask endless questions, which seem to tumble out unbidden: *How do I live into a future without them? Who am I now, and who will I become? What if more loss is waiting for me?*

For many, even simple rituals of timekeeping become painful. A new year, once a symbol of possibility, becomes a marker of absence and the foreshadowing of another year without someone you love. New Year's Eve can feel unbearable, because the calendar insists on a future in which the person you love no longer exists. Each month, each season, each anniversary reminds you of what's missing.

One woman described dreading the New Year after her husband's death. She said, "I didn't want the year to start. It meant leaving him behind, and I couldn't bear the thought of living in a world that kept going without him." For her, the future felt like betrayal.

The fear that accompanies grief can show up in your relationships too. A surviving parent might hover anxiously over their children, terrified of losing them as well. You might panic every time a loved one leaves the house, clinging tighter at each goodbye. Friendships may shift because fear makes vulnerability harder. People in the clutches of fear might also find themselves retreating, worried they'll be abandoned again.

Sometimes fear leads you to hold people too close. Other times it convinces you to keep your distance. Both are ways of trying to protect yourself. At times you may even grieve those who are still alive, rehearsing losses in your mind as if preparing for the inevitable. This is your mind's way of bracing, normalizing fear's response to devastating loss.

The Body's Response to Fear

The body's response to shock is well researched, and it is also where our capacity to cope with devastating loss lives. With fear, the amygdala, your brain's alarm system, becomes overactive.[1] Your body responds as if danger is right in front of you, even when you're safe at home. Cortisol courses through your system, keeping you awake at night.[2] Your breath can become shallow, your muscles tense, your digestion uneasy.[3] You may become hypervigilant, constantly on guard, which is your nervous system's way of trying to prevent another unbearable shock.[4]

Other times, fear can pull you into collapse. You may notice yourself unable to leave the house or frozen still in the face of tasks that once felt simple. A grieving parent may stop driving after a fatal accident. Another person may go numb with fear, their body shutting down in protection.[5] Fear can live in restlessness and agitation or in stillness and paralysis. Both are the body's ways of trying to keep you safe.[6]

Ancient traditions echo this truth. In Traditional Chinese Medicine (TCM), fear is rooted in the kidney system, which houses your *jing*, the essence that governs your deepest vitality.[7] When your kidneys are strong, you feel grounded and able to face uncertainty. When grief depletes them, fear arises.[8]

Sudden shock scatters kidney qi, leaving you trembling, collapsed, or feeling as if the ground is gone. Prolonged anticipatory loss, which can happen in diagnoses such as cancer or dementia, gradually drains kidney yin, leading to exhaustion, insomnia, and dread. When jing is weakened, fear is no longer just an emotion—it becomes a loss of rootedness itself.[9]

Your kidneys are in close relationship with your heart and lungs. When fear disturbs the kidneys, the heart's Shen, or spirit, becomes restless, bringing palpitations, anxiety, and sleeplessness. The kidneys also anchor the breath. When they are depleted, the lungs cannot root properly, and you may feel the shallow, anxious breath that so often accompanies grief.[10]

The body responds in kind to experiences of devastating loss. Coping at these depths requires a tenderness that can meet the chaos and disorientation that are profoundly present. There is no quick fix here. Rather than dramatic interventions, the body responds to what is slow and steady: a deeper breath, a moment of connection, a quiet sense of sweetness that begins to replenish what has been depleted. It is often the simplest moments that nourish jing, restoring the body's deeper reserves and softening the tension of constant bracing.

TCM teaches that fear is a signal of depletion of your deepest reserves.[11] This is why rest and permission are so necessary when you are grieving. By nourishing yourself with breath, warmth, grounding, and gentle movement, you begin to restore a quiet balance inside the body. In this way, safety begins to take root again from within.

An Encounter with the Mystery

Fear in grief is not only a symptom of trauma or a matter for the nervous system. It is also an encounter with mystery, where dissolution reveals what lies beneath our identities and the stories we have created about ourselves and our lives. What remains is not certainty but a fragile presence that feels closer to truth than anything you held before. This is a deeply spiritual dimension of grief, a threshold beyond culture or doctrine, spoken of by poets and mystics and known most intimately by those who have been broken open by loss.

When you know devastating loss and you also know deep fear, you may be met by the great abyss of life, what the psychotherapist Francis Weller, who writes so eloquently about grief, calls the "wild edge of sorrow."[12] It isn't simply fear of what has already happened or what is yet to come. It's fear before the vastness of existence itself. You stand at the threshold where all that you thought you knew dissolves.

In that place, words often fail. Mystics have referred to it as ego annihilation, the stripping away, the cloud of unknowing.[13] In myth it is the descent into the underworld, where every layer of self is taken until only essence remains. We can feel naked and exposed, raw and bare to a reality few seem to understand. It is not an obvious passage to growth but an undoing. It can leave us trembling, present, and alive in a way that defies explanation. The very annihilation we fear often becomes the threshold to our deepest spiritual opening—the moment when aliveness no longer depends on certainty but on our willingness to stay awake within the mystery.

Myth and archetype offer images when ordinary words cannot. The phoenix is consumed by fire before rising from ashes. Persephone descends into the underworld and returns each spring with new knowing. Inanna is stripped of every possession before standing naked before the throne of death. These stories echo what you may feel in your body: Through devastation you have been undone, yet something unseen still holds you.

Sufis call this fana, the annihilation of self, which is the greatest form of surrender.[14] Christian mystics speak of the cloud of unknowing, a strange grace that comes to us when we are brave enough to walk through the uncertainty.[15] Buddhists can see fear as the gate to emptiness, which is not a void but the ground of all being.[16] Sikh tradition speaks of *hukam*, the incomprehensible divine order in which all things rest.[17] Yogic philosophy gestures to *pratyahara*, the withdrawal of the senses into a reality beyond form. Each of these systems points to a shared truth: Grief can bring you into a realm where ordinary ground disappears and you are carried by something vast and unnamable.

This is not a place of disorientation alone, though it may feel unbearable, especially at first. It is also a place where our intrinsic interconnectedness is revealed. Within surrender a subtle nectar of universal love flows. Within annihilation a hidden oneness shines. In the absence of knowing, the realm of unknowing opens, asking only for listening and our receptivity.

Few are willing to walk this path, and those who have rarely wish it on another—even their worst enemies. Yet for those taken into its depths, it is an initiation through life, death, and rebirth that unveils the indestructible, deathless, perhaps unshatterable aspect of reality. It is held in the spaciousness between atoms, the empty reality through which all things move, the sacred power at the heart of being.

If this is the place where you find yourself in grief, my heart goes out to you. You may feel utterly alone. Please know that as an initiate from these depths, you're held in a fellowship, both celestial and earthly, by those who came before you, those who walk beside you now, and the unseen mystery that holds us all. In the darkest abyss, you are not abandoned. You are profoundly accompanied. The great irony is that while loss is universal, few of us are taught to face it directly. The brave work is to walk toward what most people turn away from—because this is where transformation lives.

Fear teaches that nothing is guaranteed. Strangely, that teaching, when met with compassion, awakens a deeper appreciation of the present. It's often why I share in classes that grief is one of the purest forms of mindfulness practice. Grief and fear are unexpected teachers, pulling us back into love, back into presence. When you know the deepest loss, love remains.

If you have lived through a sudden loss or one that came without warning, you may be carrying grief and fear. This is the human truth of loving and losing. The invitation is not to let fear lead your life but to learn to walk beside it. Mindfulness, presence, breath, and ritual can guide you into the unknown. They remind you that while the future may be uncertain, this moment is here and enough.

Below are practices to soothe your spirit as you walk through this sacred threshold. For whatever layer of fear your grief holds, these practices can ground your spirit, regulate your nervous system, and perhaps even unveil a light within the tunnel of darkness.

TECHNIQUES FOR WORKING WITH FEAR

Exercise: Prostrations for Meeting the Abyss

Prostration is bowing the body, a gesture of surrender and reverence. Each variation in this exercise brings your forehead to the ground, inviting humility, grounding, and the release of fear. You can modify these variations to match your level of ability.

VARIATION 1: BOW OF STILLNESS

1. Sit on your heels with your knees together.
2. Bend forward, resting your torso over your thighs.
3. Extend your arms out in front of you with palms together and place your forehead on the ground.
4. Remain in stillness. Let your body soften as you bow. Breathe gently, resting into the ground that holds you.

VARIATION 2: FLOWING BOW

1. Begin seated on your heels.
2. Place your hands on the floor in front of you for support.
3. Inhale as you rise slightly upright, then exhale as you bow forward, bringing your forehead to the ground.
4. Use your hands to press up gently as you inhale and relax down as you exhale.
5. Continue in this flowing rhythm, rising and bowing in a graceful cycle.

VARIATION 3: EXPANSIVE FLOWER BOW

1. Start seated on your heels.
2. Inhale and rise onto your knees, raising your arms to the sky. Open your chest as if you're blossoming like a flower.
3. Exhale and gently return, lowering your hips to your heels, folding forward until your forehead meets the ground, your hands resting downward.
4. Continue inhaling as you rise and expand, exhaling as you bow and return to the earth.

VARIATION 4: FULL-BODY GLIDE

This variation is best practiced on a smooth floor.

1. Begin standing.
2. Place a cushion in front of you on the floor, and just beyond that, a small towel.
3. As you kneel on the cushion, place your hands on the cloth in front of you.
4. Glide forward across the floor, extending your arms fully, lowering your body completely flat and extended, touching your forehead to the ground.
5. Use your hands to glide yourself back to your heels, then rise up to standing again.
6. Repeat this cycle, letting the movement be steady and prayerful.

WHY THIS HELPS

Ancient traditions recognize the quiet power of surrender. What may feel like failure or giving up is, in truth, a deep act of humility and an opening to the unknown. Each variation of bowing and prostration invites you to embody reverence through motion. These gestures become somatic prayers as you meet grief, fear, and uncertainty with presence. They teach your body to bow and rise, to expand and contract, and in doing so, to reconnect with the pulse and rhythm of life itself.

Research echoes this wisdom: Gentle postures of forward folding, such as the ones you might find in yoga, have been shown to calm the autonomic nervous system, reduce cortisol, and enhance parasympathetic activity, which fosters relaxation and emotional regulation.[18]

Qigong Practice: Nourishing the Water Element

1. **Establish your anchoring hand.** Place your left hand on your lower back. Let the palm rest gently, with your forearm relaxed against your back. This hand remains still for the entire practice and acts as your anchor.
2. **Prepare your circling hand.** Hold your right hand in front of your lower belly, palm facing upward, about six to eight inches away from your torso, as if you are about to scoop water from a small pool in front of you.
3. **Make a circle.** With your right hand, begin making a clockwise circle in front of yourself. Lift your hand upward in front of your body. Imagine you're gathering water in your right palm. Lift your palm smoothly upward in front of your torso. Keep the motion close enough to feel the air near your body but do not touch yourself.

   At the top of the circle, rotate the palm outward, just above your forehead; then lower your hand gently in front of you, releasing the imaginary water back into the pool below as your hand traces a downward arc in front of your torso.

   Return your hand to the starting point near the lower belly, then turn the palm upward again and begin the next circle. Repeat ten times.

   Let the circles be loose and relaxed. Do not overextend the arm or shoulder. The movement should feel natural and fluid. There is no need to force it—softness is the goal.
4. **Repeat on the other side.** Switch hands so your right hand anchors on your lower back. Extend your left hand in front of your lower belly. Your left hand will move in a counterclockwise circle, the mirror of the previous movement. Repeat ten times, keeping the motion relaxed, smooth, and close to your body without strain.
5. **Close the practice.** Place one hand over your lower belly and the other on your lower back. Breathe into the space between both hands. Imagine a deep, calm blue ocean filling your lower back and belly. Rest here for one to two minutes.

WHY THIS HELPS

In TCM, the lower back is the home of kidney energy, which holds the body's deepest reserves of vitality, or jing. Grief, fear, and exhaustion can deplete this vital energy, affecting your inner emotional reserves and creating imbalance in the heart and Shen, or spirit. This movement practice replenishes, brings warmth, and restores balance. Placing your hands on your belly and back creates a circuit of attention, while the imagery of a vast blue ocean (reflecting the kidney's association with the water element) calms your mind and nourishes your body from within. Breathing into this space replenishes what feels emptied, offering steadiness, grounding, and renewal.[19]

Breath Practice: Filling the Deep Void of Emptiness

1. Sit comfortably and take a few slow, deep breaths.
2. Allow your body to settle and your energy to ground.
3. Place the fleshy part of your thumb at the center of your chest, midway between the base of your throat and the bottom of your sternum. It doesn't matter which hand you use. Just keep your thumb centered and press firmly into this point.
4. Inhale deeply, directing the breath into the center of your chest. Hold the breath for as long as feels comfortable, without straining. Keep steady pressure on your chest as you hold.
5. Exhale forcefully through your mouth.
6. Continue this cycle of inhaling deeply, holding with pressure, and exhaling powerfully for five to seven times.
7. When you've completed the repetitions, relax. Release your hand and let it rest by your side. Take a deep, natural breath. Notice the fullness of your breath and the sense of relaxation and centeredness that fills your body.

WHY THIS HELPS

This practice connects the lung channel with the lung organ system, creating a network that helps release grief and sadness. In TCM, the lungs are said to house grief, and they are often deeply affected by the emptiness and breathlessness that grief can bring. The thumb naturally stimulates acupuncture point Lung 10, while the pressure on the chest activates Ren 17, a point that opens and expands the breath. Linking these points through touch and breath allows the chest to soften, creating spaciousness where it may have once felt void and numb. Breath retention also gently supports the kidneys, which are associated with fear. This offers support and grounding when emotions feel overwhelming.

From a Western scientific perspective, pressing on the chest while slowing and holding the breath stimulates the vagus nerve, which runs through the thorax. This helps activate the parasympathetic nervous system, lowering stress and calming the body. Research shows that slow, regulated breathing and vagal stimulation improve emotional regulation and support recovery from stress.[20]

Writing Exercise: Meeting Fear as a Sacred Messenger

1. **Prepare a sacred space.** Find a quiet place and bring your journal or some writing paper. Sit with your spine supported and place one hand over your heart or belly. Take three slow breaths and whisper inwardly, *I am held. I am here. I am safe enough for this*. Let the space become a small sanctuary inside your day. You are not trying to get rid of fear. You are preparing to meet it with reverence.
2. **Invite fear to appear in sacred form.** Allow fear to arrive in your imagination as a presence, guide, or guardian. In many spiritual traditions, fear is not an enemy. It is a messenger standing at the threshold, pointing toward what matters most.

Begin writing with one of the following openings:

- "Fear came to me as a guide and said . . ."
- "I met fear at the edge of my path, glowing with . . ."
- "Fear appeared clothed in . . "
- "Fear placed something in my hands and whispered . . ."

Let the image form gently. Do not force meaning. Let fear appear as it wishes: animal, angel, ancestor, wind, shadow, light.

3. **Enter into sacred dialogue.** Allow the story to unfold slowly. Let the presence of fear speak first. Let it show you why it came, what it sees, what it guards, or what it tries to protect within you. Then let your own voice respond. Write "What I say to fear in this sacred meeting is . . ."

   This is not a confrontation. It is a prayerful conversation. Two truths meeting: the part of you that trembles and the part of you that remembers.
4. **Transform the image gently.** Fear shifts when something in the image softens—the light grows warmer, the guide steps back, the landscape opens, the shadow reveals a face. Ask inwardly, *What single change would help this fear feel less threatening and more like a companion on my path?*

   Make that change in your writing. Let the story turn slightly toward compassion.

   This is not about control. It is about allowing the sacred intelligence of fear to be revealed.
5. **Close with a blessing.** End your writing with one final line: "The blessing fear left with me was . . ."

   This blessing may come as a word, an image, a sensation, or a memory. It may be clear or subtle. Either way, it is enough.

   Place your hand back on your heart or belly and take one gentle breath, as if sealing the encounter with gratitude.

WHY THIS HELPS

Spiritually, fear is often a threshold guardian, pointing toward your deepest values and most vulnerable truths. By imagining fear as a sacred presence rather than an intruder, you reclaim relationship instead of resistance.[21] This transforms the energy of fear from contraction into meaning, from overwhelm into guidance, from trembling into a quiet inner knowing.[22]

Exercise: Restoring Resiliency Through the Lower Back

1. Lie on your back on the floor or in bed. Keep your head resting on the surface beneath you as you gently bring your knees toward your chest and hold them with your hands. Allow your shoulders and face to soften.
2. Holding on to your knees, slowly rock your body from side to side. Move at a gentle, steady pace. Feel your lower back massaging against the floor or mattress. Let the breath stay natural. Continue for about thirty seconds to one minute.
3. Lift your face toward your knees while drawing your knees slightly toward your face. Inhale once you are in the squeeze. Hold the breath softly as you gently hug your body into itself. Then gently release your head back down on the exhale, keeping hold of your knees.
4. Repeat this squeeze and release three times. Move gently. The motion should feel compact, contained, and comforting.
5. Continuing to hold on to your knees; let your head rest. Bring your awareness to your lower back. As you breathe, imagine a deep ocean-blue color filling this area. With each inhale, picture the color expanding gently. With each exhale, imagine it settling and calming you. Stay here for one to two minutes, allowing your body to soften.
6. Release your legs to the floor and take a few deep breaths before getting up.

WHY THIS HELPS

In Traditional Chinese Medicine, the kidneys govern the water element, which supports resilience, grounding, and emotional steadiness, with the lower back as the physical home of this energy. Gentle rocking and squeezing can warm and release this area, relaxing the psoas, soothing the lumbar spine, and supporting the kidneys, while the imagery of deep ocean blue reinforces water's quiet, restorative quality.[23] This simple, restorative practice is especially helpful when you feel fear, overwhelm, fatigue, or emotional numbness. It invites the body to feel held from within and nourishes the deep reserves of energy that grief often drains, offering comfort and grounding by helping you rest into life rather than brace against it.

Exercise: Forest Bathing

1. **Enter with intention.** Find a quiet natural space, such as a forest, park, or grove of trees. Before beginning, pause at the entrance. Take a slow breath and silently set the intention to be fully present.
2. **Walk slowly.** Move through the space at a gentle pace. Do not rush or try to get anywhere. Let your steps be light and unhurried.
3. **Awaken your senses.**
   - **Sight:** Notice the patterns of leaves, branches, and light. Allow your eyes to soften and take in the colors and textures.
   - **Sound:** Listen to birds, rustling leaves, or the silence between sounds.
   - **Touch:** Run your fingers along the bark of a tree, touch a leaf, or feel the earth beneath your feet.
   - **Smell:** Breathe in the scent of pine, soil, or flowers. Notice how each fragrance shifts your body.
   - **Breath:** Inhale deeply, imagining the oxygen released by the trees filling your lungs. Exhale, offering your own breath back to the forest.

4. **Rest and receive.** Find a comfortable spot to sit or lean against a tree. Let yourself simply be, without any agenda. Feel the steadiness of the earth supporting you and the quiet presence of the forest holding you.
5. **Close with gratitude.** Before leaving, pause to thank the forest. You might touch a tree, bow your head, or silently whisper gratitude for its nourishment and companionship.

WHY THIS HELPS

Forest bathing, or *shinrin-yoku*, originated in Japan as a way to restore health, calm the mind, and reconnect with the natural world.[24] The practice invites you to slow down, awaken your senses, and allow the living presence of trees, plants, and the earth to soothe and renew you. The gentle presence of trees, fresh air, and birdsong can settle the nervous system and quiet the mind. Research shows that time spent in forests lowers cortisol, reduces blood pressure, and lifts mood.[25] But beyond the science there is a deeper gift: a sense of being held by something much bigger than ourselves. In grief, when life feels fractured and unstable, forest bathing offers a grounded way of belonging and a reminder that you are supported by larger mysteries that are always compassionately present, even when you can't see or feel them.

Summary

If fear has shattered your sense of safety, begin with the body—breathe, press your hand to your chest, and remind yourself that you are here, in this moment, alive. If you find yourself bracing for the next loss, recognize this as the nervous system's attempt to protect you; grounding, rest, and rhythm help rebuild trust in life. If fear closes you off from others, remember that love also lives in this vulnerability; connection restores what fear constricts. If you find yourself at the edge of the abyss, know that this descent—terrifying as it is—is often the very doorway through which spiritual aliveness and transformation emerge.

Fear is not a sign that you've failed to be brave. It is the threshold between the life you knew and the deeper truth waiting to be lived through you.

15

Coming Up Against Guilt

When Laura lost her baby in a late-term miscarriage, she turned all the blame inward. Layer upon layer of "if onlys" and "I should haves" stacked against her heart. "I'm the mom. I should've known better," she told me. The weight of responsibility was unbearable.

Unlike shame, which says, *I am bad*, guilt says, *I did something bad.* It's the mind's attempt to make sense of the senseless, to claim control where there was none. In grief, guilt often rushes in to fill the void that loss leaves behind. It gives the illusion of order: *If I caused it, maybe I can prevent it from ever happening again.*

Because miscarriage is rarely recognized in the same way as a "death," Laura was not given time to grieve. The ER staff checked for internal bleeding and told her there was nothing more to be done. She was *discharged*, a word that felt brutal to her. The nurses kept her a few hours longer, knowing how wrong it felt to send a mother home empty-handed. Even they carried guilt for not being able to do more.

By Monday, Laura was expected to be back at work, teaching as though nothing had happened. Standing in front of her class, she swallowed tears as children asked gently, "Ms. Laura, are you okay?" She wiped her face and kept moving.

Her grief was covered in judgment. She replayed every moment of the pregnancy, punishing herself for imagined mistakes. Even with her partner, she withheld much of her pain, afraid of burdening him, of being too much. Guilt told her that needing care would make her weak, that the loss was her fault, that she had to hold it all together.

The truth was her colleagues would have supported her. Her partner would have grieved alongside her. But guilt distorts perception. It disguises tenderness as failure and keeps love at a distance, when what it most needs is witness and rest. Guilt can be even more devastating than shame when it traps you in a loop of imagined responsibility. You can't undo what has already happened, yet your mind keeps trying. Where shame attacks identity, guilt attacks agency; it convinces you that you had control when you didn't, that you could have saved what was never yours to save. It masks itself as morality, as care, even as love, while quietly chipping away at your capacity to receive any support. In this way, guilt becomes its own form of exile: You banish yourself from compassion in the name of responsibility.

Guilt as Distortion of Reality

Laura's story shows how guilt can become the prison guard of grief. Instead of giving space for sorrow, it turns grief inward, silencing emotional honesty and making healing feel impossible.

You know that feeling when sadness wells up and your throat tightens into a lump? Grief often brings us into that space of raw, constricted suffocation. Alongside the heaviness of sadness, guilt often threads its way in.

In the courtroom, guilt means one thing: intention to harm. But in daily life, we use the word *guilt* far more loosely: "I feel guilty for not calling" or "I feel guilty for being angry." Rarely do we mean that we intended harm. More often we are describing judgment about our emotions, needs, or grief.

I once sat with a woman whose husband died suddenly. "I feel so guilty," she told me. "I should have stopped him from going out that night. I should have been kinder." Yet when I asked if she'd intended to do harm, she shook her head. Of course not. Her guilt was not about intent. It was judgment punishing her for not being perfect, for not being able to control the uncontrollable.

We rarely feel guilty because we set out to harm someone. We feel guilty for being emotionally honest; for resenting, raging, feeling relief, or simply being human. Judgment, too, often disguises itself as guilt.

Anna, who cared for her father with advanced dementia, whispered to me, almost as if she were afraid of someone overhearing, "Sometimes I just wish it was over. Then I hate myself for even thinking that." Her guilt was not intent to harm. It was exhaustion and longing for rest, tangled in judgment.

Guilt in the Body and Mind

When judgment is silent, it can lodge itself in the body. Traditional Chinese Medicine (TCM) calls this plum-pit qi: a lump in the throat that can't be swallowed or spit out.[1] Physiologically, the larynx tightens. Psychologically, the unsaid words choke us.

A father who lost his teenage son pointed to his throat as he told me, "I keep replaying the last argument we had. I yelled at him. And now I can't breathe without feeling that fight stuck here."

There's a simple practice to help assuage this pain: Place a hand gently on your throat. Take a slow breath in. As you exhale, soften your jaw and let your shoulders drop. Whisper quietly, *I am allowed to speak my truth without judging myself. I am allowed to feel what I feel.*

Unexpressed emotions demand performance. We act how we are "supposed to," but performance drains vitality, which is essential to grieving well. The suppression fragments authenticity, creating invisible barriers to emotional honesty.

Charlotte's husband had lived with chronic illness for nearly a decade. When he finally passed, she was devastated but also relieved. "I feel like I can finally sleep," she admitted. "But then I feel terrible, because what kind of wife is relieved that her husband is gone?" Grief and relief coexisted, yet guilt rushed in to split them apart.

Grief has no interest in tidy categories. It is messy, human, contradictory. When we try to split grief into categories, we don't eliminate the "bad" parts. We push them underground, where they tighten our throats, weigh on our chests, and haunt our thoughts.

If you notice yourself dividing or categorizing emotions into "good" and "bad," pause. What if both can be true? What if the emotional honesty of claiming our wholeness can dispel our judgments and restore our vitality?

Guilt as Prison Guard

Grief might feel like a life sentence, but it isn't. It's a portal into love, loss, and renewal. But guilt can act as a prison guard for grief. It shackles us to judgment and whispers, *Don't be real. Hide your true feelings.*

One mother who lost her child in stillbirth shared through tears, "I feel guilty for wishing I could move on. What kind of mother thinks that?" What she really longed for was freedom to live again while still carrying love. Naming that truth—"I want to live"—was her first act of unlocking the prison cell.

I often share the following simple practice with clients: Breathe into your chest and imagine a small key resting in your heart. With each exhale, it's possible to unlock a bit of space for honesty, grief, and life.

Sometimes guilt is the most honest expression of our life energy. Sometimes we act from jealousy, envy, anger, or spite. Sometimes we intend harm. In those cases, guilt is not distortion but a signal guiding the way forward to accountability.

A man once told me, "When my brother died, I smashed his guitar in anger. It was the one thing he loved most. I wanted to hurt him for leaving me." Afterward, he couldn't look at the broken pieces without feeling sick. His guilt wasn't about the object itself—it was about the love it represented, the bridge he'd destroyed in his pain. Together we explored amends: acknowledgment, accountability, repair, and change. He wrote a letter to his brother, restored the instrument as best he could, and donated it to a youth music program. Facing that truth and taking action released him from the loop of punishment that guilt had become.

Guilt and Empaths: The People-Pleasing Trap

Another face of guilt complicates grieving: how it shows up in empaths. Empaths are highly sensitive people who often feel the wounds and pains of others as if they were their own. I'm one of them, so I know this pain all too well. Empaths grow up learning to fawn, to people-please, to constantly seek approval. But what might feel like a natural attunement to others can actually be a survival mechanism.

When emotional needs go unmet in childhood, the psyche adapts. This is often called "small-*t*" trauma, to distinguish it from the "big-*T*" trauma, which are the large, explosive events that overwhelm the nervous system. Small-*t* trauma is the steady drip of emotional abandonment. It's the subtle experience of not being seen, heard, or validated. In response, some learn to fawn, lavishing attention on others and none on themselves. They anticipate the needs, moods, and wants of those around them in the hope of receiving love or belonging in return.

Over time, this survival pattern hardens into identity. The constant vigilance to others' needs—while neglecting your own—trains the nervous system to equate safety with self-erasure. Gradually personal wants and desires recede from awareness, as if they no longer matter. The self learns to survive by disappearing, becoming "needless" and "wantless." But a life organized around minimizing one's own needs quietly corrodes self-worth because it denies the truth that you, too, are meant to be cared for.

Then grief arrives. Grief demands attention. It demands rest, boundaries, slowness, and self-care. For empaths, these very things can trigger guilt. Guilt shows up when prioritizing personal needs, when saying no, when not having the same energy to perform as before. In this way, guilt is again a distortion. It whispers that caring for yourself is harming others, that self-care is selfishness.

I worked with Leila, a social worker who showed up for families every day, even as migraines and exhaustion consumed her. "If I don't show up, who will?" she asked. Rest felt like betrayal. Her guilt wasn't truth but the fawn response that had been shaped long ago.

Another griever, Paul, came to me after the death of his brother. Friends and relatives constantly called on him to help with funeral arrangements and paperwork. Paul confessed, "Every time I wanted to say no, I felt like I was abandoning them. But inside I was drowning." When he finally set a boundary and told his family he needed a day to himself, he was met with disappointment. He told me, "It felt like I had committed a crime." In reality, that one act of saying no allowed him to rest and cry for the first time in weeks. The guilt didn't vanish overnight, but with practice he learned that boundaries weren't the same as abandonment. They were an act of love toward himself.

This is one of the hardest lessons for empaths in grief: putting oneself first. Grief will ask for boundaries—for rest when the impulse is to push, for speaking when silence has been the default. It will ask for help rather than constant giving. At first this may feel uncomfortable.

People pleasers often feel remarkably alone in grief. Secondary losses appear when friends who once received their care don't show up in return. This can awaken deep anger at the injustice of it all. The learning curve is steep: to voice your needs clearly, risk misunderstanding, and accept that others may not be attuned in the same way.

The gauntlet of guilt is grueling. But guilt is not stronger than grief. Love is always stronger. You have already survived what you thought you couldn't. Grief is heavy enough. Don't let guilt chain you further.

Your voice matters. Your truth matters. And your grief deserves compassion, not the prison of distortion. May you remember that compassion—toward yourself and others—is the greater truth. And may guilt give way to the deeper wisdom of love.

TECHNIQUES FOR WORKING WITH GUILT

Exercise: Releasing the Lump in the Throat

1. **Prepare your posture.** Stand tall with your feet grounded. Interlace your fingers and place your hands behind your head, your elbows flared wide.
2. **Expand and contract.** Inhale deeply as you lift your chest upward, opening your throat and extending your elbows wider. Feel as if your heart is reaching toward the sky. Exhale as you gently contract forward, elbows drawing in, body folding slightly. Repeat this expansion and contraction several times, finding a steady rhythm of breath and movement.

3. **Add a twist.** On your next inhale, expand your chest and hold the open posture. Slowly twist your torso to the left, keeping your elbows lifted and your armpits open. Return to center, then twist to the right. Move gently from side to side for several breaths.
4. **Release your neck.** Relax your arms down at your sides. Begin slow neck rolls, first in one direction, then the other. Keep the movements small and gentle, noticing the relationship between the muscles of your neck and the sensation in your throat.
5. **Integrate.** Pause in stillness, your shoulders soft, your chin slightly tucked. Notice any shifts in your throat, chest, or breath.

WHY THIS HELPS

When grief is unspoken, it often gathers as tightness in the throat and chest, creating the sensation of a "lump in the throat."[2] This practice gently restores movement and circulation to the neck, throat, and upper chest, releasing tension that builds from suppression.[3] As breath and posture open the channel between head and heart, the body finds more space for expression. With this openness, what once felt blocked can begin to soften, making room for honesty, voice, and authentic release.

Exercise: Creating Energetic Boundaries

1. Place your palms together in a prayer position at the center of your chest. Press gently but firmly, with elbows open wide. Bow your head slightly so your chin moves toward your chest and your nose leans toward your hands, as if honoring yourself.
2. Inhale deeply as you extend your palms forward, then open your arms out to the sides. Imagine you are creating a spacious boundary around your chest and heart. Lift your head as your chest expands.
3. Exhale as you bring your palms back together at your chest, gently bowing your head once more.

4. Continue this cycle of expansion and contraction for a few minutes, coordinating breath and movement. Inhale as you expand, exhale as you return and bow.
5. As your arms move, sense that you are shaping a sacred bubble around you. This boundary is not about shutting people out. Instead, it is a field of honor that acknowledges your grief, your story, and your needs.
6. Conclude the practice and rest in the spaciousness you have created, feeling safe and connected.

WHY THIS HELPS

This practice supports you in forming a sacred sense of space around yourself. Boundaries are not barriers meant to isolate but circles of honor, recognition, and care. By combining breath, movement, and visualization, you remind your body and heart that it is safe to take up space. These boundaries allow your grief to breathe, soften the pull of outside pressures, and affirm that your well-being matters. They help you hold your experience with dignity while remaining open to connection.[4]

Writing Practice: Mental Dump Freewriting

1. Grab a pen and paper. Set a timer for fifteen minutes. Begin to write.
2. Let the words pour out without stopping. Don't worry about punctuation, grammar, or spelling. It doesn't even matter if you can read it later. Think of it as word vomit—a release of whatever's been locked inside.
3. Write feelings, frustrations, annoyances, fears, or regrets. Focus on one person or many. Explore something happening now or something from years ago. Let your mind jump around like a monkey. No need to make sense.
4. When you finish, release what you've written. Crumple it, burn

it, or create a simple ceremony of letting it go. This seals the practice as a ritual of release.

5. Do this each day for a week. Afterward, take a few minutes to reflect on how you feel. Notice whether the practice helps you build freedom, honesty, and the courage to honor what is real.

WHY THIS HELPS

When you need to get it out, this is your practice. No judgment, no shame, no guilt—just raw emotion and expression. Swear if you need to; research even shows that swearing can be an effective form of emotional release.[5] Writing without rules or pressure helps bypass self-censorship and opens the door to honest truth. Releasing the pages turns the act into a ritual of letting go, signaling to your nervous system that the weight has been acknowledged and set down. Practiced regularly, this builds emotional freedom, clarity, and the courage to meet grief with openness rather than suppression.

Creative Project: Putting Down a Burden

Obligation-based guilt often comes from old stories we tell ourselves—that we need to be good, be responsible, carry everyone's needs, never disappoint. These stories weave themselves into your identity so deeply that the guilt feels moral even when no harm was done. Allowance means giving yourself permission to let these inherited burdens go. This creative project lets you see the burden, shape it with your hands, and transform it into something that no longer weighs on you.

You might mold a small object out of clay, wrap stones or wool in fabric, crumple and tie paper with string, paint a shape on a piece of cardboard, or draw the guilt and fold it into a small bundle.

1. **Gather your materials.** Choose any material you'd like to work with, such as paper, clay, cardboard, twine, leaves, cloth scraps, small stones, markers, or paints.

2. **Name the obligation**. On a small slip of paper, write the belief you have been carrying:

    - "I have to keep everyone happy."
    - "I must always say yes."
    - "If I rest, I'm letting people down."
    - "My needs come last."

    Fold this slip and tuck it inside or under the object you created. This gives the burden its voice.
3. **Give the burden a texture, color, and story.** Decorate or mark your creation in whatever way feels expressive. Let it be messy. Let it be raw. Let it be honest. Ask yourself as you create:

    - What color does this obligation feel like?
    - What texture matches the weight of it?
    - What shape does the pressure take?
    - You are externalizing the internal.

4. **Create a place of release.** Choose where the burden will go when you set it down: a corner of the yard, a bowl of water, a compost heap, a drawer you rarely open, a small hole in the earth, a box marked "not mine to carry." This becomes the sacred place of release.
5. **Place the burden down with intention.** Hold the object in your hands for a moment. Say quietly,

    - "This does not belong to me anymore."
    - "I allow myself to release what I no longer need to carry."
    - "I can care for myself while also holding responsibilities of care."
    - "My needs don't have to compete with others' needs—they can coexist."

    Then put the object in its chosen place. Let your hands open. Feel the absence of its weight.
6. **Create a symbol of allowance.** After placing the burden down, create or choose one small symbol of permission, such as a feather, a ribbon, a small drawing, or a word written on a card or

stone with the word *Allow*. Keep this near you. It represents the new truth.

7. **Close with a statement of freedom.** Place your hand on your chest and speak one line:

    - "I am allowed to let this go."
    - "My worth is not tied to obligation."
    - "I am free to choose what I carry."
    - "My needs also matter."

    Let the creative act do its quiet work.

WHY THIS HELPS

Creative transformation engages the emotional brain more powerfully than thinking alone.[6] By shaping the burden with your hands and then placing it down, your body learns the truth of allowance. This practice interrupts the cycle of obligation-guilt and creates a new story: one where you are worthy of rest, boundaries, and freedom from inherited expectations.

Writing Practice: Crafting an Apology Letter

1. **Grab a piece of paper or use a computer to type your letter.** Use whatever is most comfortable to you that helps you relate to the emotional experience of this writing exercise.
2. **Acknowledge the harm.** Begin by clearly naming what happened, without excuses or justifications—such as "I see that I spoke harshly to you" or "I recognize that I ignored your needs." The goal is to validate the reality of the harm with simple clarity.
3. **Offer a sincere apology.** Move directly into an apology that communicates responsibility, using language such as "I apologize for . . ." Avoid minimizing, explaining, or being defensive. Let

your apology be direct and heartfelt. Remember, "I'm sorry" alone often feels incomplete because it expresses a feeling rather than addressing the action. True repair requires both acknowledgment and changed behavior.

4. **Acknowledge your inner landscape.** Recognize the feelings or circumstances that contributed to your actions—not to justify but to understand. For example, you might say, "I acted from a place of hurt" or "I was overwhelmed and did not express myself well." This step invites self-compassion while maintaining accountability.
5. **State your commitment to change.** Share the steps you're taking to repair the pattern within yourself, such as learning to pause before reacting, working on honest and calm communication, or practicing healthy boundaries. This demonstrates your integrity and willingness to grow.
6. **Offer space for the other person's experience.** Acknowledge that the other person may need time and has their own feelings and boundaries. You might say, "I understand you may need time" or "Your feelings matter." This honors their experience and the relationship.
7. **Close with humility and care.** End with a sincere, gentle closing, such as, "Thank you for reading this" or "I am committed to growing from this." Let your closing reflect genuine respect and care.

WHY THIS HELPS

Guilt asks for repair and apology asks for truth—both require courage. Writing an apology letter allows you to face the guilt you carry and honors your inner moral compass. This practice can restore your sense of alignment and begin to release emotional weight held in your body. When approached with honesty, humility, and compassion, writing an apology letter creates space for forgiveness, understanding, and renewed integrity.

Whether you should send the letter depends on the situation. Sometimes the act of writing is for your own healing—it helps you face the truth, soften guilt, release shame, and reclaim integrity. Other times, sharing the letter can be healing for everyone, especially when the relationship is safe, both parties are willing, or reconciliation is possible. If you feel unsure, seek guidance from a therapist, spiritual director, or trusted guide. Remember: Safety, reciprocity, and emotional readiness are essential. You do not owe access to someone who has harmed you, nor do you have to open yourself to further harm.

Summary

If guilt shows up as endless self-judgment, recognize it as the mind's attempt to find control in what was uncontrollable. Awareness, not punishment, brings freedom. If you replay what you "should have" done, pause. Guilt freezes grief in the past; compassion allows it to move and metabolize. If you feel responsible for everyone else's pain, remember that this is not virtue—it is survival. Boundaries and rest restore perspective. If guilt tells you that care must always flow outward, turn some of that tenderness inward. Tending to yourself is an act of repair, not neglect.

Guilt dissolves when you stop measuring love by sacrifice. Grief's teaching is to reclaim your right to feel, to need, to want, and to be.

16

Disentangling from Shame

Simone reached out to me through a friend. On our very first call she blurted out, "I don't even know why I'm here. It's not even real grief." She explained that her only daughter had just left for college, and although she was proud and supportive, she felt an aching sadness she just couldn't seem to shake. Her friend had noticed and gently suggested, "This is grief. I have just the person you should talk to."

At first Simone dismissed it. She told herself she was being dramatic. Other parents had endured far worse: death, illness, divorce. Who was she to feel sad about something as ordinary as a child going off to school? Beneath her words was the quiet drumbeat of shame: *I should not feel this way. I should be stronger. This isn't real grief. Something must be wrong with me.*

Shame is one of the most universal human emotions yet the least discussed. Everyone has a shame story. It may not begin in grief. It might have started with a childhood moment of humiliation, such as being told to "man up" or to quit crying, or hearing that your feelings made you too sensitive. It may come from growing up in a family where silence felt safer than truth, or from a culture that taught you worth is measured by achievement, perfection, or control. Whatever its origin, shame carries the message that *something is fundamentally wrong with me* or *I must constantly make up for what I lack.*

Unlike guilt, which says, *I did something wrong*, shame collapses your entire sense of self into a defectiveness that declares, *I am wrong.*

It thrives in secrecy, hides in your body, and attaches itself to your very identity. Shame is learned, reinforced, and often passed down through generations. At its core, shame tells a story that you don't belong and that you're unworthy of love, acceptance, and home.

If grief disorients because love has lost its anchor, shame disorients because belonging feels threatened. Grief says, *I lost something I love.* Shame says, *I am unlovable.* Both leave you unmoored. Both live in your body. Both can be inherited. And both create suffering when silenced.

The Shame Spiral

The truth is that we swim in an ocean of grief and that ocean is often polluted by shame. Shame makes grief feel heavier than it already is. It is opportunistic. It slips in when emotions are big, when your heart is raw, or when you feel uncertain about your pain. Shame is not an emotion in itself. Like guilt, it distorts reality, but the distortion is deeper, sharper, and far more wounding.

Shame spirals and hijacks the grieving process. When you feel your grief is a burden that must be carried alone, that is a shame story. When you believe you have to be strong for everyone else, that is a shame story. When you worry you are not grieving the "right way," as if such a thing existed, that too is a shame story. When grief is suppressed, shame begins to breed. It thrives in secrecy, silence, and separation, in the places where you feel most alone.

Grief is already heavy, but when shame settles on top of it, the whole experience becomes twisted. *I grieve because I loved* quietly becomes *I grieve because I am weak, broken, or failing.* In that distortion, you may stop trusting your feelings. You may stop reaching toward others. You may begin to withdraw and collapse inward. What could be a natural unfolding of sorrow becomes entangled with secrecy, perfectionism, and self-blame. Instead of compassion, shame whispers judgment. Instead of connection, it fuels isolation. In this spiral, your grief becomes harder to carry, not because it is wrong but because shame has convinced you that you are.

The Power of Words

Words carry potency that we don't always recognize but often internalize. Phrases such as *breaking down*, *falling apart*, *losing it*, or *having a meltdown* carry unspoken shame that says feeling deeply means we're falling apart. These statements weaponize pseudo-strength against what is most natural and human. They turn emotions into the enemy and cast grief as weakness rather than love in motion.

When such words come from parents, teachers, elders, or faith leaders, they set a trajectory for how you believe you should grieve. They shame you into silence, whispering that your way of grieving is wrong, that there must be a right way, and that you can't trust your own experience. Shame in grief doesn't just say, *Your pain is wrong*. It says, *You're wrong for feeling pain at all.*

This distinction matters. Embarrassment and humiliation are emotions related to self-consciousness, a normal human experience, but shame is uniquely corrosive because it fuses identity with failure. Guilt often moves you toward repair, whereas shame often leads to hiding and withdrawal.[1] Research shows that shame is strongly associated with self-criticism, avoidance, depression, and rumination, all risk factors for complex or prolonged grief.[2]

The words you use are intimately connected to the beliefs you form. Beliefs aren't abstract concepts floating above you. They're embodied patterns wired into the brain through repeated experience and interpretation. Neuroscience shows that when you tell yourself a story such as *I'm weak* or *I should be over this by now*, the brain's predictive networks, including the medial prefrontal cortex, anterior cingulate, and insula, activate to anticipate and filter reality through that lens.[3] These regions shape attention and perception, making you more likely to notice evidence that confirms the belief while ignoring what contradicts it. Over time, neuroplasticity—the capacity of the brain to change—strengthens these circuits, so the story becomes easier to access and feels truer.[4]

This is how shame-based narratives become self-fulfilling as the body and brain learn to expect rejection or unworthiness, and behaviors such as withdrawal and self-silencing begin to conform to those expectations.

The good news is that the way out of shame mirrors the way through grief, which we can hold with compassion, expression, and belonging. This is the "why" of Compassionate Grieving: Just as grief can be a compass pointing you back to love, shame can become a compass pointing you back to worthiness. It asks you to unlearn the old stories of defectiveness and reclaim your right to be seen, to feel, and to belong, especially in your pain and especially when you grieve. To do effective grief care also asks you to look at shame because of how prevalent it is within our society. The freedom from shame provides the alleviation of the sting in grief.

Disenfranchised Grief and Isolation

Shame breeds secrecy, and shame thrives when grief is invisible. *Disenfranchised grief*, a term coined by the grief expert Kenneth J. Doka, as shared in chapter 3, describes losses that are not socially recognized or validated.[5] Miscarriage, infertility, pet loss, estrangement from a friend, the death of an ex-partner, or subtle identity changes are often met with silence or dismissal. Abstract losses such as safety, trust, innocence, or faith, as well as collective and intergenerational grief and loss of dreams, hopes, and visions, often go unnamed yet are profoundly felt in the body and spirit.

Death-related grief can eclipse non-death-related grief, or it can feel as though only traumatic grief is worthy of attention. A false sense of competition forms around what counts as grief and over whose grief counts. When worthiness enters the story of grief, shame is not far behind.

Messages such as "It wasn't really a baby yet," "Why are you upset about someone you divorced?," or "It was just a job; you'll find another one" reinforce the idea that your unique grief doesn't count and undermine the complexity of love expressed through loss. When we oversimplify grief, we reduce it to tight spaces and weaponize it through minimization and invalidation to suggest that grief is unworthy.

Doka's work highlights that disenfranchised grievers internalize these invalidations, producing shame scripts such as *My type of loss doesn't matter* or *Something is wrong with me for still caring.* The deepest wound of shame is the erosion of trust in your own emotions. Shame tells you, *Don't believe what you feel. Don't believe your body. Don't believe your love.* This creates a grief beneath the grief, layered with a loss of identity and belonging within yourself. Healing asks you to restore trust in your inner compass.

Shame is not only internal. As we discussed in chapter 4 on letting go, it's also a form of cultural and social enforcement. Societies use shame to dictate how long, how deeply, and how publicly people may grieve. "You aren't over it yet?" reflects collective discomfort more than individual care. Left unchallenged, these rules perpetuate isolation and suffering.

Simran and her partner had been through four rounds of IVF. Each cycle carried the fragile rhythm of hope and devastation. Well-meaning friends told her to "just relax" or "keep trying; it'll eventually happen," but their words deepened her loneliness. Simran's grief wasn't only about not becoming pregnant. It was about invisible losses few could see: the embryos that never implanted, months structured around treatment, and the dream of holding a child slipping further away. Most painful of all, she began to believe there was something fundamentally wrong with her. Each time she tried to talk about it, people minimized her pain. The lack of recognition made her grief heavier, layering sorrow with shame.

Ancestral and Intergenerational Grief and Shame

In some cultures, stoicism is praised, tears are hidden, and strength is measured by silence. These messages are passed down generationally, creating lineages of ungrieved pain suppressed through shame.

For many communities, the weight of history is even heavier. Cultures that have endured war, famine, slavery, colonization, and systemic dehumanization carry ancestral wounds that extend beyond individual memory. Survival often required silence, endurance, and sheer force of will. Families learned to push through narratives of unworthiness imposed by oppression to build better lives for future generations.[6]

Yet survival came at a cost. On the backs of that sacrifice, trauma and countless layers of loss were often left unhealed and silently transferred to children and grandchildren. Studies of Holocaust survivors, for example, show measurable changes in stress physiology among their children, including altered cortisol regulation, which suggests that trauma can be biologically imprinted across generations.[7] Researchers describe this as an epigenetic effect, where trauma changes how certain genes are expressed without altering the genetic code.[8] These biological changes shape how the body responds to stress, carrying forward echoes of past suffering into the present. When survival opens into opportunities for thriving, distortions can surface in those who inherit stories of neglect and isolation. Shame can be imprinted, making belonging and visibility feel almost impossible. Intergenerational transmission of shame results in families where emotional suppression is normalized, leaving descendants disconnected from their own grief.

I remember a young man who came to me after the sudden death of his father. He spoke of his grief in whispers, apologizing for his tears. His family had immigrated to the United States two generations earlier, escaping political violence. He grew up hearing stories of survival, sacrifice, and hard work, but never stories about sorrow. In his family, crying was a weakness and silence, a strength. When grief came for him, it collided with this inherited narrative, and he felt ashamed for even needing comfort.

It can sometimes feel as if we're born already carrying an invisible grief backpack, weighed down by wounds from the past. When new grief arrives, whether death-related not, it may strike with greater intensity. The pain of the present is amplified by unacknowledged sorrow of the past, and shame's quiet grip tightens.

Gender, Identity, and Shame

Shame is not distributed evenly. Men are often told to "man up," suppress tears, and avoid vulnerability, while women may be shamed as too emotional or too sensitive. For LGBTQ+ and BIPOC communities, systemic oppression can compound grief shame, requiring people to appear strong for survival, denying space for visible mourning, or even pressuring early forgiveness.

William had just lost a close friend to suicide. His friend's father had always disapproved of his son's sexuality, and though the young man had come out years earlier, the shame, isolation, and alienation he carried lingered for a long time. There was anger in William's tone, especially toward his friend's father, but also a quiet echo of his story with his own father. "It feels like I have a grief closet I want to come out of now," he told me. William's words revealed not only the heaviness of his loss but the deeper layers of shame tied to identity, family, and belonging.

Grace was a trans woman in the hospital after surgery for a broken leg. She was furious because the medical staff constantly referred to her as "he." She confided that she could hear whispers about her identity from the staff who gathered outside her room each day. Already feeling vulnerable in the hospital, Grace also felt exposed and judged. The shame of being seen through others' disapproval collided with her own personal story, leaving her isolated at the very moment she needed connection.

On Grace's behalf, I confronted the medical staff and reminded them of the importance of honoring Grace's identity. I referred to her by the name she had chosen, even though it was not yet legally changed or listed in the chart. The staff seemed surprised, but the effect was immediate and humanizing. She was no longer an object of gossip and whispers but a person restored to her full and rightful dignity.

The sense of being forced into culturally acceptable shapes of identity can bear down heavily on people who have already been marginalized due to their sexuality and gender. They're now beset by an inner war to secure the right to exist authentically. The grief of lost expression and the shame of conforming to avoid being targeted can create complex layers of existential pain tied to identity, acceptance, value, and worth.

Healing Shame in the Body and Mind

When grief becomes entangled with shame, healing is not only about empathy and compassion. It also requires a courageous confrontation to reclaim worth and value. Shaming thoughts are distortions, yet when believed, they can pull you into spirals of self-attack that feel endless. The result is the ache of loss and a corrosive narrative that insists you're the problem. For those whose lives have been shaped by shame, grief can easily trigger old wounds, deepening pain and isolation.

Thankfully the mind and body do not have to suffer silently. Pain is inevitable, but suffering is not. Shame fuels suffering by silencing grief, while compassion creates freedom by allowing grief to move and be expressed. Clinical trials confirm this reality: Shame fuels self-criticism and rumination, while compassion-based interventions reliably reduce shame and improve adaptation.[9]

Shame is not something that disappears through the usual forms of letting go. It does not release simply by crying, venting, or naming it. It requires more because of how insidious it is. Shame requires a different kind of healing, one that centers on building an inner ecosystem of self-worth and self-compassion. When you cultivate deep internal value, shame loses the conditions it needs to survive. Shame breeds in the shadows of self-doubt; in a field of love, it cannot continue to grow. As you strengthen your relationship with yourself through tenderness, honesty, and care, shame is gradually pushed out. It cannot take root where there is spaciousness, compassion, and a steady sense of your own worth.

Healing shame is less about fighting it and more about nurturing what makes you whole. Think of it like tending to a garden. You do not attack the weeds; you enrich the soil. You bring in warmth, nourishment, sunlight, and care. Over time, the weeds have nowhere to root. In the same way, when you practice small acts of self-respect, speak to yourself with kindness, and allow your emotions to be seen without judgment, you create an inner environment where shame cannot thrive. This is the steady work of reclaiming dignity. As your internal landscape becomes more loving, shame begins to loosen, soften, and dissolve. It cannot thrive in an ecosystem of deep internal value. Saying it another way, shame doesn't have to be something you push out; it's something to grow beyond.

Some of the following methods are powerful ways to dispel shame:

- *Compassion:* Speak to yourself as you would to a beloved friend.
- *Witnessing:* Safe community and ritual transform secrecy into belonging.
- *Embodiment:* Breath, posture, and movement counter shame's collapse.

- *Storytelling:* Sharing grief narratives dismantles stigma and restores dignity.
- *Self-forgiveness:* Forgiveness practices reduce corrosive self-blame and support post-traumatic growth.

When you honor grief with compassion instead of shame, you not only heal personally but help reshape culture. Grief is synonymous with change; it reshapes our internal world. Ritual, community, and compassion transform shame's secrecy into the visibility of belonging.

To let go of shame in grief is to say, *I am not broken. My grief is not wrong. My emotions are not weaknesses. They are love alive in me.* This act of permission may be one of the most loving things you ever do.

TECHNIQUES FOR WORKING WITH SHAME

Exercise: Unfolding from Shame

1. **Begin in the posture of shame.** Sit or stand comfortably. Let your head drop slightly, your shoulders round, and your chest soften inward. Allow your hands to come together or rest in your lap. This posture is not meant to reenact shame but to meet your body where it already goes. Take two slow breaths, and whisper inwardly, *I am safe enough to notice this.*
2. **Bring warmth to the center of your chest.** Place one hand, then the other, over your heart space. Let your elbows drop inward and feel the warmth of your hands slowly soften any tightness beneath them. Breathe into the space under your palms, with no need to fix anything—just let warmth meet tension.
3. **Begin a slow unfolding.** On an inhale, let your elbows open just one inch, allowing your chest to lift slightly toward your hands. Exhale and pause. On the next inhale, open another inch and let your spine grow a little taller. Exhale and pause again. Repeat this gentle unfolding three or four times, keeping the movement

small and dignified. This is your body remembering it is allowed to take up space.

4. **Lift your gaze gently**. Without raising your chin too high, let your eyes rise to a soft, neutral place—not directly at someone but just enough that you are no longer hiding. Imagine looking toward a gentle horizon, a place that welcomes you.
5. **Open your arms into a receiving shape.** From your heart space, slowly open your arms outward, your palms facing slightly up. Only go as far as feels safe. This is not a power pose but a receiving pose—an offering of readiness rather than exposure. Hold this open shape for one soft breath, then bring your hands back to your heart. Repeat this opening and returning two or three times, teaching your body that it can open and still be safe.
6. **Root into the ground.** Place your feet firmly on the floor and feel the weight of your body supported through your legs. With each exhale, imagine releasing the residue of shame into the earth—not pushing it away but letting it move downward. With each inhale, imagine drawing up steadiness, dignity, and quiet presence.
7. **Close with a gesture of worthiness**. Bring both hands back to your heart or to the sides of your face and let your body stand or sit tall. End with a quiet inner phrase such as *I belong*, *I am worthy*, or *My body is safe here*. Rest in this shape for one minute.

WHY THIS HELPS

Shame pulls the body inward, collapsing the spine, lowering the gaze, rounding the shoulders, and making you want to disappear. It also restricts breath and closes off the sense of worthiness. This practice meets your body in that collapsed place and gently invites it to unfold, not by forcing confidence or expansiveness but by helping you remember your dignity and presence. Through warmth at your chest, gradual unfolding of posture, lifting your gaze, and gentle receiving gestures with your arms, your body learns to hold itself with dignity again. In this way, movement becomes a gentle restoration of worthiness, expanding the space that shame once closed.[10]

Exercise: Holding Softness and Restoring Worthiness

1. **Choose your source of touch.** Select what feels safest and most accessible to you in this moment. It might be a soft stuffed animal or blanket; your own hands resting gently on your chest or belly; a beloved pet beside you; or a trusted partner, friend, or family member offering a comforting hand. Choose whatever brings the least resistance.
2. **Create a gentle environment.** Soften the lighting and sit or lie down comfortably. Let your breath arrive naturally, without trying to shape or control it. While shame tends to quiet the body, this practice is meant to offer gentle support in return.
3. **Make contact.** Bring the soft object, your hand, or someone's supportive hand into contact with your body. Notice the temperature, pressure, and texture, as well as any subtle shifts in the breath or your shoulders. Let the contact be simple—you do not need to earn it.

   If touch feels difficult due to trauma, cultural boundaries, or past experiences, try using a soft object, placing your hand on it instead of your body, keeping the session brief or pairing the practice with grounding or breath. Move at your own pace—your body gets to decide what feels safe.
4. **Stay with the sensation.** Allow yourself to settle into the touch. You do not have to feel comfort right away; simply let yourself be held in some small way. If you are with someone you trust, you might softly say, "Stay with me" or "This is enough." If you are alone, you can whisper inwardly, *This touch is here for me*, *My body is allowed to feel supported*, or *Even this part of me deserves care*. Shame loosens when worthiness is offered gently.
5. **Notice any changes.** After a few minutes, you may notice a deeper exhale, a slight softening in your chest, your face relaxing, or a small sense of relief or quiet. Or you may feel nothing at

all—this is also a valid response. Your body is simply learning to trust again.

6. **Close with care**. Thank the source of support, whether it is a person, a pet, your hands, or a soft object. Then offer your body one simple line: *I am here with you. You are worthy of this care*. Let that be enough.

WHY THIS HELPS

This practice helps your body feel grounded, warm, and worthy through gentle touch, offering a quiet countermessage to shame, which often pulls you inward and tells you that you do not deserve care or connection. Whether the touch comes from your own hands, a soft object, a pet, or a trusted loved one, it can help your body remember that it is still lovable, deserving, and safe. Touch awakens the body's natural chemistry of comfort—particularly oxytocin, which supports bonding, calm, and a sense of inner belonging. Research shows that gentle touch activates the parasympathetic nervous system, quieting the stress response and supporting your sense of safety.[11] When touch comes from someone you trust, the body often releases oxytocin, creating feelings of comfort, connection, and worthiness. While shame insists you do not deserve tenderness, this practice gently challenges that belief by offering real, felt care—not to fix shame but to remind your body that it does not have to hold shame alone.

Exercise: Meditation for Expanding Internal Value

1. Clap your hands together, palm to palm, fingers to palms, in different playful ways until sensation builds. Shake out your hands a few times to bring circulation into your wrists.
2. Sitting or standing, bring the bases of your palms together in front of your heart. Spread your fingers wide so thumbs and pinky fingers touch, forming a flower shape with your hands. Close your eyes.

3. Imagine a radiant golden light glowing between your palms. Feel it warm and bright, radiating outward through your fingers.
4. With your palms at your heart, gently tuck your chin and feel the golden light shining onto your face. Imagine a circuit forming: heart to hands, hands to face, back to heart. Rest in this loop.
5. Remain for a few minutes, breathing calmly and allowing the golden light to flow. Let your heart, hands, and face feel connected in this radiant exchange.

WHY THIS HELPS

This practice awakens a sense of inner nobility and a quiet recognition of dignity and worth that comes from within. It is not about command or superiority over others but inhabiting your personal power with grace. The imagery of golden light nourishes your heart, evoking warmth, radiance, and vitality.[12] The hand-and-heart connection fosters a circuit of self-recognition, while the upright posture grounds and steadies you. Together these elements help expand your sense of internal value, reminding you that even in times of grief, you carry a light that is both steady and sacred.

Exercise: Earth and Sky Grounding

1. Connect with the earth outside. Stand barefoot if possible. Walk slowly and notice the sensations beneath your feet.
2. Root into the ground. Stand comfortably with soft knees and parallel feet. Imagine roots growing from your soles into the earth. With each exhale, let tension, shame, and heavy thoughts travel down the roots to be received and transformed by the earth.
3. Sense the earth offering back strength and vitality. Feel energy rise through your legs into your belly and chest.
4. With your eyes closed, imagine a vast sky above. Feel a gentle, supportive light from the sky entering through the crown of your head.

5. Unite heaven and earth within you. Let the sky's radiance meet the earth's nourishment inside your torso. Rest in their meeting place within your heart.

WHY THIS HELPS

Grounding through direct contact with the earth activates both physiological and psychological mechanisms that restore stability after loss. Barefoot contact with natural surfaces—sometimes called earthing—can reduce inflammation, balance cortisol rhythms, and support parasympathetic nervous system activity, which helps counter the hyperarousal common in grief and fear.[13]

Slow, mindful movement enhances proprioceptive awareness, signaling safety to the brain through the vagus nerve and lowering heart rate and blood pressure. Visualization practices that connect sky and earth engage bilateral integration across the brain's hemispheres, helping regulate emotional processing and restore coherence between body, mind, and breath. Together these actions reestablish orientation in space and time, reawaken sensory presence, and remind your nervous system that safety and support still exist here in the living world.

Writing Practice: Self-Praise as a Path to Worthiness

1. **Create a gentle space**. Find a quiet place with your journal. Sit comfortably and take three slow breaths. Place one hand on your heart or belly as a gesture of friendliness toward yourself. Whisper inwardly, *I am allowed to speak to myself with kindness*. Let your body settle before you begin.
2. **Choose a prompt that feels accessible**. Select a prompt such as "I am proud of myself for . . . ," "These are things I love about who I am . . . ," "Life has been hard, yet here are the ways I have shown up . . . ," "What my heart longs to be thanked for is . . . ," or "Today, I

offer myself praise for . . ." If one feels too difficult, choose another. The go-to start for this practice is "I'm proud of myself for . . ."

3. **Write without shrinking.** Let yourself write in a steady, honest flow. You are not trying to impress anyone—simply telling the truth about who you are and how you have lived. Name small efforts no one saw, moments of courage, ways you have cared for others and yourself, quiet endurance on impossible days, and love you offered even while grieving. If discomfort or self-doubt arises, write through it; this is part of the healing.
4. **Add one line of deep praise**. When you finish your first round of writing, end with a final line that begins "Despite everything, I am grateful for my ability to . . . ," "One beautiful thing about me is . . . ," or "What I am learning to honor in myself is. . . ." This line becomes the seed of internal value that grows with time.
5. **Close the practice**. Place your hand over your heart again. Take a slow breath and read your words out loud or silently. Let them land. You may feel warmth, resistance, or nothing at all—any response is normal. Whisper inwardly, *I am worthy of this praise*. Let the practice close gently.

WHY THIS HELPS

Shame and self-judgment often operate silently, shaping how you see yourself. Writing praise interrupts this pattern.[14] It activates loving-kindness, helps you reclaim dignity, and challenges the belief that self-love is egoistic. For many, self-praise feels uncomfortable at first; that discomfort signals old, internalized messages rising to the surface. With time, this practice strengthens your sense of internal value and shifts the story you tell about yourself within grief. By naming your goodness, you make space for self-love, gentleness, and recognition, even in the midst of sorrow, and remind yourself that you are—and always have been—worthy of care.[15]

Art Practice: Releasing Shame Through Expression

1. Use a blank piece of paper and any art supplies you have on hand.
2. Ask, "If my shame had a color, what would it be?" Use that color, or a similar one, and let your hand move freely across the paper.
3. Write phrases shame has whispered to you or words that left you feeling small.
4. When the page feels full, crumple, rip, or safely burn it. Throw it away or bury it as a ritual of release.
5. Place a hand on your heart and whisper, "I am worthy. I am more than shame."
6. Take three slow breaths to close this practice.

WHY THIS HELPS

Shame often hides in silence, where it grows heavier and more isolating. By giving shame a color, form, and even words, you draw it out of hiding and make it visible. This externalization breaks its hold inside and begins to loosen its power.[16] The act of destroying or releasing the artwork creates a ritual of letting go, signaling to the body and mind that you no longer need to carry this weight. Closing with compassion plants a new truth—you are worthy, whole, and more than shame—which helps you replace judgment with self-love.

Summary

If shame tells you that you don't belong, begin by creating a sense of home within yourself—through breath, compassion, and truthful self-regard. If you've withdrawn from others, practice rebuilding home alongside them. Let trusted connection and the sharing of grief narratives soften the edges of isolation. If you feel lost, turn toward what, who, and where help you remember safety and love and anchor you in your authenticity. If grief feels disorienting, find simple ways to show yourself compassion—the kind you'd give a beloved friend.

Belonging—both inward and outward—regulates the body, restores truth, and dissolves shame's illusion of separation. This is how grief begins to return you to yourself and to the larger circle that has held you all along.

17

Reconciling with Regret

HOLDING HER FRAIL HAND, Suzanne spoke through a body more bone than flesh, her jaw so stiff that each word was a small labor. Sunlight poured through the windows of the palliative-care floor, its brightness in stark contrast to the heaviness of the moment. She was dying. Treatment had ended and all that remained was comfort care. That day, she wanted to talk about her regrets.

Regret is often misunderstood as guilt or shame, but it is much quieter—and in some ways, more tender. Shame says, *I am wrong*. Guilt says, *I did wrong*. Regret says, *I wish it had been different*. Unlike shame or guilt, regret doesn't demand punishment or atonement; it asks only for witnessing—for the chance to acknowledge love that could not be expressed, choices that could not be lived, and roads that could not be taken.

Suzanne lay sunken into the hospital bed, wrapped in layers of blankets because she was always cold. "I wonder what would have happened if I had run off with that boy who wanted to take me away in his fancy car," she said, remembering her youth in the 1950s, when greasers in hot rods ruled the streets. "But I married Carl. He was the safe choice."

As a chaplain, I knew this was the kind of moment when silence mattered most. My role was not to fill the air but to be present—to let her speak at her own pace, to let my hand in hers do the listening.

Suzanne told me she had worked hard and done what was expected. She had also carried the unbearable loss of her son, John, who had died in his twenties. She regretted how busy she had been during those years, how little time she had given him. "But you worked in those days," she said softly. "You soldiered on."

She also spoke of dreams left behind. She had wanted to travel. Instead, she and Carl bought a big house they didn't need. As she stared toward the sunlight in the far corner of the room, her gaze seemed to drift into the horizon of what might have been. I squeezed her hand a little tighter, a gesture to say, *I hear you. I'm with you.*

Suzanne died two days later. Her words have never left me. They carried a transmission—a blessing whispered through time. They taught me that regret is not simply about the past; it is the past still alive in us, asking to be acknowledged before we go.

I wish . . .

Suzanne's words echoed what I would hear again and again at people's bedsides: regrets of roads not taken, time not given, and dreams left behind. They mirror what the hospice nurse Bronnie Ware later described in her book *The Top Five Regrets of the Dying*:[1]

> I wish I had lived a life true to myself, not the life others expected of me.
> I wish I hadn't worked so hard.
> I wish I had expressed my feelings more.
> I wish I had stayed in touch with my friends.
> I wish I had let myself be happier.

While regret near the end of life often seeks closure, regret in the living can linger without resolution. It can reshape your relationship to yourself, to others, and to the loss.

If you're grieving, there's rarely an easy resolution. Many people feel locked in time, replaying moments and ruminating on the should'ves, would'ves, could'ves.[2] Just as we sometimes take grief apart into smaller pieces to make it more bearable, you can do the same with regret. When you bring awareness to how regret shows up, the words it uses, and how your heart feels within it, you create room for life-force energy, qi, to circulate again. The dense layers of regret soften and begin to flow.

One of the most powerful faces of regret is words left unsaid.[3] When you're in the midst of grief, you may hear yourself thinking:

I wish I had told them . . . (I love them, I'm proud of them, etc.)
I regret not saying . . . (how much they meant to me, etc.)
If only I had said . . . (I'm sorry, etc.)

There is a deep ache around what was never said, around the fact that there will never be another conversation, accompanied by the excruciating pain of "too late," as if the door has closed on what mattered most. Please hear this: The door is not truly closed and it is not too late. The exercises at the end of this chapter offer ways to speak those words now and honor what remained unsaid. Often the deepest pain in grief is love that never got a chance to be expressed or wasn't expressed as frequently as one would have liked. Grief is love looking for a place to go. Regret carries the wound of the unspoken. It's a signal that it's time to let love flow freely now.

Regret also lives in what you didn't do but wish you had: the events you missed; the trip you never took; the visit you kept putting off; the hugs, the time, the conversations you wanted but never seemed to have time for. Sometimes you wish you had done things differently. You may wish to have led with more patience, understanding, or compassion. Perhaps you spoke in anger, pushed someone away, let a grudge linger, or left an estrangement unresolved.

Turning Your Attention to Regret

Regret can feel like a prison that locks you into self-blame, guilt, and self-punishment over perceived mistakes or failures, sometimes over long periods of time. The finality of death can leave you feeling incomplete, without closure, unable to reconcile what was lost.

People sometimes say in a blasé manner, "I don't have any regrets." I wonder how many have faced profound loss or their own mortality. Regret is part of life and a deeply painful part of grief. We receive little guidance on how to work with it, so we suppress it, push it away, or tell ourselves we're capable of just letting it go.

Regret requires attention. Like shame or guilt, it's both an emotional and a mental state. It can be buried so deeply that you barely notice it until it surges back. If unacknowledged, regret can harden from a feeling into a belief system, shaping how you see yourself. In many ways, regret can make grief feel unbearable or chronic.

When suppressed or denied, regret shows up in many unrecognized ways:

- **POOR SLEEP AND INCREASED STRESS.** Regret is linked with insomnia and often peaks at night when you try to fall asleep.[4] The more you try to push regret away, the more it disrupts sleep. Intense regret is also associated with higher overall cortisol and a sharper spike in the morning.[5] As a stress marker, this pattern suggests more strain on the body that can amplify pain and lower immunity.
- **SECOND-GUESSING AND FREEZING.** Regret can cast a shadow of doubt over your decision-making, leading to hesitation and indecision.[6] When faced with a significant choice, your body may enter a freeze state, making it hard to move forward.[7] You may begin avoiding big decisions about work, finances, or home.

  Like Billy, who made a major move with his financial portfolio. He had just bought a new home, become a new father, and started a strong position at his firm. In that moment of change, he received advice that seemed wise at the time, but it cost him dearly. That single decision began to eat at him. Each time a new opportunity arose, the memory of that regret whispered in his ear, holding him back. He second-guessed himself, hesitated when he might have stepped forward, and his work began to suffer. The regret was not just about money. It had taken root in his confidence, shaping how he saw himself and what he believed he could risk.
- **SELF-SABOTAGE AND A SENSE OF UNWORTHINESS.** Past regrets can feed a quiet belief that you don't deserve something good. Regret layers on low self-worth and the feeling of not being enough. Second-guessing and self-doubt are invisible expressions of regret.

- **INNER CRITIC AND PERFECTIONISM.** Regret magnifies insecurities. The harshest bully can be your own voice. Regret can hold you captive in moments you revisit with the clarity you did not have back then.[8] It pairs easily with perfectionism. Because regret is anchored to the past, it insists you should have known better. Pain from the past resurfaces and can eclipse your strengths and successes.[9]
- **ERODED SELF-TRUST.** Perhaps the most damaging effect is that regret teaches you not to trust yourself. It makes you doubt your gut, dismiss your intuition, and ignore your instincts. You begin to look outside yourself for validation, handing your power to others. This is how regret steals your confidence.
- **TIMELINES AND COUNTERFACTUALS.** Regret often pulls you out of the present into what's known as upward counterfactuals—mental movies about what could have been.[10] You may replay a scene from years ago until it fragments your sense of self. Part of you lives in a storyline that never happened, leaving less of you here now. The cost is steep: It robs you of love, connection, and presence that are available today.

As you've seen, regret is a major player in grief. Sometimes it isn't the grief itself that feels most overwhelming but the regret around it. The self-blame, the doubt, the locked-in-time loops—all of these make this moment heavier than it needs to be.

Turning Regret into Medicine

Thankfully there are many ways we can turn regret into one of our greatest teachers. Regret can motivate wiser choices and clarify our values. Just as grief exists in proportion to love, regret exists in proportion to value. When you work through regret, you can emerge with compassion, forgiveness, and a clear sense of what matters most.

One potent form of regret is the error of omission, the pain of what you did not do.[11] This often surfaces when facing mortality and can open a rare window of fearlessness, though that window does not stay open for long.[12] In that sacred space, you can reverse engineer your life from your values and commit to living with meaning now.

During my years in end-of-life care, I heard countless stories of what people wished they had done differently or more. Their honesty shaped me. It widened my window and keeps me asking how I am living today. By living with value and gratitude, I honor their lives. This connects to what I call the unscripted life, which I talk about in chapter 19. Grief strips life down to what matters; regret can become a compass for the life you still have to live.

We can begin by honoring that regret is different. Without awareness, we only keep burying our feelings, and they cast a long shadow over our lives.

When you acknowledge regret, you will face perceived mistakes. The word *perceived* matters. You are human, and perfection is not the standard. Perfection insists there is only one right way. That belief creates constant failure and fuels regret. Self-compassion is central to grief work and helps soften the suffering caused by self-judgment, isolation, and rumination.[13] It does not erase regret, but it changes your relationship to it, builds resilience, and can even improve sleep by reducing self-blame.

If self-compassion feels hard, self-forgiveness can feel impossible. Guilt and self-blame are the weapons of regret. You may hear yourself say, "I will never forgive myself for . . ." Yet research shows that self-forgiveness reduces rumination and improves well-being.[14] It offers a new narrative: You deserve to feel good. You are worthy of love and joy. People who practice self-forgiveness report greater resilience and life satisfaction, while those who do not carry higher levels of depression and anxiety.[15] Neuroscience even suggests that self-forgiveness relates to changes in brain regions involved in perspective-taking and empathy.[16]

Self-forgiveness does not mean letting go of the love in grief. It means letting go of perfectionism, self-doubt, and the beliefs that keep you small. It loosens rumination and self-punishment and opens a more compassionate vision of self.

Grief, regret, and loss will visit every life. How you meet them makes the difference. Self-compassion is not a way out of pain. It is a way through.

By softening self-blame, loosening the grip of rumination, and building resilience, self-compassion allows you to carry grief not as a crushing burden but as a sacred weight infused with love. In this way, regret becomes a teacher and grief becomes a companion.

Let's ground regret in the body and process it somatically so that compassion and forgiveness can be lived, not just understood.

TECHNIQUES FOR WORKING WITH REGRET

Qigong Practice: Cloud Hands

1. Stand with your feet shoulder-width apart, your knees slightly bent.
2. Relax your shoulders and soften your gaze.
3. Shift your weight to your right foot, raising your right hand in front of your chest (palm inward) while the left hand rests near your waist (palm down).
4. Breathe naturally as you move.
5. Shift your weight to your left foot and let your hands switch positions smoothly, keeping movements slow and circular, like clouds.
6. Inhale as you shift and lift; exhale as you cross to the other side.
7. Continue for two to five minutes, imagining your hands moving through soft clouds, clearing heaviness and creating inner space.
8. To close, rest your hands on your lower belly, take three full breaths, and notice the grounded calm.

WHY THIS HELPS

Cloud Hands is a flowing qigong practice that synchronizes breath, body, and energy in a gentle rhythm. Its side-to-side motion helps dissolve tension, clear heaviness from the chest, and restore balance between the left and right sides of the body. For those carrying regret or self-judgment, the movement becomes a physical metaphor for softening and forgiving, with the hands brushing away what no longer needs to be held. Each circular sweep creates space for compassion, allowing the heart to open with greater ease. Practiced regularly, Cloud Hands soothes the nervous system, promotes smooth circulation of qi, and invites calm presence where grief once felt stuck.[17]

Exercise: Primal Scream

1. Choose a private place where you won't be disturbed—your car, a secluded outdoor spot, or a quiet room.
2. If noise is a concern, scream into a pillow or towel.
3. Stand with your feet hip-width apart and your knees soft. Sit if standing feels unsteady.
4. Place a hand on your belly and take a few deep breaths.
5. Inhale into your belly, and on the exhale, let sound rise from deep within—screams, growls, cries, or sobs.
6. Repeat two or three times, or until you feel a shift, then shake your arms and legs to discharge energy.
7. Place your hands over your heart or belly, breathe gently, and rest until your body settles.
8. Notice sensations of lightness, warmth, or fatigue as the energy releases.

WHY THIS HELPS

The primal scream is a somatic release practice that allows raw emotion to move through the vocal and respiratory systems—the body's primary channels for energetic discharge. Primal sound gives form to intensity that words can't hold. It activates a natural release, reduces internal pressure, and reconnects you with calm afterward. Sometimes grief, regret, anxiety, overwhelm, and anger live so deeply in the body that language cannot reach them.[18]

Breath Practice: Pursed-Lip Breathing

1. Breathe in smoothly through your nose. Let the breath be steady and natural.
2. Pause for a gentle moment at the top of the inhale and stay in the brief stillness.
3. Exhale slowly through pursed lips, as if blowing through a straw. Feel the coolness of the breath across your lips. Make the exhale at least twice as long as the inhale.
4. Repeat this cycle for several rounds. With each breath, notice your mind becoming quieter and your body more at ease.

WHY THIS HELPS

Pursed-lip breathing is one of the simplest and most effective ways to quiet rumination and calm an overactive mind.[19] By extending the exhale, it activates the parasympathetic nervous system, signaling the body to relax.[20] This shift slows the heart rate, steadies the breath, and eases mental agitation.[21] This breath is a physiological hack for relaxation. It's especially useful when you need a quick reprieve for a pause or clarity, grounding, and quiet presence.

Exercise: Loving-Kindness Visualization

1. Find a comfortable position, either seated or lying down. Close your eyes and take a few slow breaths, softening your body with each exhale.
2. Bring to mind someone who truly adores you—a dear friend, family member, mentor, or beloved pet—someone who loves you simply for being you.

3. Imagine they are with you now, especially in a moment when you have been hard on yourself. Picture them witnessing how you treat your heart when caught in self-judgment.
4. Ask yourself:
    - What would this friend do if they saw me in this state?
    - How would they look at me?
    - What would they say?
    - How would they love me through this moment?
5. Allow yourself to receive that love—through their eyes, words, or embrace. Feel it as if it is happening now. Notice how it feels in your body to let it in, even if it feels vulnerable or unfamiliar.
6. When you are ready, say, "I can treat myself the way others treat me—with love, kindness, and respect."
7. Remain like this for a few breaths, resting in the feeling of being loved and held. When complete, place your hands over your heart and carry this warmth with you into what comes next.

WHY THIS HELPS

When self-blame or self-punishment gives rise to an inner bully, imagining someone who loves you unconditionally can help soften its voice. Loving-kindness meditation draws on this image, inviting compassion to replace harshness. Well-researched and widely practiced, loving-kindness has been shown to reduce stress, ease symptoms of anxiety, and strengthen self-compassion.[22] In grief, it offers a way to sit with sorrow while also holding love, easing the weight of rumination and opening space for tenderness to be part of the healing journey.

Art Practice: Rumination Release—a Funeral for Your Past Selves

1. **Reflect and journal.** You might wish to reflect on and journal about the following questions:
   - What heaviness am I carrying that I wish to let go of?
   - What parts of me keep me linked to the past?
   - Which storylines, regrets, or what-ifs no longer serve me?
   - What identity or behavior wants to be released so I can step into a new phase?
2. **Gather symbolic items.** Choose objects, writings, or images that represent what you are ready to let go of. For example: photographs that symbolize a phase you are releasing, journal pages filled with negative self-talk or regret, letters or gifts tied to relationships that ended or were harmful, work artifacts from roles that no longer fit, or mementos that anchor you to unworthiness or smallness.
3. **Create the funeral space.** Prepare a safe fire in a firepit or fireplace. If fire isn't possible, tear, bury, or submerge items in water as an alternative act of release.
4. **Engage a ritual of release.** Hold each item before placing it in the fire. Take a breath and silently say, *I honor who I was. I release what no longer serves me. I carry forward what is true.* Place the item into the flames with intention and watch it transform.
5. **Integrate.** Sit quietly with the fire. Notice the spaciousness within. Place your hands on your heart or belly. Breathe deeply and welcome renewal.

WHY THIS HELPS

Rituals for grief and regret work because they engage both the body and brain in symbolic completion. Releasing past selves, in particular through ritual, creates space for new paths. It frees energy bound in judgment, guilt, shame, regret, and old stories so you can live more fully now.

Neuroscience shows that the mind struggles with open loops—unfinished emotional experiences that keep the stress response activated.[23] When regret or grief has no outlet, the brain's default mode network repeatedly replays the event, fueling rumination and emotional exhaustion. A ritual provides the body and psyche with a clear marker of transition, helping to close those loops and signal to the nervous system that the moment has passed.

Sociologically, rituals have long served as containers for communal acknowledgment of loss. Even in private practice, the symbolic act of release restores meaning and coherence, reconnecting the individual to the universal human experience of change and impermanence. Ritual allows emotion to move through structure—transforming pain into understanding and helping the body and mind remember that life continues.

Summary

If you find yourself replaying the past, remember that regret is the mind's attempt to finish an unfinished story; awareness and expression help close the loop. If self-blame becomes relentless, distinguish regret from guilt and shame: Guilt seeks atonement, shame attacks worth, but regret invites reflection and renewal. If you feel haunted by what was left unsaid or undone, give those feelings voice through ritual—speak, write, move, or create to translate emotion into release. If you fear that regret means you have failed, remember that it signals what matters most. It is a teacher pointing you toward the values you want to live now.

Regret is an unfinished conversation between love and loss. When you meet it with honesty and self-forgiveness, it becomes a compass, guiding you toward a truer, more compassionate way of living.

18

Meeting Joy

KEISHA DIDN'T KNOW IT WAS OKAY, and even normal, to feel joy in the midst of grief. She had hidden from it for so long. On the surface, Keisha's life was thriving. She was a brilliant paralegal at a top law firm in a major city: successful, dependable, and a good friend to many. But joy was missing. That spark, that deep sense of aliveness, had been absent for Keisha since the age of sixteen.

The tragedy of losing her best friend to suicide when they were both teenagers had left her with questions about life and death, sorrow and grief, that she didn't know how to navigate. The school was kind and brought in counselors and social workers to help students process the loss of this bright, beloved classmate. Many took advantage of the monthlong support the school offered, including Keisha. She told me she hadn't known what to do with the overwhelming emotions she felt. Her friend wasn't just a classmate; they had grown up together through elementary school and shared activities and after-school play. They'd known and loved each other's families and had countless sleepovers and dinners. They had a wider group of friends, but the two of them were especially close, almost like sisters.

When Keisha came to see me years later, it was because of her grandmother's recent death. Her grandmother had been a special anchor in her life, and Keisha wanted support in honoring her story. As our work together unfolded, we discovered that the grief of her best friend's death fifteen years earlier was still quietly present in her.

The way it showed up was through the absence of joy. She didn't feel like she was allowed to experience it, and even small moments of pleasure were immediately quashed in order to "honor" those who were no longer with her. To Keisha, joy felt like a betrayal of her friend's memory. She feared that feeling joy meant she'd moved on, forgotten, or abandoned her beloved friend. Underneath, she carried not just grief but also anger and frustration about her friend's death. Those emotions felt familiar because she had processed some of them, alongside guilt, with the school counselors long ago. Joy, however, was different. It felt totally undeserved and almost dangerous.

Her grandmother's final words made this even more complicated. Before she died, as Keisha sat beside her hospice bed in their family home in Illinois, her grandmother reached out, touched her cheek, and whispered, "Enjoy, my darling. Enjoy this life." Retelling that moment in our session brought tears to Keisha's eyes, just as it had when it first happened. She wanted to honor her grandmother's wish, yet she had no idea how to actually hold joy.

In our time together, we began to normalize joy as a practice. She slowly befriended it, learning how to welcome it, cultivate it, and give it space in her life. She realized that joy is not only spontaneous but also something that can be nurtured, especially in the presence of grief. To her surprise, joy became one of the scariest emotions she had ever faced. She knew grief, sadness, anger, and guilt. But joy was the hardest to allow in.

One day she said something that captured the heart of her journey: "When my best friend died, joy died with her. I didn't realize I lost two things that day: my best friend and joy."

Our work became about reclaiming joy and learning that it was not a betrayal but a birthright. Through this process, Keisha discovered what so many people in the throes of grief can unexpectedly stumble upon: that joy and grief can coexist, that holding on to love does not mean letting go of joy, and that allowing joy is in fact another way of honoring the ones we have lost.

The Complexity of Joy After Loss

Each chapter in part two invites you to see an emotion through new eyes and to help meet it in the body, where it tells the truth. With emotions such as anger, anxiety, and numbness, the work has been to soften resistance. With joy, the work is different. Joy invites an unlearning about what we've been taught about happiness. For the grieving heart, joy can feel complicated, even threatening. To meet joy in the face of grief does not mean you force it or chase positivity. It is about rediscovering the quiet, authentic joy that can live alongside sorrow, a kind of joy that breathes with grief rather than against it.

Joy and grief can feel like opposites, as if they are competing for space. When grief is present, joy often feels subdued, reduced to microbursts or fleeting flashes. When joy does surface, grief may loom like a dark cloud, dimming its light. Many of us are taught to use joy to push grief away, to replace it, or to avoid the discomfort grief brings. We are told, "They'd want you to be happy" or "They wouldn't want you to be sad." These words are often meant kindly, but they can make grief feel unseen, as though joy is a correction rather than a companion.

In a culture that worships happiness, joy is often confused with positivity, performance, or denial. We are taught to smile through pain, that happiness is the goal, that sadness is weakness, and any discomfort should be fixed rather than felt. Grief is labeled as something to "get over" or "move past." Social media amplifies this by offering us images of curated perfection, a constant highlight reel that leaves little room for the complexity of human emotion. Quotes from thought leaders and spiritual figures are often reduced to one-line slogans, stripped of their original depth, shaped for likes and shares. Even spiritual teachings are sometimes co-opted into a quiet epidemic of toxic positivity—where every hardship must have a silver lining, every tear a lesson, every loss a hidden blessing. While meaning making is important, the demand to find light too soon becomes another form of avoidance. This reflex to fix discomfort co-opts joy as a feel-good medicine, disregarding the authentic joy that arises naturally and organically from within.

When joy is forced, it becomes a performance that isolates rather than connects. When grief is denied, the body tightens and the soul grows weary. Performative joy can look convincing on the surface, coming across with a forced smile, a reassuring "I'm fine," or a quick deflection away from deeper feeling; but inside, something feels hollow. When joy becomes a mask, it creates distance from not only others but also your own heart. You might feel unseen, even in a room full of people. The pressure to appear "okay" becomes its own kind of grief, one that hides behind politeness.

Politeness, from the Latin *polire*, means "to polish." It was once a word for shining a surface until it gleamed. In many ways, that is what we are taught to do with our emotions—to polish them until they appear presentable. We smooth over our grief, quiet our tears, and refine our raw edges so that others will not be disturbed. But what looks like grace on the outside can be disconnection on the inside. Beneath the surface, the nervous system stays on alert, the shoulders stay lifted, and the breath remains shallow. The body knows the truth even when the face cannot show it. When you become too polished, you may lose the texture of your truth. Politeness can easily become a form of self-erasure, a quiet unkindness toward what is real within you. True kindness is an invitation to be human. The heart does not need polish. It needs presence.

At other times, joy can feel like an undeserved luxury. As in Keisha's story, joy can feel unallowed, even foreign. Feeling joy might be construed as betrayal, abandonment, or "moving on." Persistent grief becomes the altar of remembrance, while joy is treated as disregard. Suffering begins to feel synonymous with love. Many people unconsciously equate the depth of their sorrow with the depth of their devotion. They fear that if the pain softens, the memory of the person or the meaning of the loss will fade too. The ache becomes a kind of proof that love was real, that it mattered, that the bond still exists. In this way, pain becomes sacred territory, guarded and preserved as a sign of fidelity.

When modern society co-opts joy as feel-good medicine, the consequence is equating grief with suffering. It creates a permission, even a steadfast demand, to grieve indefinitely as a way to stay loyal to pain as an act of love. The binary between "good" and "bad" emotions, or "light" and "dark" feelings, turns the heart into an emotional minefield. Because grief and pain are often suppressed, the opposite can occur: Joy becomes the emotion that is avoided and pushed away.

How Joy and Grief Can Coexist

So, can joy and grief coexist? Can there be authentic expressions of joy that are not performative or betraying? Is there room in the heart for a natural emergence of joy when grief is also present?

A joy that coexists with grief is a joy that honors truth. It is the joy that comes after a long cry—the relief of realizing you can still laugh, still feel warmth, still notice beauty without betraying your sorrow. This is the kind of joy that mends rather than masks, a heart response that whispers to joy, *You belong in my heart, even here, even now.*

The kind of joy that brings healing is not an escape from sorrow but an awakening within it. True joy is not a bypass; it is a pulse of life that reminds you that you are still here, still capable of feeling, still connected. This joy doesn't demand that your grief disappear. It arises softly, like light filtering through clouds, reminding you that even in heartbreak, the world still offers moments of beauty. You may catch it in the way the sun touches your skin, in the laughter of a friend, or in a song that reaches the ache in your chest and somehow lifts it. Joy and grief can share the same breath. They both belong to the same heart.

Joy does not mean you are "better" or "healed." It means that even amid sorrow, life is moving through you. It is the body remembering its capacity for pleasure and the soul remembering its ability for delight. In this way, joy becomes a companion to other emotions—such as despair—in grief, not its cure. It reminds you that the heart's wholeness is not found in one emotion competing with another but in the fullness of them all. Just as the heart can hold what the mind cannot understand, the heart can also hold multiple truths at the same time. Suffering is perpetuated by suppression and separation. These divisions, born of binary thinking, fragment our understanding of grief. The heart knows a wisdom beyond duality.

Grief is love looking for a place to go. When it begins to move again, joy is often what carries it forward. In Traditional Chinese Medicine, joy helps to alleviate stagnant qi. When qi becomes blocked and unmovable, joy helps to jump-start its flow. Allowing joy is not abandoning what was lost; it is allowing love to express in its many forms. Still, the heart resists, because joy can feel disorienting after long sorrow. It can feel unsafe to relax, to laugh, to feel warmth in the chest again. The nervous system, accustomed to bracing, does not yet trust ease. Healing asks for that trust to be rebuilt slowly. Joy may return quietly, like a bird testing the branch before landing. It asks for permission, not performance.

Grief opens the heart to the depths of loss; joy is also present within the heart of grief. Both are sacred teachers. Both are revealed through love. When joy returns, it does not erase grief; it sits beside it, breathing quietly, reminding you that the heart is vast enough to hold both sorrow and delight at the same time.

Joy as Courageous Vulnerability

It's important to note that when joy becomes unfamiliar, it can feel as triggering as anger, sadness, or pain. The researcher and storyteller Brené Brown calls this "foreboding joy," the reflex to shut down joy in order to protect yourself from vulnerability.[1] It is the impulse to brace for impact, to flinch before anything even goes wrong. It's the quiet whisper that says, *Don't get too happy; something bad is about to happen.* When things go up, they must come down—so the nervous system, still wired for loss, prepares for the fall even in moments of beauty. Joy, then, becomes associated with danger. The body learns that opening to goodness is unsafe because goodness was once followed by devastation.

This reflex is common in grief. When someone you love has died, or when life as you knew it has ended, the mind begins to equate joy with loss. You might remember a joyful memory only to feel a surge of pain that it's now gone. The nervous system links pleasure to threat, love to loss, joy to disappointment. Over time, joy itself becomes suspect. The heart hesitates to open because it fears what comes after—the crash, the emptiness, the ache of impermanence. It's a form of emotional conditioning: a protective strategy learned through heartbreak.

Psychologists describe this as *cherophobia*—an aversion to happiness, often rooted in the belief that joy invites misfortune. It's as if allowing yourself to feel good will summon pain back to your door. Studies show that this fear of happiness is associated with depression, insecure attachment, and emotional numbing.[2] But long before the research confirmed it, grievers already knew it in their bones: Joy can feel dangerous. To feel joy again asks you to risk tenderness, to risk opening the heart that was once broken. The nervous system must learn, slowly, that joy is not a setup but a sign of life returning.

Suppression and the Loss of Innocence

Sometimes joy is confused with pleasure, which is perhaps why those who are grieving might resist it. In our culture, joy is often associated with hedonism. It's also sought through food, sex, shopping, or exercise, which can all be ways to mask difficult emotions and chase a temporary "high." We are, after all, a "dopamine nation," as the psychiatrist Anna Lembke so eloquently pointed out in her book of that name. When pursued this way, joy can become self-centered, reckless, or destructive.

But suppression of emotion is equally destructive. Studies show that when we habitually suppress grief, anger, or sadness, we also suppress joy.[3] Suppression may blunt pain for a time, but it also silences joy, leaving mourners emotionally flat and disconnected from others. Healthy grieving requires oscillating between facing pain and restoring life, but suppression interrupts this rhythm and prolongs suffering.[4]

Keisha's deeper grief revealed another truth: When her friend died, she lost not only her best friend but also her sense of innocence. What vanished with her friend was the quiet assurance that life unfolds fairly, that love protects us from devastation, that goodness guarantees safety. That innocence—our first, unspoken faith in the benevolence of life—is a kind of sacred bubble that lets us move through the world with openness and trust. When it bursts, joy itself can feel dangerous, as if to feel good again is to risk another fall. Naming this secondary loss matters deeply. It allows mourners to understand why joy can feel treacherous, and, over time, to reclaim it—not as denial or betrayal but as a sign that the heart is strong enough to live again.

The Science of Joy in Grief

For many, the return of joy can feel confusing or even threatening. After months—or years—of contraction, the body has learned to associate safety with vigilance, not openness. When moments of lightness or laughter arise, they can trigger guilt, as though joy dishonors the loss or forgets the one who is gone. This tension between the body's innate capacity to rebalance and the heart's fear of moving on is one of grief's quiet paradoxes. It's what Keisha discovered in her own healing—the realization that joy was both what she longed for and what she feared most.

Physiology confirms what many grievers notice in their own bodies: Joy restores balance.[5] When people recall positive emotions, their heart rhythms become more flexible and their breathing steadier.[6] This is measured as increased heart rate variability, a sign of nervous system regulation.[7] Neuroimaging shows that positive affect engages brain regions involved in both pleasure and pain modulation, suggesting joy can directly ease suffering.[8]

The psychology professor Barbara Fredrickson's broaden-and-build theory affirms that these emotions expand awareness and build long-term psychological and social resources.[9] In grief, even moments of laughter can predict better adjustment over time.[10] Emotions such as gratitude and awe not only buffer stress but also promote resilience and recovery, especially in older adults.[11] Post-traumatic growth research confirms that joy can reemerge after loss as part of a transformed outlook on life.[12]

The Role of Play and Innocence

As Keisha allowed joy to reenter her life, she noticed it came not through grand revelations but through moments of levity—small flashes of curiosity, humor, and connection. At first these felt almost disloyal, as though laughter betrayed the gravity of her loss. Yet over time, she began to sense that these playful impulses were not signs of forgetting but of integration. They marked her nervous system's gradual return to balance, a reawakening of the aliveness that grief had muted.

In this way, joy and play became the language through which her body relearned safety, reminding her that innocence is not something lost forever but something that waits beneath sorrow to be remembered.

Play is not frivolous; it is healing. The English pediatrician and psychoanalyst Donald Winnicott taught that play creates a transitional space where children and adults can symbolically process experience and reengage with life.[13] Within this imaginative territory—half real, half make-believe—the nervous system rehearses safety, flexibility, and trust. Studies show that playful adults report higher life satisfaction, stronger coping skills, and more resilience during stress.[14] During the COVID-19 pandemic, playfulness was found to buffer against adversity, reducing anxiety and promoting healthier adaptation to uncertainty.[15] Physiologically, play activates the parasympathetic branch of the nervous system and releases endorphins, oxytocin, and dopamine—all biochemicals linked to connection, pleasure, and creative problem-solving.

Children embody this wisdom intuitively. They can weep with full abandon and, moments later, dissolve into laughter. They don't pathologize emotion or treat joy and sorrow as opposites; both flow through them as part of being alive. In grief, reclaiming joy means returning to this natural rhythm. It asks us to reconnect with the innocence that grief may have fractured—the capacity to trust life again, to be surprised by delight, to risk wonder even after devastation.

For Keisha, rediscovering that innocence was not naïveté but renewal. It marked the moment her healing deepened—when joy no longer felt like betrayal but like proof that the heart can break open and still choose to love the world.

Joy as a Natural Part of Grief

The Dual Process Model that we learned about in chapter 4 on letting go situates joy on the restoration side of grieving—the essential counterbalance to loss-oriented pain, where we begin to reengage with life and rebuild meaning. The grief expert and researcher Robert Neimeyer emphasizes that meaning-making is central to healthy adaptation,[16] and research confirms that positive affect and meaning reconstruction work synergistically to support integration after loss.[17] In this light, joy is not a distraction from grief but one of its most powerful medicines.

Joy within grief is not denial; it is a tender act of survival. It coexists with sorrow, creating enough space in the psyche and body to metabolize pain without being consumed by it. Physiologically and psychologically, joy protects against despair, stabilizes the nervous system, and reopens pathways to connection and creativity. Suppressing joy constricts this natural rhythm and keeps grief frozen. Embracing it reintroduces movement, coherence, and the possibility of transformation.

Grieving fully leaves us room for the entire range of being—to weep and to laugh, to rage and to rest, to remember and to begin again. The invitation is not to choose between sorrow and joy but to recognize them as companions. When you allow joy to return, you are not betraying the one you lost—you are honoring the pulse of life that continues through you.

TECHNIQUES FOR WORKING WITH JOY

Exercise: Allowing Lightness

1. Stand with your feet shoulder-width apart and your body relaxed.
2. Let your arms move like pendulums, gently swinging from side to side. Keep the motion loose and easy, as if your arms are soft noodles. Allow your arms to flow without twisting your torso.
3. Once the motion feels natural, begin adding the sound *weeeeeee* on your exhale, like the joyful cry of being on a roller coaster. Inhale as your arms swing to one side, and exhale with a long *weeeeeee* as they swing to the other.
4. Experiment with higher pitches or different lengths of sound. Notice if laughter bubbles up naturally. Allow yourself to be a little silly.

WHY THIS HELPS

This simple practice engages the body's natural stress-release systems through rhythm, movement, and sound. The gentle swinging motion encourages bilateral coordination, synchronizing both brain hemispheres and calming overactive neural circuits associated with grief and anxiety. The fluid movements release tension, allowing lightness. Together, the long exhale and vocal vibration stimulate the vagus nerve, activating the parasympathetic response that lowers heart rate and reduces cortisol.[18]

Exercise: Laughing Yoga

1. Stand or sit in a comfortable position. Take a few deep breaths to center yourself.
2. Stretch your mouth into a big smile, even if it feels silly or unnatural. Hold it for a few breaths and notice how your body responds.
3. Place your hands on your belly. Inhale deeply and exhale with a soft chuckle: "Ha, ha, ha." Repeat a few times, letting the sound come from your belly rather than your throat.
4. Inhale and then exhale with a longer, louder laugh: "Ha, ha, ha, ha, ha." Swing your arms or clap your hands as you laugh. Let the rhythm of your body encourage the laughter.
5. Walk around, make eye contact with others if you're practicing in a group, and laugh together. If practicing alone, look in a mirror or imagine laughing with a friend. Allow yourself to exaggerate, make silly faces, or raise the pitch of your laugh.
6. After a few minutes, let the laughter naturally taper off. Take a slow breath in and sigh it out. Place a hand on your heart and notice the sense of lightness, warmth, and release that laughter has created.

WHY THIS HELPS

Laughter is medicine. Even when it feels forced at first, the body does not always know the difference between pretend laughter and spontaneous laughter. Both stimulate the release of endorphins, reduce stress hormones, and soften emotional heaviness. Laughing yoga combines breath, playfulness, and sound to bring lightness into the body.[19]

Exercise: Allowing Joy to Feel Familiar

1. Place both your hands over the center of your chest and take a few slow, steady breaths. Close your eyes and notice the warmth beneath your palms.
2. Bring to mind a moment when you felt genuine joy—whether recent or long ago—and allow whatever arises to be enough.
3. Engage your senses: Recall what you saw, heard, or felt in that moment, letting the memory fill your body with its texture and light.
4. If grief appears, welcome it. This practice is not about replacing sorrow but allowing joy and grief to coexist.
5. Stay with the sensations of joy for a few minutes, feeling it in your body here and now, even if it feels tender or new.
6. When ready, take a deep breath, open your eyes, and rest quietly before returning to your day.

WHY THIS HELPS

Joy can feel frightening after loss. Yet this practice helps you open to joy not as a fleeting moment but as something you can return to again and again. With practice, you build a kind of muscle memory for joy, inviting it more fully into your life and developing confidence in its presence.

Sensory Practice: Essential Oil Meditation for Joy

1. Choose a high-quality, therapeutic-grade essential oil or blend appropriate to your stress level.
    - Level 1 Stress (tiredness, irritability, mild depression): *Eucalyptus citriodora*, 10 drops; geranium, 15 drops; lavender, 5 drops
    - Level 2 Stress (anxiety, persistent tension): Clary sage, 10 drops; chamomile, 5 drops; lavender, 5 drops; geranium, 10 drops
    - Level 3 Stress (fear, despair, withdrawal): geranium, 6 drops; *Eucalyptus citriodora,* 14 drops; mandarin, 10 drops
2. Dilute the oils with 30 milliliters of base oil for massage or use in a bath or diffuser.
3. Apply one to two drops to your palms, rub them together, and inhale deeply to begin your meditation.
4. Breathe slowly as you focus on the aroma. Imagine the scent filling your body with warmth and light.
5. Visualize yourself in a joyful, peaceful place—let the fragrance guide your attention there.
6. Repeat an affirmation such as "I welcome joy" or "I allow lightness in."
7. Rest in the sensations for ten to fifteen minutes, then take a deep breath, open your eyes, and notice how you feel.

WHY THIS HELPS

Aromatherapy works through both the body and the mind. When you breathe in the fragrance of essential oils, tiny molecules travel directly to the brain's limbic system, the center that processes memory, mood, and emotion.[20] Certain oils—such as lavender, geranium, or citrus—are known for their calming and uplifting effects, helping shift the nervous system from stress toward relaxation and ease. Blended into massage oils, baths, or diffusers, aromatherapy can soothe tension, lighten heavy moods, and awaken a sense of joy. In grief, it offers a gentle way to invite comfort and warmth back into the body, reminding you that even small sensory experiences can nurture moments of lightness.

Summary

Grief and joy are not opposites but companions. Allowing joy to coexist with sorrow honors the full spectrum of love rather than betraying it.

Suppression of pain also suppresses joy. Healing requires restoring the natural rhythm between contraction and expansion—between mourning and reengaging with life. Joy asks for courage. It requires reopening the heart after devastation, trusting that delight and wonder can return without erasing loss. Play, innocence, and laughter reawaken the body's innate capacity for safety, connection, and vitality—reminding us that aliveness is part of grief's integration.

When we welcome joy, we remember that grief and love are two movements of the same wave. Joy does not mean forgetting—it means you have survived enough to feel life again.

19

Awakening to What Matters Most

When the diagnosis came, Johanna spent the next several hours with her family, trying to take in the news. What began as a random headache, the kind she thought would pass, had become their worst fear. The pain had grown in intensity and pressure, accompanied by weakness in her arms and legs, slurred speech, and moments of forgetfulness. After a series of scans, the MRI and PET confirmed it: a rapidly growing brain tumor.

To those around her, Johanna put on a brave face. She smiled, reassured her loved ones, and tried to sound confident that she would fight or at least make the best of whatever lay ahead. But when we met alone, the truth surfaced. Her eyes softened and her composure began to tremble. "The future is not welcomed," she said quietly. Then she began to cry. I held her hand and we cried together.

In that moment, the armor of strength fell away. What remained was something more human—raw, scared, and beautifully real. She was no longer being brave for anyone. She was simply being herself, meeting the truth of her life with both fear and grace.

Over the next several weeks, I continued visiting her as she underwent treatment. Her hair thinned from chemotherapy and radiation left small patches across her scalp, but none of that mattered to her anymore. Our conversations often circled around her memories, the people she loved, the things she had once worried about. Increasingly they turned toward the future—not the imagined one of plans or achievements but the narrowing one she now faced.

Yet within that small horizon, something opened. With clarity and tenderness, she began to live differently. She wrote letters, told people she loved them, offered forgiveness, and made amends where she could. Her time was short, but her presence was vast. One afternoon she said to me, "Why don't we all live like this? Why does cancer have to make us finally live?"

Johanna passed away less than a year later. Thankfully she was able to spend her final days at home, surrounded by her family and her dog. Still, she made regular visits to the oncology floor, and each time we would sit together and talk. Those moments were not about dying; they were about living honestly, without pretense.

When Johanna said "The future is not welcomed," she gave voice to a truth that lives deep inside grief. Time no longer moves forward in the same way. The plans once made seem irrelevant, the shape of life unrecognizable. Grief is a time-bending reality. At once you are in the future and at the same time in the past. When loss comes, time folds in on itself. The past feels both close and unreachable, and the future feels like a place you no longer belong.

This is what makes *purpose* such a complicated word in grief. Purpose is a future-oriented concept. It leans forward. It imagines, plans, and builds. But when grief collapses time, purpose can feel unreachable or even cruel. The question "What's next?" becomes unbearable when what you most want is impossible.

The future is not what it once was. Dreams, hopes, and aspirations shift within the narrative of grief. After a divorce, the vows, home, and life you were building are no longer the same. After losing someone important, they are no longer there to share the momentous occasions. After a personal change or loss of identity, you arrive in a reality unclear of who you are becoming. Regardless of circumstance, grief disorients.

It makes sense, then, why there is such a cultural tendency to fill this space with urgency—to transform pain into purpose. The pain can be unbearable, and something inside you insists that something must be done. In the powerlessness of loss, doing feels important. Yet the push to find a lesson, a meaning, or a redemptive reason for suffering often arises from discomfort with uncertainty. Purpose becomes a project to repair or replace what was broken or to control what feels uncontrollable. But genuine purpose—the kind that grief invites—cannot be manufactured through avoidance or suppression. It must be revealed slowly, within the unknown.

When everything familiar has fallen away, purpose begins not as a mission but as a posture. It starts with the courage to remain, to breathe, and to stay present to what is incomprehensible. It is less about doing and more about being. In this space, time begins to shift from something linear to something circular. Each moment becomes its own small eternity, each breath a return to life as it is.

Grief teaches this kind of new time. It teaches that the future cannot be forced and that purpose does not always appear as direction. Sometimes it arrives as devotion and the willingness to stay with what is difficult. It invites you to keep tending the small acts of love and care that make life possible again. Purpose, then, becomes less about fixing the future and more about living faithfully with what remains here in the present.

The Revelation Within Grief

Maya had always imagined herself as a mother. She and her partner spent years hoping, trying, and praying for a child. Each failed attempt felt like a small death, yet she kept the dream alive.

When the doctor finally told her that pregnancy would not be possible, she felt the floor disappear beneath her. "I am not only grieving a child I never had," she said. "I'm grieving the life I thought I would live."

Her grief stretched into the future, into birthdays that would never be celebrated, graduations she would never attend, and grandchildren she would never hold. In a single conversation, the future she had pictured for decades vanished.

For months, she walked through fog. Friends suggested hobbies or urged her to move on, but nothing could replace the dream that had shaped her sense of self. She could not substitute it or silence it. She had no choice but to sit with the raw ache of what would never be.

When I began seeing Maya, I offered grief support for the losses that were present. I could hear many layers in her story—loss not only of motherhood but of identity, purpose, and the imagined future that had once given her life direction. In one session, several months in, I asked her why she wanted to be a mother. She spoke about raising children, teaching them, and creating a family; ordinary things said with extraordinary longing. I asked, "What did you want from being a mom?" She paused, reflected, and answered. Then I asked, "What is underneath being a mom?"

She grew quiet. Her eyes softened, and for the first time in months, her shoulders lowered. "I wanted to give love," she said softly. "To nurture something. To see life grow."

There it was: the truth beneath the dream. Her grief was about not only the loss of motherhood but also the impulse to love, care, and create. That impulse was still alive within her; it had simply lost its form.

We sat together in silence, both aware that something sacred had just surfaced. Naming the loss, the grief underneath the grief, revealed something. We were both surprised. While this naming didn't take away her grief, it provided her with an insight and a revelation she was longing for.

Over the next several months, her relationship to grief began to change. She still mourned the life she thought she would live, but she also began to sense a quiet wisdom forming within her. By tending to her grief, Maya discovered something unexpected: a deeper orientation toward life. She was learning to live from the essence beneath the role, from love itself rather than the identity that once held it.

When time shifts from linear to circular, something else begins to happen. Within the stillness of presence, inside the unbecoming, a kind of knowingness awakens—a wisdom not learned from books or teachers but uncovered through being.

Grief has a way of revealing what lies beneath the surface. It strips away illusion and exposes the raw, unguarded places of the soul. There is a reveal within grief, an exposure through the hollowing—as if within the dark chambers of your being, a faint light begins to shimmer. It is not the light at the end of the tunnel, promising escape. It is a gentler light, soft and interior, the kind that glows when all outer brightness fades.

This light does not arrive with confetti and fanfare. It flickers like the reflection of hidden jewels—subtle colors, quiet vibrations—shining within the dense soil of your being. In the dry, heavy earth of sorrow, something crystalline begins to form. Like solar energy crystallized in matter, grief reveals a sort of brilliance that has been buried. This is not an alchemy of loss; it's the excavation to what's hidden beneath the loss.

The ancient Greeks called this kind of unveiling *apokálypsis*—the word we now know as *apocalypse*. At its heart, apocalypse does not mean destruction; it means revelation. Grief can be a form of personal apocalypse. The life you imagined falls apart, the timelines dissolve, and the future you were walking toward disappears. Yet within that collapse, something enduring shows itself. It is the moment when the outer structures of certainty crumble and the deeper truth of life stands exposed.

This was what Johanna seemed to discover in her final months. It's also something Maya uncovered. While their stories are different, neither could welcome the future, yet both were able to see what truly mattered. Pretenses fell away. Johanna wrote letters, spoke her love aloud, and forgave what once felt unforgivable. Maya began using love and nourishment as a motivating force, caring for animals that had been sheltered and abandoned when the pandemic was over. She revealed her motherhood could exist in many ways. Grief had stripped them both down to their essence, and within that raw bareness of spirit, they found something. There's a kind of light in that darkness. This is not the light of recovery but the light of inner truth; the light that emerges when you see, perhaps for the first time, what is real and enduring.

Grief, when met with presence that doesn't push toward productivity and purpose right away, has a way of being a revelation. It shows you what cannot be taken, what remains when everything else is gone. In the circular rhythm of time, where each moment holds eternity, this light becomes your compass. It guides you not toward escape but toward meaning—toward what matters most.

The Unscripted Life

Listening to the heart requires courage. The heart speaks in intuition, sensation, and resonance. When you begin to listen, you align with a force far greater than your individual will. You connect with a power akin to the gravitational pull that keeps the earth in orbit around the sun. It is a force ever-present and quiet, a constancy of energy that holds everything within the coherent chaos of life.

This is the force of love, the animating energy that sustains life itself. It is not sentimental or fragile. It is the same intelligence that guides the tides, that draws the moon and earth into harmony, that brings seedlings toward the light. It moves through every breath, every pulse, every expression of care.

To live from what matters most is to live in rhythm with this force. You begin to feel life moving through you rather than you moving through life. Decisions arise from resonance rather than reason. You are no longer driven by external pressures but drawn, called, even pulled by an interior gravity. It is this force of love that organizes the fragments of your being into coherence.

This is the same power that steadies you when everything else falls apart. When you listen to the heart, you attune to the universal rhythm that underlies grief and growth. You begin to sense that you are part of something vast, and that the same force that turns the planets also turns you toward wholeness.

To live with such personal revelation is to live unscripted. It means following the quiet instructions of the heart rather than the conditioned plans of the mind. It is a path defined not by certainty but by authenticity, a path of deep listening. When you begin to trust what is arising within you, life begins to take on a new congruence. The outer life starts to reflect the inner truth. What once felt fragmented begins to align and life itself begins to look different.

This is not easy. When you start to live from what has been revealed, when you begin to act from your heart rather than from habit, the landscape of your life changes. You see differently, move differently, relate differently. The world you once knew may not recognize you anymore.

There is loss in this too. The people who once felt closest may not understand your change. You may also long for normalcy, to go back to the way things were before the loss. For some this may be possible, but for others that world is gone. You are no longer the same. In grief's shattering, a becoming takes place. It can feel remarkably isolating, even as it feels profoundly true.

Such living is not about fixing or returning but allowing. You begin to move in accordance with your values rather than external validation. You create a new normal shaped by an internal revelation and guided by love, presence, and truth.

Researchers have long observed this phenomenon through different lenses:

The regret-and-opportunity principle suggests that encounters with loss awaken an awareness of limited time, motivating people to align life choices with what feels meaningful rather than obligatory.[1]

Mortality salience studies show that when confronted with impermanence, people are more likely to live with intentionality and authenticity, reprioritizing relationships and purpose.[2]

Post-traumatic growth describes how individuals can experience greater appreciation for life, deeper compassion, and a redefinition of priorities after trauma.[3]

Self-determination theory emphasizes that well-being arises when life is guided by intrinsic motivation—autonomy, competence, and relatedness—rather than external approval.[4]

Cultural lenses remind us that how one integrates loss depends on the meanings their culture offers; some emphasize endurance and faith, others renewal and transformation.

In the Compassionate Grieving model, this awakening is understood as the unscripted life. It is the movement when you begin to live from the trust of an internal revelation. The unbecoming of a personal apocalypse unveils a new reality. Purpose is no longer associated solely with a plan but with a presence and a compass guided by love, truth, and the courage to live from what was uncovered. Grief, then, in a powerful sense, becomes not an interruption to life but an initiation into a deeper one.

It is not only the uncertainty of the future that feels so difficult after loss. It is the uncertainty of who you are within it. Grief reshapes identity as much as it rearranges time. The familiar self no longer fits, and the old markers of meaning fall away. Purpose, then, is not a destination waiting in the distance. It is a posture of presence, a way of standing in the mystery of your own becoming. It is the willingness to live from what has been uncovered within your heart, guided by the quiet authority of essential truths and values. When you move from this place, the future is no longer something to be solved or controlled. It becomes something you can meet with openness, reverence, and trust.

When loss becomes part of your life and you give yourself permission to grieve, you begin to honor with reverence the love that has been shaped, moved, and revealed through that loss. In that surrender, as you enter the apocalyptic unknown and the deeper revelations of your life unfold, new dimensions of your being begin to emerge. Over time, this awareness weaves through your days like a golden thread, guiding you toward what is real and true. It draws you into alignment with the essence of who you are becoming—someone living from love, anchored in presence, and faithful to what matters most.

TECHNIQUES FOR WORKING WITH PURPOSE

Qigong Practice: Clearing the Way

1. Stand with your feet shoulder-width apart, your knees soft, and your shoulders relaxed.
2. Bring your palms together, facing upward in front of your chest, pinkies close.
3. Inhale and extend your arms forward at heart level, your palms turning outward.

4. Exhale as you circle your arms wide to the sides, clearing the space in front of you, then return to center.
5. Continue this clearing motion for two to three minutes, matching breath and movement.
6. Reverse the motion: Inhale as you draw your palms toward your chest, exhale as you extend and circle them outward.
7. Repeat for another two to three minutes, moving slowly and fluidly.
8. End by resting your palms over your lower belly. Take a few calm breaths and notice the sense of openness and ease.

WHY THIS HELPS

The first sequence clears obstacles from the heart's path. The second draws in what you long for. Practiced together, breath, movement, and intention help you release what is no longer needed and receive what supports your future.

Exercise: Morning Alignment for Focus and Clarity

1. Place your fingertips two finger-widths below your belly button and press gently.
2. As you inhale, keep awareness here for about one minute. (Add an optional affirmation: *I am grounded, clear, and aligned.*)
3. Keep one hand on your belly and place the other on the center of your chest.
4. Breathe into both areas together for about one minute, repeating the affirmation.
5. Keep one hand on your belly and move the other to the point between your eyebrows.
6. Synchronize breath and awareness at your belly, chest, and brow for one minute.

7. Keep one hand on your belly, and move the other hand to the top of your head, breathing with awareness of your belly, chest, and crown for one minute.
8. Place both your hands at the crown for one minute, then release and rest.

WHY THIS HELPS

This sequence activates key acupressure points that regulate energy flow and emotional balance.[5] Ren 6 (Sea of Qi), located below the navel, strengthens vitality and centers the body. Ren 17, at the chest center, opens the chest and relieves emotional heaviness. *Yin Tang,* the brow point between the eyebrows, quiets the mind and calms the spirit. Finally, Du 20, at the crown of the head, supports mental clarity, focus, and a balanced mood.[6] Together these points harmonize the body's qi, fostering grounding, openness, and calm integration.

Breath Practice: Box Breathing for Facing Uncertainty

1. Sit or lie comfortably. Take a few natural breaths.
2. Inhale through your nose to a count of four.
3. Hold the breath for a count of four, keeping your shoulders relaxed.
4. Exhale through your nose to a count of four.
5. Pause at the bottom of the exhale for a count of four.
6. Repeat for four to six rounds, visualizing a square as you breathe.
7. Return to natural breathing and notice how your body feels.

WHY THIS HELPS

Box breathing balances the autonomic nervous system by synchronizing inhalation, retention, and exhalation. This rhythmic pattern activates the parasympathetic response, lowering heart rate and calming the stress response.[7] It steadies the mind, reduces cortisol, and increases heart rate variability—a key indicator of emotional regulation and resilience. When the future feels uncertain, this simple breath practice anchors awareness in the present and restores clarity through physiological balance.

Art Practice: The Unscripted Life Vision Board

1. Ask yourself the following questions; perhaps even journal on them:
    - What matters now?
    - What no longer deserves my time?
    - What feels essential in this season of my life?
2. Gather images, quotes, colors, or natural items that align with your values.
3. Arrange them on a poster board, gluing or taping them into place. Allow creativity and emotion to guide you.
4. Include symbols of impermanence—such as leaves, clocks, moons, or candles—to honor life's transience.
5. Add visuals or words that represent courage, risk, and stepping into the unknown.
6. Place your vision board somewhere visible, as a daily reminder to live intentionally and unscripted.

WHY THIS HELPS

Vision boards combine visual imagery, emotional intention, and repetition—three powerful drivers of motivation and neural change. Research in psychology and neuroscience shows that visualizing goals activates similar brain regions as actually pursuing them, strengthening motivation and follow-through.[8] When anchored in personal values rather than external success, vision boards support self-determination and coherence, helping bridge grief's uncertainty with a renewed sense of direction. By weaving images of impermanence and boldness, this practice transforms longing into purpose, reminding you that the future is not a replacement for what was lost but an invitation to live more fully and truthfully.

Summary

Grief does not only ask what you have lost—it asks what you will choose now. Purpose cannot be rushed, but it can be allowed to emerge from what is true for you in this moment, especially in the wake of lost or shattered dreams. The unscripted life lets grief sculpt you into someone more aligned, awake, and real. Boldness to live the unscripted can be quiet or fierce, but it always emerges from love and a willing yes to the life that now calls you forward.

Grief clears the ground for awakened purpose. It asks you to companion your sorrow rather than escape it, and to let new congruence—between inner truth and outer life—emerge in its own time.

20

Coming Alive Again

Honey came to me for grief support after the death of her mother. Her loss had undone her in ways she never expected. What surprised her most was not just the grief itself but how it unraveled her faith.

For years, Honey's faith had been the anchor of her life. She read scripture daily, prayed with discipline, and was deeply involved in her church community. She was even part of an outreach ministry that helped others through life-changing events. She believed she was prepared for grief when her mother died, but nothing could have prepared her for the emptiness that followed.

In her sorrow, Honey's faith felt hollow. The scriptures that once brought peace now felt distant and heavy. Prayer, once her comfort, turned into silence or inner arguments with God. Even her church community, which had always been her refuge, seemed impatient with her grief. People told her to "be strong" and "trust God's plan," words that deepened her shame. She began to feel judged, unseen, and eventually withdrew from her faith community.

When we met, I could sense that Honey was grieving two losses: her mother and her spiritual home. The faith that once nourished her now felt like a place she no longer belonged. The version of faith she was taught left little room for sorrow. It treated grief as weakness, something to overcome quickly rather than something sacred to honor.

We began simply, with permission: permission to feel the sorrow, to let grief become part of her spiritual life rather than a failure of it. Together we explored what faith had meant to her throughout her life, how it took shape, what it offered, and where it felt constraining.

Through these reflections Honey began to realize that much of her faith had been inherited rather than discovered. Her mother had lovingly instilled religious devotion in her through Sunday services, Bible study, and prayer groups, but these practices were bound to her mother's expression of faith, not her own. When her mother died, that connection died too. Honey had never realized how entwined her faith was with her mother's. Something new began to stir within her: curiosity.

At first she hesitated to voice her questions. She had been trained to believe doubt was dangerous. But in our sessions she found space to wonder. She admitted that sometimes in church her mind wandered, that guilt shadowed her when she didn't feel inspired, and that she longed for something more alive. As she gave voice to these feelings, something unexpected emerged: a gentle spark of awe.

Honey found herself drawn to angel cards and the stories of Mary Magdalene. She felt intrigued by ideas once considered "off-limits," such as crystals, energy healing, and sacred places such as Sedona, Arizona. She laughed at herself for these new interests, calling them "silly," but beneath the laughter was wonder. Awe became her new compass.

With time and permission, Honey's faith began to breathe again. Exploring new expressions did not take her away from God; it led her deeper into that relationship. Church, once an obligation, became a place of renewal. Her spirituality no longer felt confined to what she was taught but expanded into something personal and alive.

When her mother died, the version of faith Honey had inherited died too. In its place, a living faith began to grow, one rooted in experience rather than expectation. In grief, she rediscovered aliveness. What once felt like loss became a doorway to something sacred: a faith infused with freedom, creativity, and awe.

When Grief Awakens the Senses

Grief makes you porous to life. What once passed by unnoticed now enters you fully. A bird's call, a child's laughter, the hum of traffic in the distance—each becomes a reminder that life continues, that the world is still turning even when yours has stopped. At the same time, paradoxically, the usual noise of the world quiets, and what remains can seem unbearably still. Time widens and your perception changes, drawing your attention to what is ordinarily overlooked.

When you lose something significant in your life—whether a person, a job, a marriage, or a faith—you lose an anchor around which you used to move. It is disorienting. You may begin to notice the world in ways you never did before. It can feel as if you have stepped into a new dimension, yet nothing mystical has happened. What has changed is not the world but the way you move within it. Your senses become attuned to what once seemed imperceptible. You may begin to recognize that beauty and sorrow are braided together—like a sunset that brings tears and also awe, or a silence that aches but also soothes. There is a paradox here: The more you allow yourself to feel, the more vivid life becomes, even when it hurts.

A subtle awakening unfolds when grief is allowed. As your capacity to feel grows, aliveness begins to blossom. Like joy, it may feel unfamiliar or even uncomfortable. Yet aliveness is not only an emotion. It is a state, a vibrancy, a relationship. It is the soul's way of reorienting when the familiar has collapsed.

Aliveness often arrives quietly at first. It arrives as the body's instinct to breathe. It arrives as the heart's ache that still longs to feel. It arrives as the spirit's unspoken desire to remain connected to life. It shows up in the "somehow": Somehow, I woke up this morning. Somehow, I got out of bed. Somehow, I managed to work. Somehow, I ate. In the early confusion of acute grief, aliveness lives in the simple instinct to survive. The body and soul join forces to keep you tethered to existence. In their own language, they whisper, *Stay. Breathe. Feel.*

Aliveness born of grief is a moment-to-moment encounter with life stripped of pretense and familiar landmarks. This new way of noticing the world is what contemplatives might call mindfulness and mystics might call divine presence. For you, in the initial throes of grief, you likely think of it as surviving the next minute. For you, it is not chosen. It's not a pursuit of enlightenment or transcendence. For you, it's almost as if you are forced into the moment because the past feels gone and the future unimaginable. What remains is the now in its raw, luminous, and trembling expression of life.

As you begin to allow grief, as it's given space to breathe, as embodiment helps to manage the intensity of emotions, and the nervous system softens through the practices that have unfolded through this book, aliveness also shifts. The heightened senses that were once part of disorientation become a new relationship with sensitivity itself. You may not have chosen this new orientation to the world, this acute sense of awareness, but it is here, asking you not to turn away.

Paradoxically, grief can also appear when the grief of the original loss begins to soften. When a sense of normalcy returns, you may realize you miss the depth of feeling that grief opened in you. Life, with all its busyness, can draw you back into numbness.

Allison, exhausted from the demands of working in health care during the pandemic, reached out to me after a sudden loss. She said she felt her light dimming. As we worked through the layers of her grief, she began to feel more like herself again. Years later, she reached out once more, this time not in crisis. Life was going well. Her job was stable, she and her partner bought a new home, and things felt steady. Yet she told me something I never expected. "I'm missing my grief," she said. I knew exactly what she meant. She did not miss the pain, but she missed what grief had invited her toward. She missed the presence. She missed the heightened awareness. She missed the richness of feeling that grief had awakened in her. What was once disorienting had become something she valued.

When all that once held you together has fallen apart, something happens that no spiritual practice can manufacture: Life itself becomes unfiltered. You are cracked open, even broken open. That openness feels unbearable at first, something you might constantly manage with anything to help avoid the pain. Yet as time moves forward, you approach this new sense of aliveness with curiosity and care. This new orientation to aliveness can help you walk the path of grief. Over time, following its cues becomes a kind of embodied prayer. You begin to sense that presence itself is what carries you.

Aliveness as a Return to Belonging to Life

This heightened sensitivity is not meant to overwhelm you, though at times it might. It is your body's way of reminding you that you are still here. As you stay close to this expansive awareness, this call to the in-between invisible moments of life, something quiet begins to stir. While the world rushes forward, you may find yourself standing still, watching life unfold with unusual clarity.

Grief may have opened your senses, but aliveness begins to open your belonging. In the wake of loss, when so much has fallen away, you may start to sense that life is still reaching for you. Like a golden retriever whose heavy body leans against you, meeting you in your sorrow, or a sweet kitty who lies on your chest, purring in moments when you feel hollow, each in their own steady presence without a need: Life meets you with tenderness. This is where aliveness truly begins—not in brightness or joy but in the simple willingness to stay connected to a world that has changed. This is the moment when aliveness becomes something more than sensation. It becomes a homecoming. You might notice this belonging in simple moments: a warm cup in your hands, a kindness offered by a friend, a sudden swell of emotion at a song you used to love, a memory that brings both tears and tenderness. These moments do not announce themselves as healing, yet they are invitations. Each one reminds you, gently, that you still have a place here.

Aliveness deepens when you begin to sense that even in your pain, you are not separate from life. You breathe the same air as everyone else. You stand under the same sky. You feel the warmth of the sun and the coolness of night. The world continues to unfold around you, not to ignore your grief but to hold you within it.

Grief teaches you that you are not carried by answers or certainty. Instead, you are carried by connection. You are carried by presence. You are carried by the small ways life meets you each day. You are carried by moments of tenderness, sensations that awaken you to the invisible miracle existing all around you.

In grief, aliveness is less like a spark and more like the steady pulse of connection to the world around you. It is the gradual noticing that even in the ache, you are still part of this world. While strokes of inspiration come, it's in the subtle moments of heightened sensitivity when aliveness is felt.

The willingness to let yourself be touched by life again, even when you cannot predict how it will feel—in allowing yourself to feel the moments of beauty, tenderness, or wonder to coexist with your pain—is miraculous.

You do not have to feel ready. You do not have to feel healed. Aliveness is beyond the duality of good and bad, light and dark. Aliveness can be cultivated, but it doesn't require effort. You only need to notice it. It is already within you. It emerges when you stop trying to push yourself into healing and instead allow yourself to be where you are.

Whole-Body Yeses

Aliveness is not just an emotional experience or a spiritual awakening. It is a physical state. It emerges through your nervous system, through the regulating shifts that happen when your body begins to move out of survival and back into connection. It is the felt sense of presence, sensitivity, and connection that arises when your body softens out of dysregulation and your heart begins to attune to life again. It expresses itself through curiosity, movement, resonance, openness, belonging, and breath.

Aliveness is not simply a mood—it is a tone of being. While moods rise and fall with circumstances, a tone of being runs deeper, forming the subtle orientation beneath your feelings. It's like a resonance or frequency, a quiet current that your heart is naturally drawn to. Your nervous system seeks entrainment with this rhythm and pulse of life; aliveness is its call.

Often, aliveness is mistaken for something bright or uplifting. In grief, however, it rarely feels that way. Aliveness is not excitement, joy, or the rush of feeling better. It is not the promise of a new beginning. Instead, aliveness is the subtle, life-giving hum of reconnecting to life, even when everything feels heavy.

Aliveness grows through this inner attunement and reveals itself as a whole-body yes. It is the way your body signals that something is true, meaningful, or life-giving for you. This yes does not shout initially. It rises quietly, often beneath the sorrow. As you grow into deeper layers of emotional safety—cultivated through embodiment and supported by practices that hold powerful emotions—the quiet vibrancy begins to make itself known.

Sometimes it arrives with a lightness or a softening where there was once tension. You may feel it as a little more energy or vitality in your body, a subtle ease that makes it possible to smile without forcing it. You may feel it in moments that bring goose bumps because something inside you recognizes truth or beauty. A whole-body yes may feel like a deeper breath that you did not realize you were holding or a warmth that spreads through your chest, belly, or spine. It can come as a sensation of settling, a groundedness that replaces the tightness you have been carrying. It may arrive as more energy, more feelings of vitality, more moments of clarity, or a breath that naturally settles deeper into your body. You may feel yourself consistently drawn toward experiences that are nourishing or meaningful. These are early signs of a whole-body yes emerging from within you.

These sensations are subtle but trustworthy. They are your body's way of saying, *This nourishes me.* They are early signals of aliveness rising within you, even when grief remains. They help you sense what is supportive, what brings coherence, and what reconnects you to the world in tender, honest ways.

Aliveness reemerges when your body finds just enough safety to soften. It doesn't require perfect safety or certainty, only a gentle easing within your system. This softening is what the psychologist Stephen W. Porges describes as the ventral vagal state: the part of your nervous system that supports connection, presence, curiosity, and gentle engagement with life. It is the physiological foundation of feeling alive—a smooth flow of qi through the body, or the harmonious balance of your doshas in Ayurveda.

Cultivating Aliveness

Aliveness naturally speaks to you through sensory experiences. The more you notice them, the more you can cultivate your connection to aliveness. Subtle moments such as witnessing a beam of light falling across the floor, the sound of rain on the window, or the softness in someone's voice when they say your name can all be opportunities to notice aliveness. These are moments of awe. Awe is like a kindling for aliveness. Like the way eating pickled ginger before a meal awakens your digestive system or how wood chips start a fire, awe is a way to stoke more aliveness in your life. It slips in through the cracks of dysregulation to offer moments of coherence.

Awe is not meant to replace grief. Throughout this book, we've looked to dissolve binary ways of thinking that create separation. Grief and awe can coexist. Awe does not erase sorrow. It sits beside it. It gives it shape. It makes space around it. Awe expands your heart just enough to let your breath flow more freely, just enough to allow life to touch you again. You may find yourself crying not only because something hurts but because something is beautiful. That is awe. It braids tenderness and ache into the same moment.

There's a growing body of research on the science of awe. The psychologist Dacher Keltner and his colleagues, who have studied awe for decades, describe it as an emotion that expands your sense of self, shifts your perspective, and connects you to something larger than your individual life.[1] In moments of awe, the brain's default mode network, the area associated with self-focus and rumination, quiets.[2] This reduction in activity allows you to feel more present, less trapped inside your pain, and more connected to the world around you. At the same time, awe activates the parasympathetic nervous system, slowing the heart rate and deepening the breath.[3]

These physiological changes ripple through the body. Research shows that awe can lower stress hormones such as cortisol and decrease pro-inflammatory cytokines that contribute to chronic illness.[4] Even brief experiences, such as watching the stars move across a night sky, standing among towering trees, or hearing music that moves you to tears, can measurably reduce inflammation and calm the nervous system.[5]

Awe, in this way, does what the soul already knows to do. It restores balance. It integrates what was fragmented. It brings coherence to your body and steadiness to your heart. It expands your capacity to hold both sorrow and wonder at once.

Studies also reveal that awe increases generosity, empathy, and connection with others. After moments of awe, people are more likely to reach out, to help, and to care for others.[6] In the isolation that grief often brings, awe becomes a medicine for both your body and spirit, widening your heart's field and reminding you that you belong to something vast and interconnected.

Nature is also one of the greatest teachers of awe. In the wake of loss, when everything feels chaotic or disordered, the abundance of the natural world reveals the quiet intelligence of continuity. Seasons turn. Leaves fall. Flowers bloom again. Life regenerates itself. When you pause to notice the slow drift of clouds, the intricate veins of a leaf, or the steadiness of a stone beneath your hand, something reorders within you. The world keeps breathing with you.

Aliveness lives in the attention of awe. It invites you to keep looking until beauty reveals itself again, not as a distraction from grief but as the soul's reminder that life continues to create even in the midst of loss.

How Creativity Renews the Soul

Wonder at the aliveness and preciousness of everything may be why so many traditions of mourning were intentionally awe-inspiring. Cathedrals soar heavenward, chants spiral upward in temples, bonfires leap beneath darkened skies. These settings not only hold grief but they also invite experiences of awe. They create a kind of digestive process for sorrow through both lamentation and devotion, inviting a return to cosmic truth.

Through awe, a subtle renewal begins to move in you. The soul, once silenced by loss, starts to hum again. That hum is the call to create in life's ongoing creation—to cook, to garden, to sing softly to yourself, to write words that no one will ever read. Creativity becomes the language through which the soul remembers itself. It is how aliveness begins to take form.

In grief, creativity is not about expression or productivity. It is about connection. It offers the soul a way to keep loving what was lost by shaping something new. When your hands make, when your body moves, when your voice sounds, you join the quiet conversation between grief and life. Creativity becomes a living prayer. Through it, sorrow finds movement and the soul finds meaning.

There are many forms of creative expression that support grief. Free-writing and journaling provide structure for meaning-making. Poetry and lyric writing give voice to sorrow through image and metaphor. Visual art practices such as drawing or painting help externalize emotions and foster continuing bonds with loved ones. Playing or improvising music provides a powerful outlet for emotional expression and regulation, engaging mind and body in release. Even the creation of spiritual rituals or personal ceremonies—whether lighting candles, crafting symbolic objects, or designing new traditions—helps transform grief into meaningful connection and communal support.

For many, however, creativity feels unfamiliar. In a world ruled by stress, busyness, and productivity, creativity is often treated as a nice-to-have. In some cultures, cultivating creativity is seen as a luxury. Yet neuroscience shows that creative engagement activates networks in the brain that foster emotional flexibility and resilience, especially under stress.[7] Creativity is a vital practice that restores flow, opens perspective, and helps carry the soul of love and loss.

Kenny told me he didn't have a creative bone in his body. He especially didn't like to journal. An engineer by trade, he felt that trying to put words on a page was strange and unnatural. After his father died, though, he found himself weighed down in ways he couldn't name. His wife noticed the light leaving his eyes, how even weekends with the kids seemed to drain him. He admitted he felt like he was just going through the motions.

In one of our conversations he mentioned, almost offhand, that he used to be in a band back in college. He had been the lead singer and wrote songs occasionally. I suggested he try writing again. But this time, instead of keeping a journal, he could keep a book where he'd jot down song lyrics. His grief could take the shape of a verse and he could sing that verse if he felt like it.

At first it was awkward, but soon he began to write. Slowly, melodies and words started to carry his feelings in ways he couldn't convey in conversation. He even shared some of his songs in our sessions. They were raw and beautiful. More important, he was processing emotions that had felt stuck for months.

Kenny rediscovered a part of himself he thought was long gone, and through his renewing creative expression, he found both release and renewal. His wife later told me she could see the change: He seemed more present, more alive. Creativity had opened a door to awe he didn't know was waiting for him.

Bringing It All Together

Aliveness is not something you force or fabricate. It grows through a natural unfolding within you, carried by three quiet companions that grief awakens: sensitivity, awe, and creativity. When these three come together, something shifts. Each one plays a distinct role in returning you to life, and together they form the pathway back to your deepest sense of belonging. Together they create the lived experience of aliveness. Not the bright, exuberant aliveness you may once have known but a deeper, steadier aliveness; a tone of being that comes from staying connected to yourself and the world in honest, tender ways.

Sensitivity is the opening. It is the softening of your inner world, the widening of your senses, the willingness to feel what is here. Grief heightens this sensitivity at first, often in painful ways. Yet over time, this very sensitivity becomes the doorway through which life begins to touch you again. Sensitivity is the heart's way of saying, *I am still capable of responding*. It is your first step back into relationship with the world.

Awe is what rises when sensitivity is allowed. When you notice a small moment of beauty, tenderness, or wonder, something in you expands. Awe does not erase grief, but it brings breath into the places that feel tight. It widens your perspective just enough for hope to have a place to rest. Awe reconnects you to the larger mystery that holds your life. It reminds you that you belong to something vast and sacred, even when your inner world feels broken.

Creativity is the expression that emerges from this widened space. It is the way your soul responds to the world. Creativity gives form to what you feel. It gives movement to what has been trapped inside. It gives you a way to participate in life again, even gently. Creativity does not require artistic skill. It simply asks you to follow the small impulses that draw you toward meaning. When you create, you give voice to your sorrow and your becoming.

"Sensitivity + awe + creativity = aliveness" is not a math equation you work to solve but a pattern that naturally unfolds as you allow yourself to feel, notice, and respond. Aliveness emerges when you participate in the world from your truth. It grows when you let your heart be enlivened by wonder, when you give yourself permission to create, and when you trust the sensitivities that grief has awakened within you. These are the conditions in which whole-body yesses begin to appear. They rise as softening, clarity, deeper breath, or a quiet pull toward what nourishes you. They are the subtle ways your body signals, *This is right for me. This is life returning.*

Aliveness is not the opposite of grief. It is the companion that rises alongside it. It is the quiet homecoming, the inner returning, the recognition that even here, even now, life is still reaching for you. When you learn to listen for these whole-body yesses, you begin to sense that life is inviting you forward again. And it is waiting to show you what makes you feel alive.

TECHNIQUES FOR WORKING WITH ALIVENESS

Exercise: Embodied Aliveness

1. Create a playlist of songs that light you up—music that gives you goose bumps, makes you smile, or makes your body want to move.
2. Set a timer for at least ten minutes and give yourself full permission to dance.
3. Move freely and without judgment—shake, sway, jump, spin, laugh. Let rhythm lead.

4. If you wish, invite friends to join in or plan a communal dance gathering.

   Afterward, take a few moments to sit quietly or journal:

   - How did joy feel in my body?
   - Where do I feel aliveness now?

WHY THIS HELPS

Dancing activates joy as a full-body experience. Movement releases endorphins, dopamine, and oxytocin—the brain's natural mood enhancers—and lowers stress hormones such as cortisol.[8] Rhythmic motion helps regulate the nervous system by balancing sympathetic arousal with parasympathetic calm. In Traditional Chinese Medicine, dancing restores the flow of qi, dispersing stagnation caused by grief or emotional overload. Psychologically, spontaneous movement interrupts rumination and restores a sense of vitality, creativity, and connection. Through dance, joy becomes embodied, reminding you that energy still moves and life continues to pulse within you.

Art Practice: Exploring Creativity

1. **Follow your curiosity.** Choose a way to step into a creative space. You might visit an art supply store and notice what materials catch your eye; spend an afternoon in a museum or gallery, letting colors, textures, and images speak to you; or sign up for a class in painting, pottery, dance, writing, or music and explore without expectation.
2. **Say yes to what calls you**. As you explore, notice what sparks interest or delight, even in small ways. Allow yourself to pick up the brush, try a color, or move your body. There is no wrong way to respond.
3. **Release perfection.** Remember that this is not about skill or

outcome. Let the process itself be the reward. The act of creating opens pathways for expression, joy, and healing.

4. **Reflect.** Afterward, pause for a moment of reflection. Ask yourself the following questions and journal on them if you choose:

    - What surprised me?
    - What felt good?
    - What do I want to explore more of?

WHY THIS HELPS

Exploring creativity is a practice of reawakening. It invites you back into a relationship with wonder, play, and the part of you that longs to express life beyond words. Grief can sometimes narrow life into routines of survival. Creativity opens it back up and gives you joyful permission to be surprised by what moves you.

Exercise: Going on an Awe Date

1. **Choose your place.** Plan a trip somewhere that stirs your sense of wonder. It might be a mountain trail, the ocean, a star-filled night, a museum, or even a concert that moves your soul.
2. **Arrive with openness.** When you arrive, slow down. Take a few deep breaths and allow yourself to simply notice. Pay attention to the sights, sounds, textures, and vastness around you.
3. **Let awe touch you.** Notice what gives you goose bumps or makes your chest expand. Allow the sensation of awe to move through your body without rushing to explain it.
4. **Reflect.** After your awe date, pause and ask the following questions, which you may wish to journal in response to: *What did I feel? What important things was I reminded of?*
5. **Translate awe to your daily life.** Awe does not always require grand adventures. It can be found in ordinary moments if we pause long enough to notice. Try these simple practices:

    - Watch the sunrise or sunset. Notice the shifting colors and how the light transforms the sky.

- Look at the stars. Step outside at night and let yourself marvel at the vastness above you.
- Observe a flower or tree. Study its intricate patterns, textures, and colors as if seeing it for the first time.
- Listen to music that moves you. Let yourself be carried by the sound until you feel goose bumps.
- Stand by water. Watch the rhythm of waves, ripples in a pond, or rain falling on the ground.
- Witness kindness. Notice small acts of generosity or love in daily life and let them expand your heart.
- Hold something meaningful. A family heirloom, a shell, or a stone—feel its story and the connection it carries.
- Look into a child's or elder's eyes. Sense the wonder, wisdom, or love reflected there.
- Make time for daily reflection (you may wish to use the following as regular journaling prompts): What moment of awe did I notice today and how did it shift me? Where did I feel it in my body and what reminder did it give me about life?

WHY THIS HELPS

Awe is a medicine of expansion. It softens the weight of grief by reminding us of the mystery and beauty still available, even in the midst of sorrow. Physiologically and psychologically, as we make intentional room for awe, we restore coherence between heart, mind, and world, allowing grief to exist within a larger field of meaning.

Summary

Aliveness is an expansion of capacity to hold tears and laughter, sorrow and wonder. Feeling alive again after loss strengthens your sensitivity to beauty and connection. Grief contracts; awe and aliveness open. One turns you inward, the other restores your orientation toward life.

Courting awe rejoins us to the vast breadth of existence and expands our awareness, humility, and capacity to hold complexity.

When we allow for the movement of our own aliveness, we let grief and vitality coexist, and each gives the other meaning. It is the body remembering that it still belongs to life.

CONCLUSION

Living the Practices, Living the Love

If you've made it this far, you've done something profoundly brave. Turning toward grief is not an easy path. It asks for courage, tenderness, and persistence. It requires you to show up for your own humanity with compassion, again and again, especially when everything in you wants to turn away.

To engage grief somatically—to meet it through breath, movement, sensation, and awareness—is an act of deep self-trust. It means believing that your body can hold the truth of what you feel and guide you through it. It is vulnerable work, but it is also sacred work. Grief asks for nothing less than your honesty and presence. In return, it gives you intimacy with your own aliveness.

There is also great courage in meeting your heart with compassion. Though it beats faithfully for you every moment, you may have forgotten how to listen to it. Meeting grief with compassion means meeting yourself in your full humanity—in your imperfections, your messiness, and your tender uniqueness.

Grief, as you've learned through these pages, is not simply an emotion to be resolved. It is a whole-body, whole-being phenomenon—an expression of love that has lost its familiar form. Your body is not your enemy here. It is your companion, your teacher, your sanctuary. It knows how to weep, how to tremble, how to open, how to rest. It carries wisdom far beyond what the mind can reason.

I hope by now you have discovered that grief and love are inseparable. Because love is complex, grief must be too. Creating compassionate spaciousness for the intimacy of both is profound work. Grief is how love continues when the world changes shape. Love is what keeps grief from collapsing into despair. Together they move in a sacred dance—a rhythm that mirrors the natural harmonies of life. Just as the heart and brain, the sympathetic and parasympathetic, yin and yang, mind and body are not opposites but partners in balance, so too are grief and love in a relationship of co-creation. In this paradox of heartbreak and heart opening, you discover your heart's astonishing capacity to hold even more love.

The practices you've encountered—breathing, grounding, sensing, moving, stilling—are ways to live within that paradox. Guided by your body, they help you reharmonize what has been disconnected. They mend the wounds of separation and empower you so that suffocating, swallowing, and suppressing no longer have to be your ways of coping. These practices help you release the myths that say you must be strong, get over it, or move on alone. They teach you how to stay present instead of suppressing, how to soften instead of hardening, how to connect instead of isolating. Grief is not something to fix. It is something to companion, witness, and honor.

As you move forward, remember that grief is cyclical, not linear. It rises and falls like the tides. Some days you will feel open and clear, and others you will feel closed and heavy. This does not mean you have gone backward. It means grief is alive, and so are you. Continue to bring tenderness to your experience.

Over time, your relationship with grief will change. What once felt unbearable may soften into tenderness. What once was only pain may uncover deep truths and insights, guiding you toward an inner conviction that lives within the loss itself. Joy may return, not as a betrayal of what you have lost but as a natural expression of what remains. The more you live the practices, the more you will find peace within your emotional body, as feelings become friends and companions in this mysterious and powerful life.

When you need support, return to these practices. Read a different chapter. Try practices that didn't speak to you before and see if they do now. This resource is yours to revisit whenever you need to remember what is true. (See the appendices for lists of all the practices by type and somatic approach.) Do not grieve alone. Seek out others who understand. Grief needs community. Healing happens in connection—with others, with nature, and with something greater than yourself.

Here is one final practice to close, or perhaps to begin again:

A PRACTICE OF BELONGING

Sit quietly and bring to mind someone you love, past or present, living or gone. Feel the warmth of that love in your body, however it appears. Now imagine extending that warmth outward, like ripples in water, until it reaches all who grieve in this very moment across the world. You are not alone in your sorrow. You are part of a vast and tender web of hearts learning to live with love and loss together.

Rest here for a few breaths. Feel yourself held. Feel yourself holding. We are doing this together.

A Blessing

May your body be a refuge when the world feels heavy.
May your breath remind you that life still moves through you.
May you trust the wisdom that rises from within.
May grief teach you how to love deeper than before.
And may that love guide you—one breath, one step, one heartbeat at a time—toward peace.

ACKNOWLEDGMENTS

First and foremost, this book could not have come into being without my beloved wife, Dr. Siri Chand Kaur Khalsa. Your steadfast support extends far beyond this book, shaping the messages and work that live within it. Our shared paths—mine in chaplaincy and yours in hospice care—have allowed us, as a unique couple, to explore the depths of human experience. You are unafraid to witness grief. Even more so, you carry insights and awareness that helped me form the structures needed to create this work. Thank you dearly.

To my parents, Kultar and Dolly Sachdev: Thank you for imagining me forward through the darkest of times. Your steadfast prayers and unrelenting devotion carried me when I could not carry myself.

To my brother, Menraj Sachdev: I have taken the road less traveled because of the brave choices you pioneered. Thank you for following your heart so faithfully and modeling what it means to live with courage.

To my dear mother-in-law, Ann Roberts, my first editor: Your spiritual gifts offered structure and clarity when this book was only an idea taking shape. Your tenderness and steady love have carried me through the long seasons of its creation.

To my dear mentor and teacher, Sangeet Kaur Khalsa: You took me under your wing and shared with me your love and heart for our beloved Guru. You guided me in how to care for the soul and I'm grateful for the decade-long meditative experiences through which the blessings of this book hope to share.

To Linda Hudnall for your steadfast encouragement. You've helped instill courageous belief that this work can come to life through the countless hours over the years of advisement and insight. Thank you.

To our beloved fur babies who have come and gone through the years, and especially to my dear Teddy. You are my heart, my friend, my angelic partner. You gave me the extraordinary experience of what it would feel like to be a daddy.

To my extended family of aunties and uncles, cousins, and lifelong friends: Thank you for seeing me. Your love and encouragement continue to give me strength and help me live the dreams our ancestors prayed over us.

To the team at Shambhala: Thank you for your guidance and care in editing and crafting this manuscript while honoring the many dimensions of what it carries. I am grateful that you saw me and this work in its fullness. Special thanks to Jenn Brown, Nirmala Nataraj, Emily Wichland, and Dianna Able, my editing team, whose diligence and precision helped to bring this work to life.

To all the grievers I have had the honor and privilege to accompany—in the hospital rooms, alongside the nursing staff and physicians, in one-on-one sessions, and through retreats and classes—it is you who have shaped the very heart of this book. Whatever goodness flows from these pages belongs also to you.

I stand on the shoulders of my ancestors, whose sacrifices allow me the privilege to research and write this work. I also stand on the shoulders of my own inner child, who carried the weight of grief without a map or compass. Dear soul, you found a way. This book is part of the offering you lived and envisioned.

Lastly, I give thanks to Grief itself. You have been my teacher since childhood. For many years, you terrified me. You still do, though in different ways. Yet you have walked beside me, bringing humanity into moments that once felt disconnected from life. You are part of my triad of great teachers: God, Guru, and Grief. I do not claim to understand you, but I honor your teachings, your majesty, and your constant presence.

In gratitude,

AmarAtma Singh Khalsa

APPENDIX A

Exercises by Chapter

2. *Reclaiming the Power of the Heart*

Developing Emotional Buoyancy 25
Experiencing the Awe of Synchronicity 30

6. *Navigating Through Brain Fog*

Walking Breath Meditation 80
Sensory Nerve Activation Practice 81
Alternate Nostril Breathing 83
Expressing Yourself 84
Ginger Pickle for Focus and Clarity 85

7. *Managing Energy*

Breathing Life into the Body 92
Spine Flex and Flow 93
Mindfulness of Breath 94
Sorting What Belongs to You 94
Reflection on What Gives Life 97
Adaptogen Teas 97

8. *Getting Better Sleep*

Sleep Meditation in Bed 105
Releasing Jaw Tension 105
Simple Acupressure to Soothe the Heart 106

Positive Appreciation Reflection Before Bed 107
Yoga Nidra at Home 108

9. Tending Digestion

Kapalabhati Breathing (Skull-Shining Breath) 116
Abdominal Massage for Digestive Regulation 117
Digesting Grief—Naming and Telling Your Losses 118
Kitchari to Ease Digestion 119

10. Working Through Anger

Deep Release to Discharge Anger 129
Standing Twists for Releasing Stagnant Energy 130
Cooling Breath for Anger (Sitali Pranayama) 131
Releasing Resentments 131
Gaze upon Beauty 132
Channeling Anger into Service 133

11. Connecting with Sadness

Pulse Breathing to Reestablish Qi Flow and Heart Coherence 139
Self-Hug When You're Feeling Overwhelmed by Sadness 140
Diaphragmatic Breathing 141
Listening to Grief 142
Grief Altar for Self-Compassion 143

12. Facing Anxiety

Grounding the Winds of the Mind 153
Rhythmic Shaking to Release Overwhelm 154
4-7-8 Breath for Calming Intensity 155
Listening to Anxiety 156
The 5-4-3-2-1 Technique 157

13. Honoring When You Feel Numb

Progressive Muscle Relaxation 169
Qi Massage to Release Emotional Congestion 170
Sound and Vibration Practice (Humming or Chanting) 171

Permission Slips 172
Drum Practice: Returning to Rhythm 172
Finding Rhythm Beyond Your Home 174
Cold Plunge or Cold Shower 175

14. Navigating the Abyss of Fear

Prostrations for Meeting the Abyss 183
Nourishing the Water Element 186
Filling the Deep Void of Emptiness 187
Meeting Fear as a Sacred Messenger 188
Restoring Resiliency Through the Lower Back 190
Forest Bathing 191

15. Coming Up Against Guilt

Releasing the Lump in the Throat 199
Creating Energetic Boundaries 200
Mental Dump Freewriting 201
Putting Down a Burden 202
Crafting an Apology Letter 204

16. Disentangling from Shame

Unfolding from Shame 215
Holding Softness and Restoring Worthiness 217
Meditation for Expanding Internal Value 218
Earth and Sky Grounding 219
Self-Praise as a Path to Worthiness 220
Releasing Shame Through Expression 222

17. Reconciling with Regret

Cloud Hands 230
Primal Scream 231
Pursed-Lip Breathing 232
Loving-Kindness Visualization 232
Rumination Release—a Funeral for Your Past Selves 234

18. Meeting Joy

Allowing Lightness 245
Laughing Yoga 246
Allowing Joy to Feel Familiar 247
Essential Oil Meditation for Joy 248

19. Awakening to What Matters Most

Clearing the Way 257
Morning Alignment for Focus and Clarity 258
Box Breathing for Facing Uncertainty 259
The Unscripted Life Vision Board 260

20. Coming Alive Again

Embodied Aliveness 273
Exploring Creativity 274
Going on an Awe Date 275

Conclusion

A Practice of Belonging 280

APPENDIX B

Exercises by Method

Grounding Exercises

Developing Emotional Buoyancy	25
Experiencing the Awe of Synchronicity	30
Walking Breath Meditation	80
Alternate Nostril Breathing	83
Breathing Life into the Body	92
Spine Flex and Flow	93
Mindfulness of Breath	94
Sleep Meditation in Bed	105
Yoga Nidra at Home	108
Kapalabhati Breathing (Skull-Shining Breath)	116
Cooling Breath for Anger (Sitali Pranayama)	131
Pulse Breathing to Reestablish Qi Flow and Heart Coherence	139
Self-Hug When You're Feeling Overwhelmed by Sadness	140
Diaphragmatic Breathing	141
Grounding the Winds of the Mind	153
4-7-8 Breath for Calming Intensity	155
Progressive Muscle Relaxation	169
Sound and Vibration Practice (Humming or Chanting)	171
Drum Practice: Returning to Rhythm	172
Nourishing the Water Element	186
Filling the Deep Void of Emptiness	187
Restoring Resiliency Through the Lower Back	190

Meditation for Expanding Internal Value 218
Earth and Sky Grounding 219
Pursed-Lip Breathing 232
Morning Alignment for Focus and Clarity 258
Box Breathing for Facing Uncertainty 259
A Practice of Belonging 280

Heart Opening Exercises

Developing Emotional Buoyancy 25
Experiencing the Awe of Synchronicity 30
Expressing Yourself 84
Spine Flex and Flow 93
Simple Acupressure to Soothe the Heart 106
Cooling Breath for Anger (Sitali Pranayama) 131
Channeling Anger into Service 133
Pulse Breathing to Reestablish Qi Flow and Heart Coherence 139
Self-Hug When You're Feeling Overwhelmed by Sadness 140
Listening to Grief 142
Prostrations for Meeting the Abyss 183
Filling the Deep Void of Emptiness 187
Releasing the Lump in the Throat 199
Creating Energetic Boundaries 200
Unfolding from Shame 215
Holding Softness and Restoring Worthiness 217
Meditation for Expanding Internal Value 218
Self-Praise as a Path to Worthiness 220
Cloud Hands 230
Loving-Kindness Visualization 232
Allowing Lightness 245
Allowing Joy to Feel Familiar 247
Clearing the Way 257
Morning Alignment for Focus and Clarity 258
Embodied Aliveness 273
A Practice of Belonging 280

Letting Go Exercises

Developing Emotional Buoyancy 25
Experiencing the Awe of Synchronicity 30
Sensory Nerve Activation Practice 81
Releasing Jaw Tension 105
Kapalabhati Breathing (Skull-Shining Breath) 116
Abdominal Massage for Digestive Regulation 117
Deep Release to Discharge Anger 129
Standing Twists for Releasing Stagnant Energy 130
Releasing Resentments 131
Rhythmic Shaking to Release Overwhelm 154
Listening to Anxiety 156
Progressive Muscle Relaxation 169
Qi Massage to Release Emotional Congestion 170
Releasing the Lump in the Throat 199
Mental Dump Freewriting 201
Primal Scream 231
Pursed-Lip Breathing 232
Laughing Yoga 246
Clearing the Way 257
Embodied Aliveness 273

Writing Prompts/Journaling Exercises

Expressing Yourself 84
Reflection on What Gives Life 97
Positive Appreciation Reflection Before Bed 107
Digesting Grief—Naming and Telling Your Losses 118
Releasing Resentments 131
Listening to Grief 142
Listening to Anxiety 156
Permission Slips 172
Meeting Fear as a Sacred Messenger 188
Mental Dump Freewriting 201
Crafting an Apology Letter 204

Self-Praise as a Path to Worthiness 220
Rumination Release—a Funeral for Your Past Selves 234

Sensory Exercises

Ginger Pickle for Focus and Clarity 85
Adaptogen Teas 97
Kitchari to Ease Digestion 119
Gaze upon Beauty 132
The 5-4-3-2-1 Technique 157
Drum Practice: Returning to Rhythm 172
Finding Rhythm Beyond Your Home 174
Cold Plunge or Cold Shower 175
Forest Bathing 191
Loving-Kindness Visualization 232
Allowing Joy to Feel Familiar 247
Essential Oil Meditation for Joy 248
Embodied Aliveness 273
Going on an Awe Date 275

Art and Creative Exercises

Sorting What Belongs to You 94
Reflection on What Gives Life 97
Digesting Grief—Naming and Telling Your Losses 118
Channeling Anger into Service 133
Grief Altar for Self-Compassion 143
Drum Practice: Returning to Rhythm 172
Finding Rhythm Beyond Your Home 174
Putting Down a Burden 202
Releasing Shame Through Expression 222
The Unscripted Life Vision Board 260
Exploring Creativity 274

NOTES

1. *Start with Compassion*

1. Giuseppe Tettamanti and Marco Casartelli, "Cell Death During Complete Metamorphosis," *Philosophical Transactions of the Royal Society B: Biological Sciences* 374, no. 1783 (2019), https://doi.org/10.1098/rstb.2019.0065.
2. Bipin Kumar Tripathi and Kenneth D. Irvine, "The Wing Imaginal Disc," *Genetics* 220, no. 4 (2022), https://doi.org/10.1093/genetics/iyac020.
3. Ivar Agrell, "Histolysis, Histogenesis, and Differentiation During Insect Metamorphosis in Relation to Metabolic Changes," *Development* 1, no. 3 (1953): 279–82, https://doi.org/10.1242/dev.1.3.279.
4. James W. Truman and Lynn M. Riddiford, "The Evolution of Insect Metamorphosis: A Developmental and Endocrine View," *Philosophical Transactions of the Royal Society B: Biological Sciences* 374, no. 1783 (2019), https://doi.org/10.1098/rstb.2019.0070.

2. *Reclaiming the Power of the Heart*

1. Brian Baillargeon, Nuno Rebelo, David D. Fox, Robert L. Taylor, and Ellen Kuhl, "The Living Heart Project: A Robust and Integrative Simulator for Human Heart Function," *European Journal of Mechanics: A/Solids* 48 (2014): 38–47, https://doi.org/10.1016/j.euromechsol.2014.04.001; Victoria L. Bautch and Kathleen M. Caron, "Blood and Lymphatic Vessel Formation," *Cold Spring Harbor Perspectives in Biology* 7, no. 3 (2015), https://doi.org/10.1101/cshperspect.a008268.
2. Perumal Thiagarajan, Charles J. Parker, and Josef T. Prchal, "How Do Red Blood Cells Die?" *Frontiers in Physiology* 12 (2021), https://doi.org/10.3389/fphys.2021.655393.
3. Joshua E. Brinkman and Sandeep Sharma, *Physiology, Pulmonary* (StatPearls Publishing, 2025).
4. Julian F. Thayer and Richard D. Lane, "Claude Bernard and the Heart–Brain Connection: Neurovisceral Integration," *Neuroscience & Biobehavioral Reviews* 33, no. 2 (2009): 81–88.
5. Fred Shaffer and J. P. Ginsberg, "An Overview of Heart Rate Variability Metrics and Norms," *Frontiers in Public Health* 5 (2017), https://doi.org/10.3389/fpubh.2017.00258.
6. Mara Mather and Julian Thayer, "How Heart Rate Variability Affects Emotion Regulation Brain Networks," *Current Opinion in Behavioral Sciences* 19 (2018): 98–104, https://doi.org/10.1016/j.cobeha.2017.12.017.

7. Laurie Kelly McCorry, "Physiology of the Autonomic Nervous System," *American Journal of Pharmaceutical Education* 71, no. 4 (2007): 78, https://pubmed.ncbi.nlm.nih.gov/17786266/.
8. Valentin A. Pavlov and Kevin J. Tracey, "The Vagus Nerve and the Inflammatory Reflex," *Nature Reviews Endocrinology* 8, no. 12 (2012): 743–54, https://doi.org/10.1038/nrendo.2012.189.
9. Elisa A. Wehrwein, H. S. Orer, and S. M. Barman, "Overview of the Anatomy, Physiology, and Pharmacology of the Autonomic Nervous System," *Comprehensive Physiology* 6, no. 3 (2016): 1239–78, https://doi.org/10.1002/cphy.c150037.
10. Mark N. Alshak and Joe M, *Neuroanatomy, Sympathetic Nervous System* (StatPearls Publishing; 2025).
11. Sarah Beutler, Yoki L. Mertens, Liliana Ladner, Julia Schellong, Ilona Croy, and Judith K. Daniels, "Trauma-Related Dissociation and the Autonomic Nervous System: A Systematic Literature Review of Psychophysiological Correlates of Dissociative Experiencing in PTSD Patients," *European Journal of Psychotraumatology* 13, no. 2 (November 2, 2022), https://doi.org/10.1080/20008066.2022.2132599.
12. Andrea Zaccaro, Andrea Piarulli, Marco Laurino, Erika Garbella, Danilo Menicucci, Bruno Neri et al., "How Breath-Control Can Change Your Life: A Systematic Review on Psycho-Physiological Correlates of Slow Breathing," *Frontiers in Human Neuroscience* 12 (2018), https://doi.org/10.3389/fnhum.2018.00353.
13. Jennifer A. Galvin, Herbert Benson, Gloria R. Deckro, Gregory L. Fricchione, and Jeffery A. Dusek, "The Relaxation Response: Reducing Stress and Improving Cognition in Healthy Aging Adults," *Complementary Therapies in Clinical Practice* 12, no. 3 (2006): 186–91, https://doi.org/10.1016/j.ctcp.2006.02.004.
14. Jacob Tindle and Prasanna Tadi, *Neuroanatomy, Parasympathetic Nervous System* (StatPearls Publishing, October 2022).
15. Shaffer and Ginsberg, "An Overview of Heart Rate Variability Metrics and Norms."
16. Kaia S. Sargent, Emily L. Martinez, Alexandra C. Reed, Anika Guha, Morgan E. Bartholomew, Caroline K. Diehl et al., "Oscillatory Coupling Between Neural and Cardiac Rhythms," *Psychological Science* 35, no. 5 (2024): 517–28, https://doi.org/10.1177/09567976241235932.
17. Ryan V. Raut, Abraham Z. Snyder, Anish Mitra, Dov Yellin, Naotaka Fujii, Rafael Malach et al., "Global Waves Synchronize the Brain's Functional Systems with Fluctuating Arousal," *Science Advances* 7, no. 30 (2021), https://doi.org/10.1126/sciadv.abf2709.
18. Paul M. Lehrer and Richard Gevirtz, "Heart Rate Variability Biofeedback: How and Why Does It Work?" *Frontiers in Psychology* 5 (2014), https://doi.org/10.3389/fpsyg.2014.00756.
19. Jaume F. Lalanza, Sergio Lorente, Ricard Bullich, Cristina García, José M. Losilla, and Luís Capdevila, "Methods for Heart Rate Variability Biofeedback (HRVB): A Systematic Review and Guidelines," *Applied Psychophysiology and Biofeedback* 48, no. 3 (2023): 275–97, https://doi.org/10.1007/s10484-023-09582-6.

20. Rollin McCraty and Fred Shaffer, "Heart Rate Variability: New Perspectives on Mechanisms and Self-Regulatory Capacity," *Global Advances in Health and Medicine* 4, no. 1 (2015): 46–61, https://doi.org/10.7453/gahmj.2014.073.
21. V. C. Goessl, J. E. Curtiss, and S. G. Hofmann, "HRV Biofeedback for Stress and Anxiety: A Meta-Analysis," *Psychological Medicine* 47, no. 15 (2017): 2578–86, https://doi.org/10.1017/S0033291717001003.
22. Shaffer and Ginsberg, "An Overview of Heart Rate Variability Metrics and Norms."
23. M. Grol and R. De Raedt, "The Link Between Resting Heart Rate Variability and Affective Flexibility," *Cognitive, Affective, and Behavioral Neuroscience* 20 (2020): 746–56, https://doi.org/10.3758/s13415-020-00800-w.
24. Hye-Geum Kim, Eun-Jin Cheon, Dong-Soo Bai, Yeon-Ho Lee, and Bong-Hyeon Koo, "Stress and Heart Rate Variability: A Meta-Analysis and Review of the Literature," *Psychiatry Investigation* 15, no. 3 (2018): 235–45, https://doi.org/10.30773/pi.2017.08.17.
25. Marc H. Bornstein and Gianluca Esposito, "Coregulation: A Multilevel Approach via Biology and Behavior," *Children* 10, no. 8 (2023): 1323, https://doi.org/10.3390/children10081323; David A. Sbarra and Cindy Hazan, "Coregulation, Dysregulation, Self-Regulation in Adult Attachment, Separation, and Loss," *Personality and Social Psychology Review* 12, no. 2 (2008): 141–67, https://doi.org/10.1177/1088868308315702.
26. Stephen W. Porges, "The Polyvagal Theory: Phylogenetic Substrates of a Social Nervous System," *International Journal of Psychophysiology* 42, no. 2 (2001): 123–46, https://doi.org/10.1016/S0167-8760(01)00162-3.
27. Etsuro Ito, Rei Shima, and Tohru Yoshioka, "A Novel Role of Oxytocin: Oxytocin-Induced Well-Being in Humans," *Biophysics and Physicobiology* 16 (2019): 132–39, https://doi.org/10.2142/biophysico.16.0_132.
28. Hans-Rudolf Berthoud and Winfried L. Neuhuber, "Functional and Chemical Anatomy of the Afferent Vagal System," *Autonomic Neuroscience* 85, no. 1 (2000): 1–17, https://doi.org/10.1016/S1566-0702(00)00215-0.
29. J. A. Armour, "Potential Clinical Relevance of the 'Little Brain' on the Mammalian Heart," *Experimental Physiology* 93, no. 2 (2008): 165–76, https://doi.org/10.1113/expphysiol.2007.041178; Laura Fedele and Thomas Brand, "The Intrinsic Cardiac Nervous System and Its Role in Cardiac Pacemaking and Conduction," *Journal of Cardiovascular Development and Disease* 7, no. 4 (2020): 54, https://doi.org/10.3390/jcdd7040054; Giuseppe Giannino, Valentina Braia, Carola Griffith Brookles, Federico Giacobbe, Fabrizio D'Ascenzo, Filippo Angelini et al., "The Intrinsic Cardiac Nervous System: From Pathophysiology to Therapeutic Implications," *Biology* 13, no. 2 (2024): 105, https://doi.org/10.3390/biology13020105.
30. B. J. Kenny and Bruno Bordoni, "Neuroanatomy, Cranial Nerve 10 (Vagus Nerve)," in *StatPearls* (StatPearls Publishing, 2025), https://www.ncbi.nlm.nih.gov/books/NBK537171/.
31. Stephen W. Porges, "Cardiac Vagal Tone: A Neurophysiological Mechanism That Evolved in Mammals to Dampen Threat Reactions and Promote Sociality," *World Psychiatry* 20, no. 2 (2021): 296–98, https://doi.org/10.1002/wps.20871.

32. Zaccaro et al., "How Breath-Control Can Change Your Life," 353.
33. Sarah N. Garfinkel and Hugo D. Critchley, "Threat and the Body: How the Heart Supports Fear Processing," *Trends in Cognitive Sciences* 20, no. 1 (2016): 34–46, https://doi.org/10.1016/j.tics.2015.10.005.
34. Hyeong-Dong Park, Fosco Bernasconi, Roy Salomon, Catherine Talon-Baudry, Laurent Spinelli, Margitta Seek et al., "Neural Responses to Heartbeats and Bodily Self-Consciousness: An Intracranial EEG Study," *Cerebral Cortex* 28, no. 7 (2018): 2351–64, https://doi.org/10.1093/cercor/bhx136.
35. Hans-Rudolf Berthoud and Winfried L. Neuhuber, "Functional and Chemical Anatomy of the Afferent Vagal System," *Autonomic Neuroscience: Basic and Clinical* 85, nos. 1–3 (2000): 1–17, https://doi.org/10.1016/S1566-0702(00)00215-0.
36. Bethany E. Kok and Barbara L. Fredrickson, "Upward Spirals of the Heart: Vagal Tone Predicts Positive Emotions and Social Connectedness," *Biological Psychology* 85, no. 3 (2010): 432–36, https://doi.org/10.1016/j.biopsycho.2010.09.005.
37. R. K. Dubey and B. Kumar, "A Comprehensive Overview of Traditional Chinese Medicine (TCM)," *Zhongguo Ying Yong Sheng Li Xue Za Zhi* 41 (2025), https://doi.org/10.62958/j.cjap.2025.015.
38. Ling-Yu Kong, Xuan-Yu Chen, Xin Lu, Qinggele Caiyin, and Dong-Hua Yang, "Association of Lung-Intestinal Microecology and Lung Cancer Therapy," *Chinese Medicine* 18 (2023): 37, https://doi.org/10.1186/s13020-023-00742-8.
39. Paul U. Unschuld, Hermann Tessenow, and Zheng Jinsheng, *Huang Di Nei Jing Su Wen: An Annotated Translation of Huang Di's Inner Classic; Basic Questions*, vol. 1 (University of California Press, 2011).
40. Yong-Shun Bei, "Shen in Acupuncture for Chronic Pain," *Chinese Medicine and Culture* 5, no. 4 (2022): 228–33, https://doi.org/10.1097/MC9.0000000000000032.
41. Giovanni Maciocia "The Treatment of Shen Disturbances with Chinese Medicine," Giovanni Maciocia, August 29, 2025, https://giovanni-maciocia.com/wp-content/uploads/2019/02/shen-maciocia-online.pdf.
42. Tejalrani Jaiswal, Babita Sharma, and Swati Nagpal, "Sādhaka Pitta: The Gatekeeper for Mental Health," *Journal of Ayurveda and Integrated Medical Sciences* 9, no. 4 (2024): 118–22, https://jaims.in/jaims/article/download/3146/4823/.
43. Pradeep Moharana and Rajesh Roushan, "Sadhaka Pitta of Ayurveda and Its Affiliates in Modern Perspective: A Review," *International Journal of Research in Ayurveda and Pharmacy* 11, no. 6 (2020): 69–74, https://ijrap.net/admin/php/uploads/2499_pdf.pdf; S. Deepika, N. R. Navoday Raju, Kulkarni Pratibha, and Kekuda TR Prashanth, "Sadhaka Pitta: Conceptual Understanding," *International Ayurvedic Medical Journal* 3, no. 10 (2015): 3057–62, https://iamj.in/posts/2015/images/upload/3057_3062.pdf.

3. Grieving in a Culture of Disconnection

1. Darcy L. Harris, *Oppression of the Bereaved: A Critical Analysis of Grief in Western Society* (Routledge, 2009).
2. Stephen W. Porges, *The Polyvagal Theory: Neurophysiological Foundations of*

Emotions, Attachment, Communication, and Self-Regulation (W. W. Norton, 2011).

3. Louise C. Hawkley and John T. Cacioppo, "Loneliness Matters: A Theoretical and Empirical Review of Consequences and Mechanisms," *Annals of Behavioral Medicine* 40, no. 2 (2010): 218–27, https://pubmed.ncbi.nlm.nih.gov/20652462/.
4. J. S. Bottomley and R. A. Neimeyer. "Avoidant and Approach-Oriented Coping Strategies, Meaning Making, and Mental Health Among Adults Bereaved by Suicide and Fatal Overdose: A Prospective Path Analysis," *Behavioral Sciences* 15, no. 5 (2025): 671, https://doi.org/10.3390/bs15050671.
5. James Gillies and Robert A. Neimeyer, "Loss, Grief, and the Search for Significance: Toward a Model of Meaning Reconstruction in Bereavement," *Journal of Constructivist Psychology* 19, no. 1 (2006): 31–65, https://doi.org/10.1080/10720530500311182.
6. Kenneth J. Doka, *Disenfranchised Grief: Recognizing Hidden Sorrow* (Lexington Books, 1989).
7. Pauline Boss, *Ambiguous Loss: Learning to Live with Unresolved Grief* (Harvard University Press, 1999).
8. Bessel van der Kolk, *The Body Keeps the Score: Brain, Mind, and Body in the Healing of Trauma* (Viking, 2014).
9. Valerie L. Jentsch, and Oliver T. Wolf, "The Impact of Emotion Regulation on Cardiovascular, Neuroendocrine and Psychological Stress Responses," *Biological Psychology* 154 (2020), https://pubmed.ncbi.nlm.nih.gov/32437903/.
10. Francisco Tausk, Ilia Elenkov, and Jan Moynihan, "Psychoneuroimmunology," *Dermatologic Therapy* 21, no. 1 (2008): 22–31, https://pubmed.ncbi.nlm.nih.gov/18318882/.
11. Rainer H. Straub and Maurizio Cutolo, "Psychoneuroimmunology: Developments in Stress Research," *Wiener Medizinische Wochenschrift* 168, no. 3–4 (2018): 76–84, https://pubmed.ncbi.nlm.nih.gov/28600777/.
12. Gregory E. Miller, Sheldon Cohen, and A. Kim Ritchey, "Chronic Psychological Stress and the Regulation of Proinflammatory Cytokines: A Glucocorticoid-Resistance Model," *Health Psychology* 21, no. 6 (2002): 531–41, https://pubmed.ncbi.nlm.nih.gov/12433005/.
13. Susan Segerstrom and Gregory E. Miller, "Psychological Stress and the Human Immune System: A Meta-Analytic Study of 30 Years of Inquiry," *Psychological Bulletin* 130, no. 4 (2004): 601–30, https://www.ncbi.nlm.nih.gov/pmc/articles/PMC1361287/.
14. Allison A. Appleton, Stephen L. Buka, Eric B. Loucks, Stephen E. Gilman, and Laura D. Kubzansky, "Divergent Associations of Adaptive and Maladaptive Emotion Regulation Strategies with Inflammation," *Health Psychology* 32, no. 7 (2013): 748–56, https://pubmed.ncbi.nlm.nih.gov/23815767/.
15. Philippe R. Goldin, Kateri McRae, Wiveka Ramel, and James J. Gross, "The Neural Bases of Emotion Regulation: Reappraisal and Suppression of Negative Emotion," *Biological Psychiatry* 63, no. 6 (March 15, 2008): 577–86, https://doi.org/10.1016/j.biopsych.2007.05.031.
16. Firdaus S. Dhabhar, "Effects of Stress on Immune Function: The Good, the Bad, and the Beautiful," *Immunologic Research* 58, no. 2–3 (2014): 193–210, https://pubmed.ncbi.nlm.nih.gov/24798553/.

4. *How to Let Go*

1. Mary-Frances O'Connor and Saren H. Seeley, "Grieving as a Form of Learning: Insights from Neuroscience Applied to Grief and Loss," *Current Opinion in Psychology* 43 (2022): 317–22, https://doi.org/10.1016/j.copsyc.2021.08.019.
2. George A. Bonanno and Stacey Kaltman, "The Varieties of Grief Experience," *Clinical Psychology Review* 21, no. 5 (2001): 705–34, https://doi.org/10.1016/S0272-7358(00)00062-3.
3. Ruth Feldman, "Oxytocin and Social Affiliation in Humans," *Hormones and Behavior* 61, no. 3 (2012): 380–91, https://doi.org/10.1016/j.yhbeh.2012.01.008.
4. Naomi I. Eisenberger, "The Neural Bases of Social Pain: Evidence for Shared Representations with Physical Pain," *Psychosomatic Medicine* 74, no. 2 (2012): 126–35; see also Naomi I. Eisenberger and Matthew D. Lieberman, "Why It Hurts to Be Left Out," *Trends in Cognitive Sciences* 8, no. 7 (2004): 294–300.
5. Dennis Klass, "Continuing Conversation About Continuing Bonds," *Death Studies* 30, no. 9 (2006): 843–58, https://doi.org/10.1080/07481180600886959.
6. Helen Hewson, Niall Galbraith, Claire Jones, and Gemma Heath, "The Impact of Continuing Bonds Following Bereavement: A Systematic Review," *Death Studies* 48, no. 10 (2023): 1001–14, https://doi.org/10.1080/07481187.2023.2223593.
7. O'Connor and Seeley, "Grieving as a Form of Learning," 317–22.
8. Daniel M. Wegner, "Ironic Processes of Mental Control," *Psychological Review* 101, no. 1 (1994): 34–52, https://doi.org/10.1037/0033-295X.101.1.34.
9. Martin A. Conway and Christopher W. Pleydell-Pearce, "The Construction of Autobiographical Memories in the Self-Memory System," *Psychological Review* 107, no. 2 (2000): 261–88, https://doi.org/10.1037/0033-295X.107.2.261.
10. Karim Nader, Glenn E. Schafe, and Joseph E. LeDoux, "Fear Memories Require Protein Synthesis in the Amygdala for Reconsolidation After Retrieval," *Nature* 406, (2000): 722–26, https://doi.org/10.1038/35021052; Almut Hupbach, Rebecca Gomez, Oliver Hardt, and Lynn Nadel, "Reconsolidation of Episodic Memories: A Subtle Reminder Triggers Integration of New Information," *Learning & Memory* 14, no. 1 (2007): 47–53, https://doi.org/10.1101/lm.365707.
11. Julian F. Thayer and Richard D. Lane, "Claude Bernard and the Heart–Brain Connection: Neurovisceral Integration," *Neuroscience & Biobehavioral Reviews* 33, no. 2 (2009): 81–88, https://doi.org/10.1016/j.neubiorev.2008.08.004.
12. Kevin P. Madore and Daniel L. Schacter, "An Episodic Specificity Induction Enhances Means–End Problem Solving in Young and Older Adults," *Psychology and Aging* 29, no. 4 (2014): 913–24, https://doi.org/10.1037/a0038209.
13. Margaret Stroebe and Henk Schut, "The Dual Process Model of Coping with Bereavement: Rationale and Description," *Death Studies* 23, no. 3 (1999): 197–224, https://doi.org/10.1080/074811899201046.
14. Margaret Stroebe and Henk Schut, "The Dual Process Model of Coping with Bereavement: A Decade On," *Omega: Journal of Death and Dying* 61, no. 4 (2010): 273–89, https://doi.org/10.2190/OM.61.4.b.

5. *Embodiment as the Path to Peace*

1. Wen G. Chen, Dana Schloesser, Angela M. Arensdorf, Janine M. Simmons, Changhai Cui, Rita Valentino et al., "The Emerging Science of Interoception: Sensing, Integrating, Interpreting, and Regulating Signals within the Self," *Trends in Neurosciences* 44, no. 1 (2021): 3–16, https://doi.org/10.1016/j.tins.2020.10.007.
2. Carolyn M. Schmitt and Sarah Schoen, "Interoception: A Multi-Sensory Foundation of Participation in Daily Life," *Frontiers in Neuroscience* 16 (2022), https://doi.org/10.3389/fnins.2022.875200.
3. Lisa Quadt, Hugo D. Critchley, and Sarah N. Garfinkel, "The Neurobiology of Interoception in Health and Disease," *Annals of the New York Academy of Sciences* 1428, no. 1 (2018): 112–28, https://doi.org/10.1111/nyas.13915.
4. Matthew D. Lieberman, Naomi I. Eisenberger, Molly J. Crockett, Sabrina M. Tom, Jennifer H. Pfeifer, and Baldwin M. Way, "Putting Feelings into Words: Affect Labeling Disrupts Amygdala Activity in Response to Affective Stimuli," *Psychological Science* 18, no. 5 (2007): 421–28, https://doi.org/10.1111/j.1467-9280.2007.01916.x.

6. *Navigating Through Brain Fog*

1. Nikolaos Statharakos, "Unraveling the Neurobiology of Grief: Insights into Brain and Behavior–Narrative Review," *Brain Science Advances* 11, no. 3 (2025), https://doi.org/10.26599/BSA.2025.905001.
2. Charles A. Hall, Charles F. Reynolds III, Meryl Butters, Sidney Zisook, Naomi Simon, Jody Corey-Bloom et al., "Cognitive Functioning in Complicated Grief," *Journal of Psychiatric Research* 58 (2014): 20–25, https://doi.org/10.1016/j.jpsychires.2014.07.002.
3. Eun Joo Kim and Jeansok J. Kim, "Neurocognitive Effects of Stress: A Meta-Paradigm Perspective," *Molecular Psychiatry* 28, no. 7 (2023): 2750–63, https://doi.org/10.1038/s41380-023-01986-4.
4. Cadu Klier and Luciano Grudtner Burrato, "Stress and Long-Term Memory Retrieval: A Systematic Review," *Trends in Psychiatry and Psychotherapy* 42, no. 3 (2020), https://doi.org/10.1590/2237-6089-2019-0077.
5. Eun Joo Kim, Blake Pellman, and Jeansok J. Kim, "Stress Effects on the Hippocampus: A Critical Review," *Learning and Memory* 22, no. 9 (2015): 411–16, https://doi.org/10.1101/lm.037291.114.
6. Robert-Paul Juster, Bruce S. McEwen, and Sonia J. Lupien, "Allostatic Load Biomarkers of Chronic Stress and Impact on Health and Cognition," *Neuroscience and Biobehavioral Reviews* 35, no. 1 (2010): 2–16, https://doi.org/10.1016/j.neubiorev.2009.10.002.
7. Mary-Frances O'Connor, "Grief: A Brief History of Research on How Body, Mind, and Brain Adapt," *Psychosomatic Medicine* 81, no. 8 (2019): 731–38, https://doi.org/10.1097/PSY.0000000000000717.
8. Margaret Stroebe and Henk Schut, "The Dual Process Model of Coping with Bereavement: Rationale and Description," *Death Studies* 23, no. 3 (1999): 197–224, https://doi.org/10.1080/074811899201046.
9. M. Katherine Shear, Naomi Simon, Melanie Wall, Sidney Zisook, Robert Neimeyer, Naihua Duan et al., "Complicated Grief and Related Bereavement Issues for DSM-5," *Depression and Anxiety* 28, no. 2 (2011): 103–17.

10. Ling-Yu Kong, Xuan-Yu Chen, Xin Lu, Qinggele Caiyin, and Dong-Hua Yang, "Association of Lung–Intestinal Microecology and Lung Cancer Therapy," *Chinese Medicine* 18, no. 37 (2023), https://link.springer.com/content/pdf/10.1186/s13020-023-00742-8.pdf.
11. Hemant Rajpurohit, Poona Nath Chouhan, Jay Prakash Gupta, Amit Gehlot, and Praveen Kumar, "Exploring the Ayurvedic Perspective of Gut Health and Its Correlation with Mental Well-Being," *African Journal of Biomedical Research* 27, no. 3s (2024), 6601–7, https://doi.org/10.53555/AJBR.v27i3S.5626.
12. Melis Yilmaz Balban, Eric Neri, Manuela M. Kogon, Lara Weed, Bita Nouriani, Booil Jo et al., "Brief Structured Respiration Practices Enhance Mood and Reduce Physiological Arousal," *Cell Reports Medicine* 4, no. 1 (2023), https://doi.org/10.1016/j.xcrm.2022.100895.
13. Balban et al., "Brief Structured Respiration Practices Enhance Mood and Reduce Physiological Arousal."
14. Zohre Rahmani Vasokolaei, Nahid Rejeh, Majideh Heravi-Karimooi, Seyed Davood Tadrisi, Kiarash Saatchi, Zahra Poshtchaman et al., "Comparison of the Effects of Hand Reflexology Versus Acupressure on Anxiety and Vital Signs in Female Patients with Coronary Artery Diseases," *Healthcare* 7, no. 1 (2019): 26, https://doi.org/10.3390/healthcare7010026; Chongjie Yao, Xinyu Zeng, Shuaipan Zhang, Bin Xao, Pingping Sun, Lingjun Kong et al., "Acupoint Massage: A Comprehensive Descriptive Review of Its Forms, Applications, and Underlying Mechanisms," *Chinese Medicine* 20, no. 54 (2025), https://doi.org/10.1186/s13020-025-01105-1.
15. Anant Narayan Sinha, Desh Deepak, and Vimal Singh Gusain, "Assessment of the Effects of Pranayama/Alternate Nostril Breathing on the Parasympathetic Nervous System in Young Adults," *Journal of Clinical and Diagnostic Research* 7, no. 5 (2013): 821–23, https://doi.org/10.7860/JCDR/2013/4750.2948.
16. Dongpeng Yao, Shuo Xu, Jiaqi Liu, Yihan Gai, and Jie Li, "Expressive Writing for Grief: A Meta-Analysis of Randomized Controlled Trials," *Research on Social Work Practice*, September 2025, https://doi.org/10.1177/10497315251371566.
17. Brynne C. DiMenichi, Ahmet O. Ceceli, Jamil P. Bhanji, and Elizabeth Tricomi, "Effects of Expressive Writing on Neural Processing During Learning," *Frontiers in Human Neuroscience* 12, no. 389 (2019), https://doi.org/10.3389/fnhum.2019.00389.
18. Vasant Lad, *Textbook of Ayurveda: Fundamental Principles*, vol. 2 (Ayurvedic Press, 2012), 135.

7. Managing Energy

1. Charles A. Hall, Charles F. Reynolds III, Meryl Butters, Sidney Zisook, Naomi Simon, Jody Corey-Bloom et al., "Cognitive Functioning in Complicated Grief," *Journal of Psychiatric Research* 58 (2014): 20–25, https://doi.org/10.1016/j.jpsychires.2014.07.002.
2. Mary-Frances O'Connor, *The Grieving Brain: The Surprising Science of How We Learn from Love and Loss* (HarperOne, 2022).
3. M. Katherine Shear, "Complicated Grief," *New England Journal of Medicine* 372, no. 2 (2015): 153–60, https://doi.org/10.1056/NEJMra1315618.

4. Lauren M. Bylsma, Asmir Gračanin, and Ad J. J. M. Vingerhoets, "The Neurobiology of Human Crying," *Clinical Autonomic Research* 26, no. 1 (2019): 63–73, https://doi.org/10.1007/s10286-018-0526-y.
5. Yuliya Richard, Nadia Tazi, Dorota Frydecka, Mohamed S. Hamid, and Ahmed A. Moustafa, "A Systematic Review of Neural, Cognitive, and Clinical Studies of Anger and Aggression," *Current Psychology* 42 (2023): 17174–86, https://www.doi.org/10.1007/s12144-022-03143-6.
6. Karin Roelofs, "Freeze for Action: Neurobiological Mechanisms in Animal and Human Freezing," *Philosophical Transactions of the Royal Society B* 372, no. 1718 (2017), https://doi.org/10.1098/rstb.2016.0206.
7. James J. Gross and Robert W. Levenson, "Emotional Suppression: Physiology, Self-Report, and Expressive Behavior," *Journal of Personality and Social Psychology* 64, no. 6 (1993): 970–86, https://doi.org/10.1037/0022-3514.64.6.970.
8. Charles R. Figley, "Compassion Fatigue: Toward a New Understanding of the Costs of Caring," in *Secondary Traumatic Stress*, ed. Charles R. Figley (Sidran Press, 1995), 3–28.
9. Figley, "Compassion Fatigue."
10. Ling-Yu Kong, Xuan-Yu Chen, Xin Lu, Qinggele Caiyin, and Dong-Hua Yang, "Association of Lung-Intestinal Microecology and Lung Cancer Therapy," *Chinese Medicine* 18 (2023): 37, https://doi.org/10.1186/s13020-023-00742-8.
11. Shilpa Das, "The Spoon Theory: A Journey into the World of Chronic Illness," in *Literary and Cultural Disability Studies: A Primer*, ed. Someshar Sati (Worldview Publications, 2025).
12. Luis Carlos Matos, Jorge Pereira Machado, Fernando Jorge Monteiro, and Henry Johannes Greten, "Understanding Traditional Chinese Medicine Therapeutics: An Overview of the Basics and Clinical Applications," *Healthcare (Basel)* 9, no. 3 (2021): 257, https://doi.org/10.3390/healthcare9030257.
13. H. C. Dung, "Acupuncture Points of the Typical Spinal Nerves," *American Journal of Chinese Medicine* 13, no. 1–4 (1985): 39–47, https://doi.org/10.1142/S0192415X85000083.
14. Kian F. Wong, James Teng, Michael W. L. Chee, Kinjal Doshi, and Julian Lim, "Positive Effects of Mindfulness-Based Training on Energy Maintenance and the EEG Correlates of Sustained Attention in a Cohort of Nurses," *Frontiers in Human Neuroscience* 12, no. 80 (2018), https://doi.org/10.3389/fhum.2018.00080.
15. Jamie Shapiro, "Burning Bright or Burning Out: A Qualitative Investigation of Leader Vitality," *Frontiers in Psychology* 2, no. 14 (2023), https://doi.org/10.3389/fpsyg.2023.1244089.
16. Paulina Mikulska, Martina Malinowska, Milosz Ignacyk, Pawel Szutowski, Joanna Mowak, Karolina Pesta et al., "Ashwagandha (*Withania somnifera*)—Current Research on the Health-Promoting Activities: A Narrative Review," *Pharmaceutics* 15, no. 4 (2023), https://doi.org/10.3390/pharmaceutics15041057.
17. Marc Maurice Cohen, "Tulsi—Ocimum sanctum: A Herb For All Reasons," *Journal of Ayurveda and Integrative Medicine* 5, no. 4 (2014): 251–59, https://pmc.ncbi.nlm.nih.gov/articles/PMC4296439/.

18. Yu-Jin Kwon, Da-Hye Son, Tae-Ha Chung, and Yong-Jae Lee, "A Review of the Pharmacological Efficacy and Safety of Licorice Root from Corroborative Clinical Trial Findings," *Journal of Medicinal Food* 23, no. 1 (2020): 12–20, https://doi.org/10.1089/jmf.2019.4459.
19. Noel M. Arring, Denise Millstine, Lisa A. Marks, and Lillian M. Nail, "Ginseng as a Treatment for Fatigue: A Systematic Review," *Journal of Alternative and Complementary Medicine* 24, no. 7 (2018): 624–33, https://doi.org/10.1089/acm.2017.0361.
20. Rizwan Ahmad, Muhammad Riaz, Aslam Khan, Ahmed Aljamea, Mohammad Algheryafi, Deya Sewaket et al., "*Ganoderma lucidum* (Reishi) an Edible Mushroom; A Comprehensive and Critical Review of Its Nutritional, Cosmeceutical, Mycochemical, Pharmacological, Clinical, and Toxicological Properties," *Phytotherapy Research* 35, no. 11 (2021): 6030–62, https://doi.org/10.1002/ptr.7215.
21. Alexander Panossian, "Understanding Adaptogenic Activity: Specificity of the Pharmacological Action of Adaptogens and Other Phytochemicals," *Annals of the New York Academy of Sciences* 1401, no. 1 (2017): 49–64, https://doi.org/10.1111/nyas.13399.

8. Getting Better Sleep

1. Thomas M. Buckley and Lesley D. Schatzberg, "On the Interactions of the Hypothalamic-Pituitary-Adrenal (HPA) Axis and Sleep: Normal HPA Axis Activity and Circadian Rhythm, Exemplary Sleep Disorders," *Journal of Clinical Endocrinology and Metabolism* 90, no. 5 (2005): 3106–14, https://doi.org/10.1210/jc.2004-1056.
2. Alexandros N. Vgontzas, Edward O. Bixler, Hung-No Lin, Paolo Prolo, George Mastorakos, Antion Vela-Bueno et al., "Chronic Insomnia Is Associated with Nyctohemeral Activation of the Hypothalamic-Pituitary-Adrenal Axis: Clinical Implications," *Journal of Clinical Endocrinology and Metabolism* 86, no. 8 (2001): 3787–94, https://doi.org/10.1210/jcem.86.8.7778.
3. Heather G. Hardison, Robert A. Neimeyer, and Kenneth L. Lichstein, "Insomnia and Complicated Grief Symptoms in Bereaved College Students," *Behavioral Sleep Medicine* 3, no. 2 (2005): 99–111, https://doi.org/10.1207/s15402010bsm0302_4.
4. Timothy H. Monk, Anne Germain, and Charles F. Reynolds, "Sleep Disturbance in Bereavement," *Psychiatric Annals* 38, no. 10 (2008): 671–75, https://doi.org/10.3928/00485713-20081001-06.
5. Way-Yee Yeung, Mei-Ling Poon, Siew-Eng Choo, and Fiona K. Y. Lam, "Chinese Herbal Medicine for Primary Insomnia: A Systematic Review," *Sleep Medicine Reviews* 16, no. 6 (2012): 497–507, https://doi.org/10.1016/j.smrv.2011.10.002.
6. Clifford B. Saper, Thomas E. Scammell, and Jun Lu, "Hypothalamic Regulation of Sleep and Circadian Rhythms," *Nature* 437 (2005): 1257–63, https://doi.org/10.1038/nature04284.
7. Steven M. Reppert and David R. Weaver, "Coordination of Circadian Timing in Mammals," *Nature* 418, no. 6901 (2002): 935–41, https://doi.org/10.1038/nature00965.

8. Andrew Huberman, "Toolkit for Sleep," Neural Network Newsletter, September 20, 2021, https://hubermanlab.com/toolkit-for-sleep/.
9. "Blue Light Has a Dark Side," Harvard Health Publishing, July 24, 2024, https://www.health.harvard.edu/staying-healthy/blue-light-has-a-dark-side.
10. Greg J. Elder, Mark A. Wetherell, Nicola L. Barclay, and Jason G. Ellis, "The Cortisol Awakening Response—Applications and Implications for Sleep Medicine," *Sleep Medicine Reviews* 18, no. 2 (2013): 215–24, https://pubmed.ncbi.nlm.nih.gov/23835138/.
11. Elder et al., "Cortisol Awakening Response—Applications and Implications for Sleep Medicine."
12. Tarja Porkka-Heiskanen, Lauri Alanko, Anna Kalinchuk, and Dag Stenberg, "Adenosine and Sleep," *Sleep Medicine Reviews* 6, no. 4 (2013): 321–32, https://pubmed.ncbi.nlm.nih.gov/12531135/.
13. Maggie Man-Ki Poon, Ka-Fai Chung, Wing-Fai Yeung, Verdi Hon-Kin Yau, and Shi-Ping Zhang, "Classification of Insomnia Using the Traditional Chinese Medicine System: A Systematic Review," *Evidence-Based Complementary and Alternative Medicine*, July 2012, https://pmc.ncbi.nlm.nih.gov/articles/PMC3414091/.
14. Huberman, "Toolkit for Sleep."
15. Mohamed H. El-Gendy, Mostafa M. Ibrahim, Emad S. Helmy, Neama H. Neamat Allah, Batool Abdulelah Alkhamis, Ghada M. Koura, and Hamada A. Hamada, "Effect of Manual Physical Therapy on Sleep Quality and Jaw Mobility in Patients with Bruxism: A Biopsychosocial Randomized Controlled Trial," *Frontiers in Neurology* 13 (2022), https://doi.org/10.3389/fneur.2022.1041928.
16. Lijun Bai, Hao Yan, Linling Li, Wei Qin, Peng Chen, Peng Liu et al., "Neural Specificity of Acupuncture Stimulation at Pericardium 6: Evidence from an fMRI Study," *Journal of Magnetic Resonance Imaging* 31, no. 1 (2010): 71–77, https://doi.org/10.1002/jmri.22006.
17. Heather R. Altier, Jameson K. Hirsch, Annemarie Weber, Niko Kohls, Jorg Schelling, Loren L. Toussaint et al., "Gratitude and Sleep Disturbance in Primary Care Patients: The Mediating Roles of Health Self-Efficacy, Health Behaviors, and Psychological Distress," *Frontiers in Sleep* 4 (2025), https://doi.org/10.3389/frsle.2025.1459854.
18. Susan Musto and April Hazard Vallerand, "Exploring the Uses of Yoga Nidra: An Integrative Review," *Journal of Nursing Scholarship* 55, no. 6 (2023): 1164–78, https://doi.org/10.1111/jnu.12927.

9. Tending Digestion

1. Herbert Mönnikes, J. J. Tebbe, M. Hildebrandt, Petra C. Arck, E. Osmanoglou, Matthias Rose et al., "Role of Stress in Functional Gastrointestinal Disorders: Evidence for Stress-Induced Alterations in Gastrointestinal Motility and Sensitivity," *Digestive Diseases* 19, no. 3 (2001): 201–11, https://doi.org/10.1159/000050681.
2. John F. Cryan, Kenneth J. O'Riordan, Caitlin S. M. Cowan, Kiran V. Sandhu, Thomaz F. S. Bastiaanssen, Marcus Boehme et al., "The Microbiota–Gut–Brain Axis," *Physiological Reviews* 99, no. 4 (2019): 1877–2013, https://doi.org/10.1152/physrev.00018.2018; Tim Vanuytsel, Sander van Wanrooy,

Hanne Vanheel, Christophe Vanormelingen, Sofie Verschueren, Elke Houben et al., "Psychological Stress and Corticotropin-Releasing Hormone Increase Intestinal Permeability in Humans by a Mast Cell-Dependent Mechanism," *Gut* 63, no. 8 (2014): 1293–1299. https://doi.org/10.1136/gutjnl-2013-305690.

3. Thomas F. S. Bastiaanssen, Sofia Cussotto, Marcus J. Claesson, Gerard Clarke, Timothy G. Dinan, and John F. Cryan, "Gutted! Unraveling the Role of the Microbiome in Major Depressive Disorder," *Harvard Review of Psychiatry* 28, no. 1 (2020): 26–39, https://doi.org/10.1097/HRP.0000000000000243; James E. Gangwisch, Lauren Hale, Lorena Garcia, Dolores Malaspina, Mark G. Opler, Martha E. Payne et al., "High Glycemic Index Diet as a Risk Factor for Depression: Analyses from the Women's Health Initiative," *American Journal of Clinical Nutrition* 102, no. 2 (2015): 454–63, https://doi.org/10.3945/ajcn.114.103846.
4. Cryan et al., "Microbiota–Gut–Brain Axis;" Bastiaanssen et al., "Gutted! Unraveling the Role of the Microbiome in Major Depressive Disorder."
5. Amina Khokhar and Faisal A. Rathore, "Psychosomatic Concepts in Traditional Medicine," *Journal of Ayurveda and Integrative Medicine* 10, no. 2 (2019): 125–31.
6. John B. Furness, "The Enteric Nervous System and Neurogastroenterology," *Nature Reviews Gastroenterology and Hepatology* 9 (2012): 286–94, https://doi.org/10.1038/nrgastro.2012.32.
7. Jessica M. Yano, Kristie Yu, Gregory P. Donaldson, Gauri G. Shastri, Pheobe Ann, Liang Ma et al., "Indigenous Bacteria from the Gut Microbiota Regulate Host Serotonin Biosynthesis," *Cell* 161, no. 2 (2015): 264–76, https://doi.org/10.1016/j.cell.2015.02.047.
8. Cryan et al., "Microbiota–Gut–Brain Axis."
9. Cryan et al., "Microbiota–Gut–Brain Axis;" Vanuytsel et al., "Psychological Stress and Corticotropin-Releasing Hormone Increase Intestinal Permeability in Humans by a Mast Cell-Dependent Mechanism."
10. Amy Seiler, Christopher P. Fagundes, and Lisa M. Christian, "Psychobiology of Bereavement and Health," *Psychosomatic Medicine* 82, no. 4 (2020): 408–17, https://doi.org/10.1097/PSY.0000000000000780.
11. Menglin Liu, Genhao Fan, Lingkai Meng, Kuo Yang, and Huayi Liu, "New Perspectives on Microbiome-Dependent Gut-Brain Pathways for the Treatment of Depression with Gastrointestinal Symptoms: From Bench to Benchside," *Journal of Zhejiang University Science B* 26, no. 1 (2025): 1–25, https://doi.org/10.1631/jzus.B2300343.
12. Raphael Enaud, Renaud Prevel, Eleonora Ciarlo, Fabien Beaufils, Gregoire Wieërs, Benoit Guery et al., "The Gut-Lung Axis in Health and Respiratory Diseases: A Place for Inter-Organ and Inter-Kingdom Crosstalks," *Frontiers in Cellular and Infection Microbiology* 10, no. 9 (2020), https://doi.org/10.3389/fcimb.2020.00009.
13. Julian F. Thayer and Esther Sternberg, "Beyond Heart Rate Variability: Vagal Regulation of Allostatic Systems," *Annals of the New York Academy of Sciences* 1088 (2006): 361–72, https://doi.org/10.1196/annals.1366.014.
14. Varun Malhotra, Danish Javed, Santosh Wakode, Rajay Bharshankar, Neha Soni, and Patrick K. Porter, "Study of Immediate Neurological and Autonomic Changes During Kapalabhati Pranayama in Yoga Practitioners," *Journal of*

Family Medicine and Primary Care 11, no. 2 (2022): 720–27, https://doi.org/10.4103/jfmpc.jfmpc_1662_21; Rana B. Budhi and Deepeshwar Singh, "The Influence of Kapalabhati on Working Memory and Phasic Heart Rate Variability," *Cureus* 16, no. 5 (2024), https://doi.org/10.7759/cureus.61027.

15. Zhangxiang Lin, Dacun Wang, Ziaoyang Fei, Dongmiao Han, and Zicai Liu, "Effect of Abdominal Massage on Constipation: A Systematic Review and Meta-Analysis of Randomized Controlled Studies," *Complementary Medicine Research* (2025): 1–30, https://doi.org/10.1159/000548699.
16. Petra Santos and Luísa Soares, "Narrative Therapy and Constructivist Perspective: An Integrative Review of Complicated Grief and Effective Therapeutic Contributions," *Psychology and Behavioral Science International Journal* 22, no. 2 (2024), https://doi.org/10.19080/PBSIJ.2024.22.556082.
17. Vasant Lad, *Textbook of Ayurveda: Fundamental Principles*, vol. 2 (Ayurvedic Press, 2012), 86–87.

10. Working Through Anger

1. Andrea Scarantino, "How to Define Emotions Scientifically," *Emotion Review* 9, no. 4 (2017): 345–57, https://doi.org/10.1177/1754073912445810.
2. Lauri Nummenmaa, Enrico Glerean, Riitta Hari, and Jari K. Hietanen, "Bodily Maps of Emotions," *Proceedings of the National Academy of Sciences* 111, no. 2 (2014): 646–51, https://doi.org/10.1073/pnas.1321664111.
3. A. D. Craig, "Interoception: The Sense of the Physiological Condition of the Body," *Current Opinion in Neurobiology* 13, no. 4 (2003): 500–505, https://doi.org/10.1016/S0959-4388(03)00090-4; Lauri Nummenmaa, Enrico Glearan, Mikko Viinikainen, Iiro P. Jaaskelainen, Riitta Hari, and Mikko Sams, "Emotions Promote Social Interaction by Synchronizing Brain Activity Across Individuals," *Proceedings of the National Academy of Sciences* 109, no. 24 (2014): 9599–604, https://doi.org/10.1073/pnas.1206095109.
4. Julian F. Thayer and Richard D. Lane, "A Model of Neurovisceral Integration in Emotion Regulation and Dysregulation," *Journal of Affective Disorders* 61, no. 3 (2000): 201–16, https://doi.org/10.1016/S0165-0327(00)00338-4.
5. Steven K. H. Aung, Heather C. Fay, and Richard F. Hobbs, "Traditional Chinese Medicine as a Basis for Treating Psychiatric Disorders: A Review of Theory with Illustrative Cases," *Medical Acupuncture* 25, no. 6 (2013): 398–406, https://doi.org/10.1089/acu.2013.1007.
6. Vasant Lad, *Textbook of Ayurveda: Fundamental Principles*, vol. 2 (Ayurvedic Press, 2012), 318–19.
7. Ted J. Kaptchuk, *The Web That Has No Weaver: Understanding Chinese Medicine* (McGraw-Hill, 2000); Aung, Fay, and Hobbs, "Traditional Chinese Medicine as a Basis for Treating Psychiatric Disorders."
8. Aung, Fay, and Hobbs, "Traditional Chinese Medicine as a Basis for Treating Psychiatric Disorders."
9. Giovanni Maciocia, *The Foundations of Chinese Medicine: A Comprehensive Text for Acupuncturists and Herbalists*, 3rd ed. (Churchill Livingstone, 2015); Kevin Chen and Yong Huang, "Principles of Yin-Yang and Five Elements in Traditional Chinese Medicine," *Integrative Medicine: A Clinician's Journal* 9, no. 4 (2010): 72–75.

10. Maciocia, *Foundations of Chinese Medicine.*
11. Kaptchuk, *Web That Has No Weaver.*
12. Elizabeth Mostofsky, Elizabeth Anne Penner, and Murray A. Mittleman, "Outbursts of Anger as a Trigger of Acute Cardiovascular Events: A Systematic Review and Meta-Analysis," *European Heart Journal* 35, no. 21 (2014): 1404–10; Murray A. Mittleman, Malcolm Maclure, Jane B. Sherwood, Richard P. Mulry, Geoffrey H. Tofler, Sue C. Jacobs et al., "Triggering of Acute Myocardial Infarction by Episodes of Anger," *Circulation* 92, no. 7 (1995): 1720–25, https://doi.org/10.1161/01.CIR.92.7.1720.
13. Daichi Shimbo, William Chaplin, Oluwaseun Akinola, Adam Harris, Dennis Abraham, Shunichi Homma et al., "Effect of Anger Provocation on Endothelium-Dependent and -Independent Vasodilation," *The American Journal of Cardiology* 99, no. 6 (2007): 860–63, https://doi.org/10.1016/j.amj-card.2006.10.051.
14. Melis Y. Balban, Eric Neri, Manuela M. Kogon, Lara Weed, Bita Nourani, Booil Jo et al., "Brief Structured Respiration Practices Enhance Mood and Reduce Physiological Arousal," *Cell Reports Medicine* 4, no. 1 (2023), https://doi.org/10.1016/j.xcrm.2022.100895; I-Ming Lin, Chia-Jung Lee, and Wen-Chin Tsai, "Heart Rate Variability Biofeedback Attenuates Autonomic Reactivity During Anger Recall in Coronary Artery Disease," *Applied Psychophysiology and Biofeedback* 47, no. 2 (2022): 131–42.
15. Aung, Fay, and Hobbs, "Traditional Chinese Medicine as a Basis for Treating Psychiatric Disorders"; Kaptchuk, *Web That Has No Weaver.*
16. Aung, Fay, and Hobbs, "Traditional Chinese Medicine as a Basis for Treating Psychiatric Disorders."
17. Christopher P. Fagundes, Julianne M. Bennett, Heather M. Derry, Janice K. Kiecolt-Glaser, "Relationships and Inflammation Across the Lifespan: Social Developmental Pathways to Disease," *Social and Personality Psychology Compass* 5, no. 11 (2011): 891–903. https://doi.org/10.1111/j.1751-9004.2011.00392.x.
18. Paul Lucian Szasz, Aurora Szentagotai, and Stefan G. Hofmann, "The Effect of Emotion Regulation Strategies on Anger," *Behaviour Research and Therapy* 49, no. 2 (2011): 114–19, https://doi.org/10.1016/j.brat.2010.11.011.
19. Paul U. Unschuld, trans., *Huang Di Nei Jing Su Wen: Nature, Knowledge, Imagery in an Ancient Chinese Medical Text* (University of California Press, 2003); Bethany Eggleston and Lisa M. Schmalzried, "'I Just Find It Easier to Let Go of Anger': Reflections on the Ways in Which Yoga Influences How Young People Manage Their Emotions," *Frontiers in Psychology* 12 (2021), https://doi.org/10.3389/fpsyg.2021.729588.
20. Lad, *Textbook of Ayurveda*, 318–19; Siddappa Naragatti, "Scientific Review of Cooling Pranayama Techniques: Efficacy in Alkalizing the Blood and Managing Acidic Conditions," *International Journal of Research Publication and Reviews* 6, no. 3 (2025): 1107–16, https://doi.org/10.55248/gengpi.6.0325.1133.
21. James W. Pennebaker and Cindy K. Chung, "Expressive Writing: Connections to Physical and Mental Health," in *The Oxford Handbook of Health Psychology*, ed. Howard S. Friedman (Oxford University Press, 2011), 417–37.
22. David Frawley, *Ayurveda and the Mind: The Healing of Consciousness* (Lotus Press, 1997), 184–201.
23. Tristen K. Inagaki and Naomi I. Eisenberger, "Giving Support to Others Re-

duces Sympathetic Nervous System-Related Responses to Stress," *Psychophysiology* 53, no. 4 (2016): 427–35, https://doi.org/10.1111/psyp.12578.

24. Iwona Nowakowska, "Volunteerism in the Last Year as a Moderator Between Empathy and Altruistic Social Value Orientation: An Exploratory Study," *Current Issues in Personality Psychology* 10, no. 1 (2021): 10–20, https://doi.org/10.5114/cipp.2021.108258.

11. Connecting with Sadness

1. Hao Liang, Songye Wu, Duo Yang, Jianhua Huang, Xiaolei Yao, Jingbo Gong et al., "Non-targeted Metabolomics Analysis Reveals Distinct Metabolic Profiles Between Positive and Negative Emotional Tears of Humans: A Preliminary Study," *Cureus* 15, no. 8 (2023), https://doi.org/10.7759/cureus.42985.
2. Elisabeth M. Messmer, "Emotionale tränen [Emotional tears]," *Der Ophthalmologe* 106, no. 7 (2009): 593–602, https://doi.org/10.1007/s00347-009-1966-5.
3. Lauren M. Bylsma, Asmir Gračanin, and Ad J. J. M. Vingerhoets, "The Neurobiology of Human Crying," *Clinical Autonomic Research* 26, no. 1 (2019): 63–73, https://doi.org/10.1007/s10286-018-0526-y.
4. Asmir Gračanin, Lauren M. Bylsma, and Ad J. J. M. Vingerhoets, "Is Crying a Self-Soothing Behavior?" *Frontiers in Psychology* 5 (2014), https://doi.org/10.3389/fpsyg.2014.00502.
5. Jaak Panksepp, Rick Meeker, and N. J. Bean, "The Neurochemical Control of Crying," *Pharmacology Biochemistry and Behavior* 12, no. 3 (1980): 437–43, https://doi.org/10.1016/0091-3057(80)90050-7.
6. Gračanin, Bylsma, and Vingerhoets, "Is Crying a Self-Soothing Behavior?"
7. Julie B. Kaplow, Polly Y. Gipson, Adam G. Horwitz, Bianca N. Burch, and Cheryl A. King, "Emotional Suppression Mediates the Relation Between Adverse Life Events and Adolescent Suicide: Implications for Prevention," *Prevention Science* 15 (2014): 177–85, https://doi.org/10.1007/s11121-013-0367-9.
8. Megan E. Renna, "A Review and Novel Theoretical Model of How Negative Emotions Influence Inflammation: The Critical Role of Emotion Regulation," *Brain, Behavior, and Immunity - Health* 18 (2021), https://doi.org/10.1016/j.bbih.2021.100397.
9. Pilleri Sikka, Jonathan Stenberg, Victor Vorobyev, and James J. Gross, "The Neural Bases of Expressive Suppression: A Systematic Review of Functional Neuroimaging Studies," *Neuroscience and Biobehavioral Reviews* 138 (2022), https://doi.org/10.1016/j.neubiorev.2022.104708.
10. Anthony Matta, Clement Delmas, Francesco Campelo-Parada, Thibault Lhermusier, Frederic Bouisset, Meyer Elbaz et al., "Takotsubo Cardiomyopathy," *Reviews in Cardiovascular Medicine* 23, no. 1 (2022): 38, https://doi.org/10.31083/j.rcm2301038.
11. Giovanni Maciocia, *The Practice of Chinese Medicine* (Churchill Livingstone, 2005).
12. *Jin Gui Yao Lue* (Essential Prescriptions of the Golden Cabinet), c. 220 C.E.
13. Paul U. Unschuld, Hermann Tessenow, and Zheng Jinsheng, *Huang Di Nei Jing Su Wen: An Annotated Translation of Huang Di's Inner Classic; Basic Questions*, vol. 1 (University of California Press, 2011).

14. Yan Yang, Yan-Kun Chen, and Meng-Zhou Xie, "Exploring the Transformative Impact of Traditional Chinese Medicine on Depression: Insights from Animal Models," *World Journal of Psychiatry* 14, no. 5 (2024): 607–23, https://doi.org/10.5498/wjp.v14.i5.607.
15. Stefano Spaccapanico Proietti, Manuela Chiavarini, Francesco Iorio, Livia Buratta, Giancarlo Pocetta, Roberta Carestia et al., "The Role of a Mindful Movement-Based Program (Movimento Biologico) in Health Promotion: Results of a Pre-Post Intervention Study," *Frontiers in Public Health* 12 (2024), https://doi.org/10.3389/fpubh.2024.1372660.
16. Rollin McCraty and Maria A. Zayas, "Cardiac Coherence, Self-Regulation, Autonomic Stability, and Psychosocial Well-Being," *Frontiers in Psychology* 5 (2014), https://doi.org/10.3389/fpsyg.2014.01090.
17. Kerstin Uvnäs-Moberg, Linda Handlin, and Maria Petersson, "Self-Soothing Behaviors with Particular Reference to Oxytocin Release Induced by Non-Noxious Sensory Stimulation," *Frontiers in Psychology* 5 (2015), https://doi.org/10.3389/fpsyg.2014.01529; Aljoscha Dreisoerner, Nina M. Junker, Wolff Schlotz, Julia Heimrich, Svenja Bloemeke, Beate Ditzen et al., "Self-Soothing Touch and Being Hugged Reduce Cortisol Responses to Stress: A Randomized Controlled Trial on Stress, Physical Touch, and Social Identity," *Comprehensive Psychoneuroendocrinology* 8 (2021), https://doi.org/10.1016/j.cpnec.2021.100091.
18. Susan I. Hopper, Sherrie L. Murray, Lucille Ferrara, and Joanne K. Singleton, "Effectiveness of Diaphragmatic Breathing for Reducing Physiological and Psychological Stress in Adults: A Quantitative Systematic Review," *JBI Database of Systematic Reviews and Implementation Reports* 17, no. 9 (2019): 1855–76, https://doi.org/10.11124/JBISRIR-2017-003848.
19. Ze Zhang, Jianning Meng, Ziyi Li, Yabing Sun, and Jing Luo, "The Role of Creative Cognitive Reappraisals in Positively Transforming Negative Emotions," *PsyCh Journal* 11, no. 6 (2022): 837–51, https://doi.org/10.1002/pchj.589.
20. A. S. Troy, A. J. Shallcross, A. Brunner, R. Friedman, and M. C. Jones, "Cognitive Reappraisal and Acceptance: Effects on Emotion, Physiology, and Perceived Cognitive Costs," *Emotion* 18, no. 1 (2018): 58–74, https://doi.org/10.1037/emo0000371.

12. Facing Anxiety

1. Stephen W. Porges, "The Polyvagal Perspective," *Biological Psychology* 74, no. 2 (2007): 116–43, https://doi.org/10.1016/j.biopsycho.2006.06.009.
2. John A. Chalmers, Daniel S. Quintana, Maree J.-Anne Abbott, and Andrew H. Kemp, "Anxiety Disorders Are Associated with Reduced Heart Rate Variability: A Meta-Analysis," *Frontiers in Psychiatry* 5 (2014), https://doi.org/10.3389/fpsyt.2014.00080; Ashvita Ramesh, Tanvi Nayak, Molly Beestrum, Giorgio Quer, and Jay A. Pandit, "Heart Rate Variability and Psychiatric Disorders: A Systematic Review and Meta-Analysis," *Psychological Medicine* 51, no. 2 (2021): 195–208, https://doi.org/10.2147/NDT.S429592.
3. Julian F. Thayer and Richard D. Lane, "A Model of Neurovisceral Integration in Emotion Regulation and Dysregulation," *Journal of Affective Disorders* 61, no. 3 (2000): 201–16, https://doi.org/10.1016/S0165-0327(00)00338-4.

4. Hari Sharma and H. M. Chandola, "Anxiety Disorders in Ayurveda with Special Reference to Chittodvega," *AYU* 32, no. 4 (2011): 569–72, https://doi.org/10.4103/0974-8520.96118.
5. *Caraka Samhita*, trans. R. K. Sharma and Bhagwan Dash (Chowkhamba Sanskrit Series, 2001).
6. Porges, "Polyvagal Perspective," 116–43.
7. Christopher A. Moyer, James Rounds, and James W. Hannum, "A Meta-Analysis of Massage Therapy Research," *Psychological Bulletin* 130, no. 1 (2004): 3–18, https://doi.org/10.1037/0033-2909.130.1.3.
8. G. K. Pal, S. Velkumary, and Madanmohan, "Effect of Short-Term Practice of Breathing Exercises on Autonomic Functions in Normal Human Volunteers," *Indian Journal of Medical Research* 120, no. 2 (2004): 115–21.
9. Penelope J Klein, Joseph Baumgarden, and Roger Schneider, "Qigong and Tai Chi as Therapeutic Exercise: Survey of Systematic Reviews and Meta-Analyses Addressing Physical Health Conditions," *Alternative Therapies in Health and Medicine* 25, no. 5 (2019): 48–53; Ann Van de Winckel, Sydney T. Carpentier, Wei Deng, Lin Zhang, Angela Philippus, Ricardo Battaglino et al., "Feasibility of Using Remotely Delivered Spring Forest Qigong to Reduce Neuropathic Pain in Adults with Spinal Cord Injury: A Pilot Study," *Frontiers in Physiology* 14 (2023), https://doi.org/10.3389/fphys.2023.1222616.
10. David Berceli, Melanie Salmon, Robin Bonifas, and Nkem Ndefo, "Effects of Self-Induced Unclassified Therapeutic Tremors on Quality of Life Among Non-Professional Caregivers: A Pilot Study," *Global Advances in Health and Medicine* 3, no. 5 (2014): 45–48, https://doi.org/10.7453/gahmj.2014.032.
11. Jaruwan Vierra, Orocahorn Boonla, and Piyapong Prasertsri, "Effects of Sleep Deprivation and 4-7-8 Breathing Control on Heart Rate Variability, Blood Pressure, Blood Glucose, and Endothelial Function in Healthy Young Adults," *Physiological Reports* 10, no. 13 (2022), https://doi.org/10.14814/phy2.15389.
12. Vierra, Boonla, and Prasertsri, "Effects of Sleep Deprivation and 4-7-8 Breathing Control."
13. Cynthia J. Price and Helen Y. Weng, "Facilitating Adaptive Emotion Processing and Somatic Reappraisal Via Sustained Mindful Interoceptive Attention," *Frontiers in Psychology* 12 (2021), https://doi.org/10.3389/fpsyg.2021.578827.
14. Simon Guendelman, Sebastian Medeiros, and Hagen Rampes, "Mindfulness and Emotion Regulation: Insights from Neurobiological, Psychological, and Clinical Studies," *Frontiers in Psychology* 8 (2017), https://doi.org/10.3389/fpsyg.2017.00220.

13. Honoring When You Feel Numb

1. Mette K. Nielsen, Kaj Sparle Christensen, Mette Asbjoern Neergaard, Pernille Envold Bidstrup, and Mai-Britt Guldin, "Grief Trajectories and Long-Term Health Effects in Bereaved Relatives: A Prospective, Population-Based Cohort Study with Ten-Year Follow-Up," *Frontiers in Public Health* 13 (2025), https://doi.org/10.3389/fpubh.2025.1619730.
2. Mai-Britt Guldin and Carlo Leget, "The Integrated Process Model of Loss and Grief: An Interprofessional Understanding," *Death Studies* 48, no. 7 (2023): 738–52, https://doi.org/10.1080/07481187.2023.2272960.

3. Nada Pop-Jordanova, "Grief: Aetiology, Symptoms and Management," *Prilozi (Makedonska Akademija na Naukite i Umetnostite)* 42, no. 2 (2021): 9–18, https://doi.org/10.2478/prilozi-2021-0014.
4. Anthony D. Mancini and George A. Bonanno, "Resilience in the Face of Potential Trauma: Clinical Practices and Illustrations," *Journal of Clinical Psychology* 62, no. 8 (2006): 971–85, https://doi.org/10.1002/jclp.20283.
5. George A. Bonanno and Stacey Kaltman, "The Varieties of Grief Experience," *Clinical Psychology Review* 21, no. 5 (2001): 705–34, https://doi.org/10.1016/s0272-7358(00)00062-3.
6. M. Katherine Shear, Angela Ghesquiere, and Kim Glickman, "Bereavement and Complicated Grief," *Current Psychiatry Reports* 15, no. 11 (2013): 406, https://doi.org/10.1007/s11920-013-0406-z.
7. Joan Didion, *The Year of Magical Thinking* (Vintage, 2007), 188–89; Laura Upenieks, Terrence D. Hill, and Christopher Orfanidis, "Crisis of Faith and Sleep Quality in the United States: A Literal Dark Night of the Soul?" *Journal of Religion and Health* 63 (2024): 3066–87, https://doi.org/10.1007/s10943-023-01958-6.
8. Terri Daniel, "Grief as a Mystical Journey: Fowler's Stages of Faith Development and Their Relation to Post-Traumatic Growth," *Journal of Pastoral Care & Counseling* 71, no. 4 (2017): 220–29, https://doi.org/10.1177/1542305017741858.
9. A. Barratt Brown, "The Dark Night of the Soul," *Journal of Religion* 3, no. 5 (1923): 476–88, doi.org/10.1086/480382; Upenieks, Hill, and Orfanidis, "Crisis of Faith and Sleep Quality in the United States," 3066–87; St. John of the Cross, *Dark Night of the Soul*, trans. E. Allison Peers (Image Books, 1991).
10. Hanan Bushkin, Roelf van Niekerk, and Louise Stroud, "Searching for Meaning in Chaos: Viktor Frankl's Story," *Europe's Journal of Psychology* 17, no. 3 (2021): 233–42, https://doi.org/10.5964/ejop.5439.
11. Stephen W. Porges, "Polyvagal Theory: A Science of Safety," *Frontiers in Integrative Neuroscience* 16 (2022), https://doi.org/10.3389/fnint.2022.871227.
12. Karin Roelofs, "Freeze for Action: Neurobiological Mechanisms in Animal and Human Freezing," *Philosophical Transactions of the Royal Society B: Biological Sciences* 372, no. 1718 (2017), https://doi.org/10.1098/rstb.2016.0206; Porges, "Polyvagal Theory."
13. Porges, "Polyvagal Theory."
14. Daniel J. Siegel, *The Developing Mind: Toward a Neurobiology of Interpersonal Experience* (Guilford Press, 1999).
15. Daniel J. Siegel and Chloe Drulis, "An Interpersonal Neurobiology Perspective on the Mind and Mental Health: Personal, Public, and Planetary Well-Being," *Annals of General Psychiatry* 22, no. 1 (2023): 5, https://doi.org/10.1186/s12991-023-00434-5.
16. Sidney Zisook and Katherine Shear, "Grief and Bereavement: What Psychiatrists Need to Know," *World Psychiatry* 8, no. 2 (2009): 67–74, https://doi.org/10.1002/j.2051-5545.2009.tb00217.x.
17. Miriam Greenspan, *Healing through the Dark Emotions: The Wisdom of Grief, Fear, and Despair* (Shambhala Publications, 2003), 67.
18. Alejandra Motiño, Jesus Saiz, Ivan Sanchez-Iglesias, Maria Salazar, Tiffany J.

Barsotti, Deepak Chopra et al., "Cross-Cultural Analysis of Spiritual Bypass: A Comparison Between Spain and Honduras," *Frontiers in Psychology* 12 (2021), https://doi.org/10.3389/fpsyg.2021.658739.

19. Sonia, "The Dark Side of Positivity: How Toxic Positivity Contributes to Emotional Suppression and Mental Health Struggles," *International Journal of Indian Psychology* 13, no. 2 (2025): 1155–64, https://ijip.in/wp-content/uploads/2025/05/18.01.104.20251302.pdf.
20. Tania Chandra, "The Interplay of Elements and Ailments in Body: Exploring Gunas and Doshas Balance in Mental Health Through Ayurveda's Perspective," *International Journal of Indian Psychology* 12, no. 4 (2024): 2422–35, https://ijip.in/wp-content/uploads/2025/01/18.01.230.20241204.pdf.
21. Taoying Lu, Mingyue Fan, Jianxiong Cai, Aolin Liu, Qianwen Xie, Xiaowen Zhou et al., "Psychometric Validation of the Dampness Syndrome Scale of Chinese Medicine for People in China," *Patient Preference and Adherence* 18 (2024): 2041–53, https://doi.org/10.2147/PPA.S468732; Sin Yee Yap, Foong Leng Ng, Menaga Subramaniam, Yang Mooi Lim, and Chai Nien Foo, "Traditional Chinese Medicine Body Constitutions as Predictors for Depression: A Systematic Review and Meta-Analysis," *Behavioral Sciences* 12, no. 11 (2022): 423, https://doi.org/10.3390/bs12110423.
22. John W. James and Russell Friedman, *The Grief Recovery Handbook: The Action Program for Moving Beyond Death, Divorce, and Other Losses, Including Health, Career, and Faith*, 20th ann. expanded ed. (William Morrow, 2017).
23. Karin Chellew, Phil Evans, Joana Fornes-Vives, Gerardo Perez, and Gloria Garcia-Banda, "The Effect of Progressive Muscle Relaxation on Daily Cortisol Secretion," *Stress* 18, no. 5 (2015): 538–44, https://doi.org/10.3109/10253890.2015.1053454.
24. Louisa M. T. Silva, Mark Schalock, Robert Ayres, Carol Bunse, and Sarojini Budden, "Qigong Massage Treatment for Sensory and Self-Regulation Problems in Young Children with Autism: A Randomized Controlled Trial," *American Journal of Occupational Therapy* 63, no. 4 (2009): 423–32, https://doi.org/10.5014/ajot.63.4.423.
25. Gunjan Trivedi, Kamal Sharma, Banshi Saboo, Soundappan Kathirvel, Ashwati Konat, Vatsal Zapadia et al., "Humming (Simple Bhramari Pranayama) as a Stress Buster: A Holter-Based Study to Analyze Heart Rate Variability (HRV) Parameters During Bhramari, Physical Activity, Emotional Stress, and Sleep," *Cureus* 15, no. 4 (2023), https://doi.org/10.7759/cureus.37527.
26. Gemma Perry, Vince Polito, and William Forde Thompson, "Exploring the Physiological and Psychological Effects of Group Chanting in Australia: Reduced Stress, Cortisol and Enhanced Social Connection," *Journal of Religion and Health* 63, no. 6. (2024): 4793–4815, https://doi.org/10.1007/s10943-023-01967-5.
27. Areum Han and Tae Hui Kim, "Effects of Self-Compassion Interventions on Reducing Depressive Symptoms, Anxiety, and Stress: A Meta-Analysis," *Mindfulness* 14 (2023): 1553–81, https://doi.org/10.1007/s12671-023-02148-x.
28. Rosie Perkins, Sara Ascenso, Louise Atkins, Daisy Fancourt, and Aaron Williamon, "Making Music for Mental Health: How Group Drumming Mediates Recovery," *Psychology of Well-Being* 6, no. 1 (2016): 11, https://doi.org/10.1186/s13612-016-0048-0; Sara Ascenso, Rosie Perkins, Louise Atkins,

Daisy Fancourt, and Aaron Williamon, "Promoting Well-Being Through Group Drumming with Mental Health Service Users and Their Careers," *International Journal of Qualitative Studies on Health and Well-Being* 13, no. 1 (2018), https://doi.org/10.1080/17482631.2018.1484219.

29. Petr Srámek, M. Simeckova, L. Jansky, J. Savlikova, and Stanislav Vybiral, "Human Physiological Responses to Immersion into Water of Different Temperatures," *European Journal of Applied Physiology* 81, no. 5 (2000): 436–42, https://doi.org/10.1007/s004210050065.
30. Ala Yankouskaya, Ruth Williamson, Cameron Stacey, John James Totman, and Heather Massey, "Short-Term Head-Out Whole-Body Cold-Water Immersion Facilitates Positive Affect and Increases Interaction Between Large-Scale Brain Networks," *Biology* 12, no. 2 (2023): 211, https://doi.org/10.3390/biology12020211.
31. Štefan Tóth, Marianna Barbierik Vachalcova, David Kasko, Martin Turek, Zuzana Gulasova, and Zdenka Hertelyova, "Effect of Repeatedly Applied Cold Water Immersion on Subclinical Atherosclerosis, Inflammation, Fat Accumulation and Lipid Profile Parameters of Volunteers," *Wiener Klinische Wochenschrift* 136 (2024): 87–93, https://doi.org/10.1007/s00508-023-02246-9.

14. Navigating the Abyss of Fear

1. J. E. LeDoux, "Emotion Circuits in the Brain," *Annual Review of Neuroscience* 23 (2000): 155–84, https://doi.org/10.1146/annurev.neuro.23.1.155.
2. Bruce S. McEwen, "Physiology and Neurobiology of Stress and Adaptation: Central Role of The Brain," *Physiological Reviews* 87, no. 3 (2007): 873–904, https://doi.org/10.1152/physrev.00041.2006.
3. Amy F. T. Arnsten, "Stress Signalling Pathways That Impair Prefrontal Cortex Structure and Function," *Nature Reviews Neuroscience* 10, no. 6 (2009): 410–22, https://www.nature.com/articles/nrn2648.
4. Stephen W. Porges, *The Polyvagal Theory: Neurophysiological Foundations of Emotions, Attachment, Communication, and Self-Regulation* (W. W. Norton, 2011).
5. Bessel van der Kolk, *The Body Keeps the Score: Brain, Mind, and Body in the Healing of Trauma* (Viking, 2015).
6. Robert M. Sapolsky, *Why Zebras Don't Get Ulcers* (Holt Paperbacks, 2004).
7. Ted J. Kaptchuk, *The Web That Has No Weaver: Understanding Chinese Medicine* (McGraw-Hill, 2000).
8. Giovanni Maciocia, *The Foundations of Chinese Medicine,* 3rd ed. (Elsevier, 2015).
9. Maciocia, *Foundations of Chinese Medicine.*
10. Maciocia, *Foundations of Chinese Medicine.*
11. Kaptchuk, *Web That Has No Weaver.*
12. Francis Weller, *The Wild Edge of Sorrow: Rituals of Renewal and the Sacred Work of Grief* (North Atlantic Books, 2015).
13. St. John of the Cross, *Dark Night of the Soul*, trans. Mirabai Starr (Riverhead Books, 2003); *The Cloud of Unknowing*, trans. Carmen Acevedo Butcher (Shambhala Publications, 2004).
14. Annemarie Schimmel, *Mystical Dimensions of Islam* (University of North Carolina Press, 1975).

15. *The Cloud of Unknowing.*
16. David Loy, *Ecodharma: Buddhist Teachings for the Ecological Crisis* (Wisdom Publications, 2019).
17. Nikky-Guninder Kaur Singh, *The Name of My Beloved: Verses of the Sikh Gurus* (HarperCollins, 1993).
18. Michaela C. Pascoe, David R. Thompson, and Chantal F. Ski, "Yoga, Mindfulness-Based Stress Reduction and Stress-Related Physiological Measures: A Meta-Analysis," *Psychoneuroendocrinology* 86 (2017): 152–68, https://doi.org/10.1016/j.psyneuen.2017.08.008.
19. Giovanni Maciocia, "The Treatment of Shen Disturbances with Chinese Medicine," online publication, accessed February 2019, https://giovanni-maciocia.com/wp-content/uploads/2019/02/shen-maciocia-online.pdf.
20. Ravinder Jerath, John W. Edry, Vernon A. Barnes, and Vandna Jerath, "Physiology of Long Pranayamic Breathing: Neural Respiratory Elements May Provide a Mechanism That Explains How Slow Deep Breathing Shifts the Autonomic Nervous System," *Medical Hypotheses* 67, no. 3 (2006): 566–71, https://doi.org/10.1016/j.mehy.2006.02.042.
21. Emily A. Holmes and Andrew Mathews, "Mental Imagery in Emotion and Emotional Disorders," *Clinical Psychology Review* 30, no. 3 (2010): 349–62, https://doi.org/10.1016/j.cpr.2010.01.001.
22. Leon Skottnik and David E. J. Linden, "Mental Imagery and Brain Regulation—New Links Between Psychotherapy and Neuroscience," *Frontiers in Psychiatry* 10 (2019), https://doi.org/10.3389/fpsyt.2019.00779.
23. Maciocia, "The Treatment of Shen Disturbances with Chinese Medicine."
24. Bum Jin Park, Yuko Tsunetsugu, Tamami Kasetani, Takahide Kagawa, and Yoshifumi Miyazaki, "The Physiological Effects of Shinrin-Yoku (Taking In the Forest Atmosphere or Forest Bathing): Evidence from Field Experiments in 24 Forests Across Japan," *Environmental Health and Preventive Medicine* 15, no. 1 (2010): 18–26, https://doi.org/10.1007/s12199-009-0086-9.
25. Chiew Jiat Rosalind Siah, Yong Shiah Goh, Jungup Lee, Sum Nok Poon, Jenna Qing Yun Ow Yong, and Wai-San Wilson Tam, "The Effects of Forest Bathing on Psychological Well-Being: A Systematic Review and Meta-Analysis," *International Journal of Mental Health Nursing* 32, no. 4 (2023): 1038–54, https://doi.org/10.1111/inm.13131.

15. Coming Up Against Guilt

1. Bob Flaws and Craig Mitchell, *Chinese Medical Qigong Therapy: A Comprehensive Clinical Text* (Blue Poppy Press, 1999).
2. Wencong Zhou, Qi Deng, Lin Jia, Hanbing Zhao, Meng Yang, Guoyuan Dou et al., "Acute Effect of Transcutaneous Electroacupuncture on Globus Pharyngeus: A Randomized, Single-Blind, Crossover Trial," *Frontiers in Medicine* 7 (2020), https://doi.org/10.3389/fmed.2020.00179.
3. Hsin-Fu Yeh, Yi-Shun Chu, Shinn-Jang Hwang, Fang-Pey Chen, Yen-Ting Lu, "Effects of Ban-Xia-Hou-Pu-Tang and Western Medicine on Patients with Globus Sensation: A Randomized Controlled Trial," *Journal of the Chinese Medical Association* 88, no. 12 (2025): 941–48, https://doi.org/10.1097/JCMA.0000000000001237.

4. Kristin D. Neff, "Self-Compassion: Theory, Method, Research, and Intervention," *Annual Review of Psychology* 74 (2023): 193–218, https://doi.org/10.1146/annurev-psych-032420-031047.
5. Richard Stephens and Claudia Umland, "Swearing as a Response to Pain-Effect of Daily Swearing Frequency," *Journal of Pain* 12, no. 12 (2011): 1274–81, https://doi.org/10.1016/j.jpain.2011.09.004.
6. Christianne E. Strang, "Art Therapy and Neuroscience: Evidence, Limits, and Myths," *Frontiers in Psychology* 15 (2024), https://doi.org/10.3389/fpsyg.2024.1484481.

16. Disentangling from Shame

1. James J. Gross and Oliver P. John, "Individual Differences in Two Emotion Regulation Processes: Implications for Affect, Relationships, and Well-Being," *Journal of Personality and Social Psychology* 85, no. 2 (2003): 348–62, https://doi.org/10.1037/0022-3514.85.2.348.
2. Maarten C. Eisma, Minita Franzen, Mabel Paauw, Anke Bleeker, and Marije aan het Rot, "Rumination, Worry and Negative and Positive Affect in Prolonged Grief: A Daily Diary Study," *Clinical Psychology & Psychotherapy* 29, no. 1 (2022): 299–312, https://doi.org/10.1002/cpp.2635.
3. Petra Michl, Thomas Meindl, Franziska Meister, Christine Born, Rolf R. Engel, Maximilian Reiser et al., "Neurobiological Underpinnings of Shame and Guilt: A Pilot fMRI Study," *Social Cognitive and Affective Neuroscience* 9, no. 11 (2014): 1508–14, https://doi.org/10.1093/scan/nss114.
4. Diede Fennema, Gareth J. Barker, Owen O'Daly, Suqian Duan, Ewan Carr, Kimberley Goldsmith et al., "Self-Blame-Selective Hyper-Connectivity Between Anterior Temporal and Subgenual Cortices Predicts Prognosis in Major Depressive Disorder," *NeuroImage: Clinical* 39 (2023): 103453, https://doi.org/10.1016/j.nicl.2023.103453.
5. Kenneth J. Doka, *Disenfranchised Grief: New Directions, Challenges, and Strategies for Practice* (Research Press, 2002).
6. Maria Yellow Horse Brave Heart, "The Historical Trauma Response Among Natives and Its Relationship with Substance Abuse: A Lakota Illustration," *Journal of Psychoactive Drugs* 35, no. 1 (2003): 7–13, https://doi.org/10.1080/02791072.2003.10399988.
7. Rachel Yehuda and Amy Lehrner, "Intergenerational Transmission of Trauma Effects: Putative Role of Epigenetic Mechanisms," *World Psychiatry* 17, no. 3 (2014): 273–85, https://doi.org/10.1002/wps.20568.
8. Rachel Yehuda, Stephanie Mulherin Engel, Sarah R. Brand, Jonathan Seckl, Sue M. Marcus, and Gertrude S. Berkowitz, "Transgenerational Effects of Posttraumatic Stress Disorder in Babies of Mothers Exposed to the World Trade Center Attacks During Pregnancy," *Journal of Clinical Endocrinology & Metabolism* 90, no. 7 (2005): 4115–18, https://doi.org/10.1210/jc.2005-0550.
9. Kristin D. Neff and Christopher K. Germer, "A Pilot Study and Randomized Controlled Trial of the Mindful Self-Compassion Program," *Journal of Clinical Psychology* 69, no. 1 (2013): 28–44, https://doi.org/10.1002/jclp.21923.
10. Marilia Lira da Silveira Coêlho, Tanja S. H. Wingenbach, and Paulo Sergio Boggio, "Social and Affective Neuroscience of Embodiment," in *Social and*

Affective Neuroscience of Everyday Human Interaction: From Theory to Methodology, ed. Paulo Sergio Boggio, Tanja S. H. Wingenbach, Marilia Lira da Silveira Coêlho, William Edgar Comfort, Lucas Murrins Marques, and Marcus Vinicius Alves (Springer; 2023), https://www.ncbi.nlm.nih.gov/books/NBK595456/doi: 10.1007/978-3-031-08651-9_3.
11. Mirjam Bonanno, Antonio Gangemi, Rosa Angela Fabio, Marco Tramontano, Maria Grazia Maggio, Federica Impellizzeri et al., "Impact of Gentle Touch Stimulation Combined with Advanced Sensory Stimulation in Patients in a Minimally Conscious State: A Quasi-Randomized Clinical Trial," *Life* 15, no. 2 (2025 Feb): 280, https://doi.org/10.3390/life15020280.
12. Leon Skottnik and David E. J. Linden, "Mental Imagery and Brain Regulation—New Links Between Psychotherapy and Neuroscience," *Frontiers in Psychiatry* 10 (2019), https://doi.org/10.3389/fpsyt.2019.00779.
13. Gaétan Chevalier, Stephen T. Sinatra, James L. Oschman, Karol Sokal, and Pawel Sokal, "Earthing: Health Implications of Reconnecting the Human Body to the Earth's Surface Electrons," *Journal of Environmental and Public Health*, January 12, 2012, https://doi.org/10.1155/2012/291541.
14. J. David Creswell, William T. Welch, Shelley E. Taylor, David K. Sherman, Tara L. Gruenewald, and Traci Mann, "Affirmation of Personal Values Buffers Neuroendocrine and Psychological Stress Responses," *Psychological Science* 16, no. 11 (2005): 846–51, https://doi.org/10.1111/j.1467-9280.2005.01624.x.
15. Ryan Hamilton, B. Miedema, L. MacIntyre, and J. Easly, "Using a Positive Self-Talk Intervention to Enhance Coping Skills in Breast Cancer Survivors: Lessons from a Community-Based Group Delivery Model," *Current Oncology* 18, no. 2 (2011): 46–53, https://doi.org/10.3747/co.v18i2.706.
16. Patricia Sherwood, "Somatically-Based Art Therapy for Transforming Experiences of Shame," in *The Bright Side of Shame*, ed. Claude-Hélène Mayer and Elisabeth Vanderheiden (Springer, 2019), https://doi.org/10.1007/978-3-030-13409-9_32.

17. Reconciling with Regret

1. Bronnie Ware, *The Top Five Regrets of the Dying: A Life Transformed by the Dearly Departing* (Hay House, 2012).
2. Neal J. Roese, "Counterfactual Thinking," *Psychological Bulletin* 121, no. 1 (1997): 133–48, https://doi.org/10.1037/0033-2909.121.1.133.
3. Jason M. Holland, Kara L. Thompson, Vincent Rozalski, and Wendy G. Lichtenthal, "Bereavement-Related Regret Trajectories Among Widowed Older Adults," *Journals of Gerontology Series B* 69, no. 1 (2014): 40–47, https://doi.org/10.1093/geronb/gbt050.
4. Ralph E. Schmidt, Olivier Renaud, and Martial Van Der Linden, "Nocturnal Regrets and Insomnia in Elderly People," *International Journal of Aging and Human Development* 73, no. 4 (2012): 371–93, https://doi.org/10.2190/AG.73.4.f.
5. Schmidt, Renaud, and Van Der Linden, "Nocturnal Regrets and Insomnia in Elderly People."
6. Carsten Wrosch, Isabelle Bauer, Gregory E. Miller, and Sonia J. Lupien, "Regret Intensity, Diurnal Cortisol Secretion, and Physical Health in Older Individuals:

Evidence for Directional Effects and Protective Factors," *Psychology and Aging* 22, no. 2 (2007): 319–30, https://doi.org/10.1037/0882-7974.22.2.319.

7. Natalie Joseph-Williams, Adrian Edwards, and Glyn Elwyn, "The Importance and Complexity of Regret in the Measurement of 'Good' Decisions: A Systematic Review and Content Analysis of Existing Assessment Instruments," *Health Expectations* 14, no. 1 (2011): 59–83, https://doi.org/10.1111/j.1369-7625.2010.00621.x.
8. Kasia Kozlowska, Peter Walker, Loyola Mary McLean, and Pascal Carrive, "Fear and The Defense Cascade: Clinical Implications and Management," *Harvard Review of Psychiatry* 23, no. 4 (2015): 263–87, https://doi.org/10.1097/HRP.0000000000000065.
9. Maarten C. Eisma, Kai Epstude, Henk A. W. Schut, Maragaret S. Stroebe, Adrianna Simion, and Paul A. Boelen, "Upward and Downward Counterfactual Thought After Loss: A Multiwave Controlled Longitudinal Study," *Behaviour Therapy* 52, no. 3 (2021): 577–93, https://doi.org/10.1016/j.beth.2020.07.007.
10. Nyla R. Branscombe, Michael J. A. Wohl, Susan Owen, Julie A. Allison, and Ahogni N'gbala, "Counterfactual Thinking, Blame Assignment, and Well-Being in Rape Victims," *Basic and Applied Social Psychology* 25, no. 4 (2003): 265–73, https://doi.org/10.1207/S15324834BASP2504_1.
11. Noel T. Brewer, Jessica T. DeFrank, and Mellisa B. Gilkey, "Anticipated Regret and Health Behavior: A Meta-Analysis," *Health Psychology* 35, no. 11 (2016): 1264–75, https://doi.org/10.1037/hea0000294.
12. Hyun-Ju Kim, Jungwa Seo, Minji Bang, and Sang-Hyuk Lee, "Self-Forgiveness Is Associated with Increased Volumes of Fusiform Gyrus in Healthy Individuals," *Scientific Reports* 13, no. 5505 (2023), https://doi.org/10.1038/s41598-023-32731-0.
13. Kristin D. Neff, "Self-Compassion: Theory, Method, Research, and Intervention," *Annual Review of Psychology* 74 (2023): 193–218, https://doi.org/10.1146/annurev-psych-032420-031047.
14. A Vismaya, Aswathy Gopi, John Romate, and Eslavath Rajkumar, "Psychological Interventions to Promote Self-Forgiveness: A Systematic Review," *BMC Psychology* 12, no. 1 (2024): 258, https://doi.org/10.1186/s40359-024-01671-3.
15. Brittany N. Semenchuk, Samantha Onchulenko, and Shaelyn M. Strachan, "Self-Compassion and Sleep Quality: Examining the Mediating Role of Taking a Proactive Health Focus and Cognitive Emotional Regulation Strategies," *Journal of Health Psychology* 27, no. 10 (2022): 2435–45, https://doi.org/10.1177/13591053211047148.
16. Ting Wang and Xicong Wu, "Self-Compassion Moderates the Relationship Between Neuroticism and Depression in Junior High School Students," *Frontiers in Psychology* 15 (2024), https://doi.org/10.3389/fpsyg.2024.1327789.
17. Roger Jahnke, Linda Larkey, Carol Rogers, Jennifer Etnier, and Fang Lin, "A Comprehensive Review of Health Benefits of Qigong and Tai Chi," *American Journal of Health Promotion* 24, no. 6 (2010): e1–e25, https://doi.org/10.4278/ajhp.081013-lit-248.
18. Waqar Husain, Samia Wasif, and Insha Fatima, "Profanity as a Self-Defense Mechanism and an Outlet for Emotional Catharsis in Stress, Anxiety, and Depression," *Depression Research and Treatment,* no. 1 (2023), https://doi.org/10.1155/2023/8821517.

19. John D. Nguyen and Hieu Duong, "Pursed-Lip Breathing," in *StatPearls* (StatPearls Publishing, 2025), https://www.ncbi.nlm.nih.gov/sites/books/NBK545289/.
20. Teruhisa Komori, "The Relaxation Effect of Prolonged Expiratory Breathing," *Mental Illness* 10, no. 1 (2018), https://doi.org/10.4081/mi.2018.7669.
21. S. Laborde, M. S. Allen, U. Borges, F. Dosseville, T. J. Hosang, M. Iskra et al., "Effects of Voluntary Slow Breathing on Heart Rate and Heart Rate Variability: A Systematic Review and a Meta-Analysis," *Neuroscience & Biobehavioral* Reviews 138 (2022), https://doi.org/10.1016/j.neubiorev.2022.104711.
22. Julia Petrovic, Jessica Mettler, Sohyun Cho, and Nancy L. Heath, "The Effects of Loving-Kindness Interventions on Positive and Negative Mental Health Outcomes: A Systematic Review and Meta-Analysis," *Clinical Psychology Review* 110 (2024), https://doi.org/10.1016/j.cpr.2024.102433.
23. Wendy G. Lichtenthal and Dean G. Cruess, "Effects of Directed Written Disclosure on Grief and Distress Symptoms Among Bereaved Individuals," *Death Studies* 34, no. 6 (2010): 475–99, https://doi.org/10.1080/07481187.2010.483332.

18. Meeting Joy

1. Brené Brown, *Daring Greatly: How the Courage to Be Vulnerable Transforms the Way We Live, Love, Parent, and Lead* (Gotham Books, 2012).
2. Mohsen Joshanloo, "The Influence of Fear of Happiness Beliefs on Responses to the Satisfaction with Life Scale," *Personality and Individual Differences* 54, no. 5 (2013): 647–51, https://doi.org/10.1016/j.paid.2012.11.011.
3. Emily A. Butler, Boris Egloff, Frank H. Wilhelm, Nicholas C. Smith, Elizabeth A. Erickson, and James J. Gross, "The Social Consequences of Expressive Suppression," *Emotion* 3, no. 1 (2003): 48–67, https://doi.org/10.1037/1528-3542.3.1.48.
4. Margaret Stroebe and Henk Schut, "The Dual Process Model of Coping with Bereavement: A Decade On," *Omega: Journal of Death and Dying* 61, no. 4 (2010): 273–89, https://doi.org/10.2190/OM.61.4.b.
5. Patrick H. Finan and Eric L. Garland, "The Role of Positive Affect in Pain and Its Treatment," *Clinical Journal of Pain* 31, no. 2 (2015): 177–87, https://doi.org/10.1097/AJP.0000000000000092.
6. Barbara L. Fredrickson, "The Role of Positive Emotions in Positive Psychology: The Broaden-and-Build Theory of Positive Emotions," *American Psychologist* 56, no. 3 (2001): 218–26, https://doi.org/10.1037/0003-066X.56.3.218.
7. Maarten C. Eisma and Margaret Stroebe, "Emotion Regulatory Strategies in Complicated Grief: A Systematic Review," *Behavior Therapy* 52, no. 1 (2021): 234–49, https://doi.org/10.1016/j.beth.2020.05.004.
8. Finan and Garland, "Role of Positive Affect in Pain and Its Treatment," 177–87.
9. Fredrickson, "Role of Positive Emotions in Positive Psychology," 218–26.
10. Dacher Keltner and George A. Bonanno, "A Study of Laughter and Dissociation," *Journal of Personality and Social Psychology* 73, no. 4 (1997): 687–702, https://doi.org/10.1037/0022-3514.73.4.687.
11. Anthony D. Ong, Cindy Bergeman, Toni Bisconti, and Kimberly Wallace, "Psychological Resilience, Positive Emotions, and Successful Adaptation to Stress

in Later Life," *Journal of Personality and Social Psychology* 91, no. 4 (2006): 730–49, https://doi.org/10.1037/0022-3514.91.4.730.

12. Richard G. Tedeschi and Lawrence G. Calhoun, "The Posttraumatic Growth Inventory," *Journal of Traumatic Stress* 9, no. 3 (1996): 455–71, https://doi.org/10.1002/jts.2490090305.
13. Donald Woods Winnicott, *Playing and Reality* (Tavistock, 1971).
14. René T. Proyer and Willibald Ruch, "The Virtuousness of Adult Playfulness: The Relation of Playfulness with Strengths of Character," *Psychology of Well-Being* 1, no. 4 (2011): 1–12, https://doi.org/10.1186/2211-1522-1-4.
15. Christopher Clifford, Ellis Paulk, Qiyang Lin, Jeanne Cadwallader, Kathy Lubbers, and Leslie D. Frazier, "Relationships Among Adult Playfulness, Stress, and Coping During the COVID-19 Pandemic," *Current Psychology* (2022): 1–10, https://doi.org/10.1007/s12144-022-02841-6.
16. Robert A. Neimeyer, ed., *Meaning Reconstruction and the Experience of Loss* (American Psychological Association, 2001).
17. Crystal L. Park and Susan Folkman, "Meaning in the Context of Stress and Coping," *Review of General Psychology* 1, no. 2 (1997): 115–44, https://doi.org/10.1037/1089-2680.1.2.115.
18. Takuya Matsumoto, Takashi Masuda, Kazuki Hotta, Ryosuke Shimizu, Akira Ishli, Toshiki Kutsuna et al., "Effects of Prolonged Expiration Breathing on Cardiopulmonary Responses During Incremental Exercise," *Respiratory Physiology & Neurobiology* 178, no. 2 (2011): 275–82, https://doi.org/10.1016/j.resp.2011.06.025.
19. Daniel Bressington, Clare Yu, Wandy Wong, Tsz C. Ng, and Wai Tong Chien, "The Effects of Group-Based Laughter Yoga Interventions on Mental Health in Adults: A Systematic Review," *Journal of Psychiatric and Mental Health Nursing* 25, no. 8 (2018): 517–27, https://doi.org/10.1111/jpm.12491.
20. Susan Earle and Jeanne Rose, "Aroma Herbal Stress Relief," *Scentsitivity: Journal of the National Association for Holistic Aromatherapy* 6, no. 1 (1996): 6–10.

19. Awakening to What Matters Most

1. Denise R. Beike, Benjamin P. Markman, and Keith D. Karakashian, "What We Regret Most Are Lost Opportunities: A Theory of Regret Intensity," *Personality and Social Psychology Bulletin* 35, no. 9 (2009): 1253–65.
2. Jeff Greenberg, Sheldon Solomon, and Tom Pyszczynski, "Terror Management Theory and Research: How the Desire for Death Transcendence Drives Our Strivings for Meaning and Significance," *Advances in Experimental Social Psychology* 52 (2015): 129–218.
3. Richard G. Tedeschi and Lawrence G. Calhoun, "Posttraumatic Growth: Conceptual Foundations and Empirical Evidence," *Psychological Inquiry* 15, no. 1 (2004): 1–18.
4. Edward L. Deci and Richard M. Ryan, *Self-Determination Theory: Basic Psychological Needs in Motivation, Development, and Wellness* (Guilford Press, 2017).
5. Luis Carlos Matos, Jorge Machado, Henry Johannes Greten, and Fernando Jorge Monteiro, "Changes of Skin Electrical Potential in Acupoints from Ren

Mai and Du Mai Conduits During Qigong Practice: Documentation of a Clinical Phenomenon," *Journal of Bodywork and Movement Therapies* 23, no. 4 (2019): 713–20, https://doi.org/10.1016/j.jbmt.2019.02.021.
6. Teruhisa Yamamoto, Jun Kawanokuchi, Nobuyuki Nagaoka, Ken Takagi, Torao Ishida, Tomoya Hayashi et al. "Antidepressant Effects of Acupuncture in a Murine Model: Regulation of Neurotrophic Factors," *Acupuncture in Medicine* 41, no. 1 (2023): 38–47, https://doi.org/10.1177/09645284221085279.
7. Melis Yilmaz Balban, Eric Neri, Manuela M. Kogon, Lara Weed, Bita Nouriani, Booil Jo et al., "Brief Structured Respiration Practices Enhance Mood and Reduce Physiological Arousal," *Cell Reports Medicine* 4, no. 1 (2023), https://doi.org/10.1016/j.xcrm.2022.100895.
8. Laura Rennie, Ayse K. Uskul, Catherine Adams, and Katherine Appleton, "Visualisation for Increasing Health Intentions: Enhanced Effects Following a Health Message and When Using a First-Person Perspective," *Psychology & Health* 29, no. 2 (2014): 237–52, https://doi.org/10.1080/08870446.2013.843685.

20. Coming Alive Again

1. Maria Monroy and Dacher Keltner, "Awe as a Pathway to Mental and Physical Health," *Perspectives on Psychological Science* 18, no. 2 (2023): 309–20, https://doi.org/10.1177/17456916221094856.
2. Michiel van Elk, M. Andrea Arciniegas Gomez, Wietske van der Zwaag, Hein van Schie, and Disa Sauter, "The Neural Correlates of the Awe Experience: Reduced Default Mode Network Activity During Feelings of Awe," *Human Brain Mapping* 40, no. 12 (2019): 3561–74, https://doi.org/10.1002/hbm.24616.
3. van Elk, Arciniegas Gomez, van der Zwaag, van Schie, and Sauter, "Neural Correlates of the Awe Experience."
4. Jennifer E. Stellar, Amie Gordon, Criag L. Anderson, Paul K. Piff, Galen McNeil, and Dacher Keltner, "Awe and Humility," *Journal of Personal and Social Psychology* 114, no. 2 (2015): 258–69, https://doi.org/10.1037/pspi0000109.
5. Andrea Chirico and David B. Yaden, "Awe: A Self-Transcendent and Sometimes Transformative Emotion," *Frontiers in Psychology* 9 (2018), https://doi.org/10.3389/fpsyg.2018.00550.
6. Paul K. Piff, Pia Dietze, Matthew Feinberg, Daniel M. Stancato, and Dacher Keltner, "Awe, the Small Self, and Prosocial Behavior," *Journal of Personality and Social Psychology* 108, no. 6 (2015): 883–99, https://doi.org/10.1037/pspi0000018.
7. Roger E. Beaty, Mathias Benedek, Paul J. Silva, and Daniel L. Schacter, "Creative Cognition and Brain Network Dynamics," *Trends in Cognitive Sciences* 20, no. 2 (2016): 87–95, https://doi.org/10.1016/j.tics.2015.10.004.
8. Young-Ja Jeong, Sung-Chan Hong, Myeong So-o Lee, Min-Cheol Park, Yong-Kyu Kim, and Chae-Moon Suh, "Dance Movement Therapy Improves Emotional Responses and Modulates Neurohormones in Adolescents with Mild Depression," *International Journal of Neuroscience* 115, no. 12 (2005): 1711–20, https://doi.org/10.1080/00207450590958574.

INDEX

acceptance, 47, 51–53, 58, 208, 213
aches, 12–13, 57, 161, 239, 253, 264, 267
acupressure points, 93, 105, 106–7, 117–18, 188, 259
agni (digestive fire), 79, 86, 114, 116
aliveness, 264–65, 277
  development of, 266–67
  intimacy with, 278
  naturally unfolding, 272, 273
  reemerging, 268
  techniques for working with, 273–76
analogies and metaphors
  backpack, invisible, 38–39
  caterpillar and chrysalis, 13–14, 15
  garden, tending, 214
  gears, 90
ancestral grief, 211–12
anger, 60, 122
  cold, 127–28
  deep, awakening, 199
  energy and, 87
  from exhaustion, 125–26
  hot, 126–27
  from internal pressure, 124–25
  physiology, 88
  purpose, 66
  regret and, 226
  sensations of, noticing, 64
  somatic experience, 123–24
  as survival signal, 123
  techniques for working with, 129–33
anxiety, 60, 146
  in daily life, 54, 147
  jaw tension and, 106
  as misguided, recognizing, 151
  physiology, 64, 148, 149
  from pressure, 36
  self-forgiveness and, 229
  See also grief-anxiety
apocalypse/revelation, 254, 256–57
apologies, 204–6
aromatherapy, 248–49
arrival fallacy, 52
attachment, 45, 47, 51, 75, 78, 85
attention, 19, 63, 97
  in aliveness, 264, 270, 275
  brain fog and, 76, 78, 80
  brain regions in, 209
  compassionate, 12, 29, 43, 50
  numbness and, 163, 169
  regret and, 226–27
  sharpening, 94
autonomic nervous system
  anxiety and, 148
  balancing, 259–60
  calming, 185
  heart rate variability and, 19–20, 24
  polyvagal theory and, 166–67
  shifting, 155–56
  suppression and, 42
  See also parasympathetic nervous system; sympathetic nervous system
awe, 165, 275–76
  aliveness and, 269–70, 272–73
  benefits, 243
  experiencing, 19, 30, 263
  sadness and, 264
Ayurveda, 17
  anger in, 124, 132
  balance in, 268
  daily rhythms in, 104
  digestion in, 86, 114
  grief fog in, 78, 79

Ayurveda *(continued)*
heart in, 29–30
tamas in, 168
vata in, 149–50, 151–52

bereavement, 38, 53, 78, 114, 148
body, 13–14, 68, 239, 278
as ally, 30–31, 43, 57, 114, 115
anger in, 123–24
anxiety in, 148
awe and, 269
Ayurvedic understanding, 29–30
communication of, 20, 31, 42, 63, 65, 72
compassion and, 11
crying and, 137
disconnection from, 59–60, 101
emotional, 15, 63–64, 279
fear in, 178–79, 180–81, 192
and grieving, role in, 15, 16, 25
healing and, 151–52, 218
joy in, 240, 243–44
and mind, relationship between, 14, 26–27, 81, 83
natural stress-release systems, 246
numbness in, 161, 166–67, 175, 176
pain in, unresolved, 40
reclaiming, 17, 22
regulating, 152
shame in, 216
sorrows in, unnamed, 39
strain from regret, 227
suppression and, 41–42, 155
See also whole-body yeses
Boss, Pauline, 39
brain, 86
amygdala, 180
attachment and, 46, 47–48
beliefs and, 209
cognitive load from grieving, 88
default mode network, 269
entrainment and, 23
executive function, 78
gut-brain axis, 114
and heart, relationship of, 26–27, 28, 31
hemispheres, synchronizing, 246
isolation and, 35
limbic system, 248
regulatory capacity, strengthening, 94
rituals and, 51
supporting others and, 133
suppression and, 42
visualization and, 260–61
Yoga Nidra and, 109
brain fog/grief fog, 75, 163
food and, 112
physiology of, 77–79
qi and, 138
techniques for working with, 80–85
breath/breathing, 13, 16, 60, 279
anger and, 127, 131
digestion and, 116–17
energy and, 92, 94
entrainment and, 22–23
fear and, 180, 187–88
for grief fog, 80–81, 83
grief-anxiety and, 155–56
heart and, 26–27
parasympathetic nervous system and, 21
regret and, 232
sadness and, 137, 138, 139–40, 141–42
shame and, 216
synchronizing with others, 24
in Traditional Chinese Medicine, 28
in uncertainty, 259–60
broaden-and-build theory, 243
broken heart syndrome, 137
Brown, Brené, 241
Buddhism, 182

caffeine, 103
caregiving professions, 89, 125, 198
cherophobia, 241–42
Christian mysticism, 182
chronic stress, 78, 112, 125–26, 128
circadian rhythms, 102–3
clarity, mental, 94, 258–59
aliveness and, 266
coherence and, 23, 27
creating conditions for, 79–80
digestion and, 86
emotional release and, 137

from freewriting, 202
gut and, 116
restoring, 80–82
coherence, 23–24, 25, 26–27, 276
restoring, 43, 138, 139–40, 220
in Traditional Chinese Medicine, 28
collective grief, 39, 89–90, 94–96, 99, 210
compassion, 10, 15, 199, 278
anxiety, responding with, 157
in befriending ache, 12–13
for cold anger, 128
collective grief and, 90
cultural narratives and, 43
emotional freedom and, 69–70
and energy, cultivating, 99
fear and, 183
for grief-anxiety, 152
interoception and, 63
with memories, painful, 50
need for, 56–57, 80
for oneself, 97, 98, 137, 223 (*see also* self-compassion)
as physiological, 11, 24
regret and, 226
reminders and, 48
for shame, reducing, 213, 214
with whatever arises, 73
Compassionate Grieving, 11, 60–61
on cultural forces derailing grief, 36–38
love in, 12
mindfulness of emotions if, 62
on shame and grief, relationship of, 210
unscripted life in, 256–57
confidence, 68, 69, 216, 227, 228, 247
continuing bonds theory, 46–48, 50, 84–85
coping
avoidant, 38
numbness as, 167–68
cortisol, 77, 98, 269
anxiety and, 151–52
digestion and, 114
fear and, 180
forest bathing and, 192
forward folds and, 185
reducing, 246, 260, 274
regret and, 227
regulation, altered, 212
sleep and, 101, 103, 109
counterfactuals, 228
courage, 10, 252, 278
facing fear with, 57
guilt and, 202, 205
in healing shame, 213
joy and, 249
in unscripted life, 255, 257
creativity, 149, 245, 260, 270–73, 274–75
cultural narratives and pressures
avoidant behaviors, 167–68
defensive responses, 49
harm from, 43
identity and, 213
joy and, 238, 239, 242
letting go and, 44
pain and, 36–37, 251–52
sadness and, 135, 136
shame and, 209–11, 213
curiosity, 55, 56, 267
toward ache, 12–13
aliveness and, 265, 274
awakening, 263
interoception and, 63, 64
in observing emotions, 68
toward suffering, 10–11
cytokines, 41, 269

dancing, 273–74
dark night of the soul, 165–66
death
of children, 52, 196, 197, 224–25
finality of, 226
grief's layers and, 39
of parent, 19, 28, 47, 75–76, 162–63, 262
of pets, 146
of siblings, 46, 134–35
of spouses, 45, 53, 59–60, 80, 87, 160–61
sudden, 29, 38, 50, 114, 177–78, 183, 212, 265
terminal illness, 224–25, 250–51

Descartes, René, 32
dementia, 39, 77, 180, 196
depression, 49, 112, 209, 229, 241–42
devotion, 10, 239, 252, 263, 270
digestion, 91, 112
  anger and, 128
  fear and, 180
  hormones and, 114
  mirror of, 111, 115
  supporting, 86
  suppression and, 41
  techniques for working with, 116–21
divorce, 38, 40, 48, 103, 122–23, 128, 162, 251
Doka, Kenneth J., 39, 210
dopamine, 175, 242, 244, 274
dorsal vagal response, 20, 166
Dual Process Model, 53, 244

embodied path of peace, 60, 107
embodiment
  compassion and, 70
  defining, 61–62
  emotional literacy, 65–67
  emotions and, 62, 68, 69–70, 265, 268
  interoception, 63–65
  natural expression of, 25
  for shame, dispelling, 214
emotional buoyancy, 21–22, 23, 24, 25, 94
emotional intelligence, 29
emotions, 9–10, 68, 125, 196
  aromatherapy for, 248–49
  balancing, 259
  and body, bridge between, 14, 63–65
  cycles, 17, 54
  distrust in one's own, 210–11
  embodiment and, 62, 68, 69–70, 265, 268
  entrainment and, 23
  expressing, 25, 145
  fitness of, 71–72
  food and, 112, 113
  gut and, 115–16
  lack of education about, 34
  mindfulness of, 62, 68
  name and analyzing, difference between, 66
  overload of, 20, 161
  physiological foundation of, 149
  regulating, 149, 188
  releasing, 137
  suppressing, 33, 41–42, 124–25
  unprocessed, 100–101, 235
  welcoming, 53
  in Western culture, 32–33, 54
  yin and yang in, 28
empaths, 197–99
empathy, 24, 34, 42, 43, 90, 133, 229, 270
endorphins, 244, 247, 274
energy, 25, 85
  balancing, 97, 154
  in grieving, 87–88, 98
  individual and shared, 91
  rebuilding, 98
  short-term energy-relieving behaviors, 168
  stabilizing, 103, 259
  suppression and, 42
  techniques for working with, 92–97, 170–71
energy mapping, 91
entrainment, 22–23, 26–27
epigenetic effect, 212
exhaustion, 10, 87, 98, 101
  anger from, 125–26
  brain fog and, 75
  caffeine and, 103
  cycles of, 38
  deepening, 36, 79
  food and, 113
  inner work and, 88
  numbness and, 167
  physiology of, 19, 25, 91
  qi and, 138

faith, unraveling, 262–63
fatigue, 10–11, 103
  causes, 14, 20, 41, 92
  chronic, 128
  food and, 112
  gut and, 115

numbness as, 162
sleeplessness and, 100–101
fear, 60, 72, 92
actualized, 178–79
brain fog and, 75
existential, 179, 181–83
facing, 57
gentleness in meeting, 157
of grief, 11
in grief-anxiety, 147, 148
of happiness, 241–42
of inner world, 64
of joy, 247
releasing, 69
reminders and, 48
sudden loss and, 178
techniques for working with, 183–92
fearlessness, 229
feelings, 35, 38, 66, 136, 168, 205, 279
in aliveness, 267, 268, 271–72
digestion and, 112–13, 115
distrusting, 208
embodiment and, 62, 63, 65, 68
expressing, 201, 225, 235, 263
and knowing, gap between, 61
listening to, 31, 32, 64, 67, 76
naming, 136
overwhelming, 22, 60, 156, 161
presence with, 135
suppressing, 2, 33–34, 36, 54, 88–89, 128, 229
unexpressed, 125
unprocessed, 14, 93
welcoming, 168
food, 112, 113–14, 168
Frankl, Victor, 166
Fredrickson, Barbara, 243
Friedman, Russell, 168

gender identity, 212–13
gratitude, 19, 23, 28, 30, 108, 229, 243
Greenspan, Miriam, 168
grief and grieving, 55, 76, 114
allowing, 264
anger, forms commonly accompanying, 124–28
awakenings within, 253–54
boundaries for, 199
causes, 9
contemporary culture and, 32–35
contradictions in, 196–97
creative expressions supporting, 271
disenfranchised, 39, 210–11
effects, 9–10
embracing, 52–53, 57, 58
emotions related to, 60, 67, 161
expressing, 12, 28–29, 41, 56–57
grief for, 265
and joy, relationship of, 237, 238, 240–41, 244–45, 249
layers of, 134–35
and love, relationship between, 11–12, 39–40, 143, 197, 278–79
as mindfulness practice, 183
as nonlinear, 54
oversimplifying, 210
paradox and, 30
personal and collective, distinguishing, 94–96
physiology, 16, 19, 138
regret and, 225–26, 227, 228
relationship with, changing, 279–80
secondary, 89–90
styles of, 164
time sense in, 251–52, 254
tools for meeting, 73–74
turning toward, 168, 278–79
types, 39
unnamed, 101, 200
See also ancestral grief; collective grief; intergenerational grief
grief fog. *See* brain fog/grief fog
grief literacy, 40, 43
grief narratives, 215, 222
Grief Recovery Handbook (James and Friedman), 168
grief-anxiety, 148
expressions of, 147
as psychological and physiological, 149
reflecting on, 152
in relationships, 150–51
techniques for working with, 153–58

guilt, 66, 69, 206
- distortion by, 194–96, 198
- empaths and, 198–99
- energy and, 87
- honesty of, 197
- jaw tension and, 106
- joy and, 243–44
- numbness and, 163
- obligation-based, 202–4
- regret and, 224, 226, 235
- releasing, 56
- and shame, distinctions in, 194, 195, 207–8, 209, 224, 235
- techniques for working with, 199–206

gut, 112, 113, 115, 116, 121, 228

Harris, Darcy, 34
healing, 15, 53, 61, 71, 80, 249, 266
- apology letters, 205–6
- as communal, 43, 90, 280
- compassion in, 10
- embodiment and, 65
- energy in, 25
- food for, 120–21
- indications of, 176
- interrupting, 50
- joy in, 240–41
- pace of, 76, 109
- relationship to, expanding, 40
- as restoring harmony, 23
- sleep for, importance of, 101
- trust and, 211

heart, 17, 31
- anger and, 127
- and brain, relationship of, 26–27, 28, 31
- coherence of, 23
- intelligence of, 57
- kidneys and, 180–81
- listening to, 255
- and lungs, relationship of, 18–19, 28, 31, 140
- and mind, relationship of, 67, 107
- reopening, 249, 267
- role of, 18–19
- sorrows in, unnamed, 39
- vastness, 240, 241

heart rate variability (HRV), 19–20, 21
- anger and, 124, 127
- anxiety and, 148
- increasing, 83, 243, 260
- influencing, 23
- observing, 24
- social disconnection and, 35
- sound and, 171
- suppression and, 42
- vagus nerve and, 26

HeartMath Institute, 23
Holocaust survivors, 211–12
hyperarousal, 42, 46, 148, 149, 220
hypoarousal, 167
hypothalamic-pituitary-adrenal axis, 114, 149

identity, 28, 48, 75, 198
- changes in, 210
- energy and, 91
- existential fear and, 179, 181–83
- guilt and, 202
- loss of, 39, 211, 251
- memories and, 48–50
- reconstructing, 119, 257
- shame and, 208, 209
- in Western culture, 32

immune system, 20, 23, 41, 101, 114, 128, 137
impermanence, 49, 235, 241, 256, 260, 261
inflammation, 43, 112, 114, 132, 175, 220, 269
intergenerational grief, 210, 211–12
interoception, 63–65, 69, 124
ironic process theory, 49
isolation, 270, 279
- creating, 35, 41, 55, 165
- disenfranchised grief and, 210–11
- reducing, 40
- regret and, 229
- shame and, 208, 212, 213
- softening, 222, 229
- from suppression, 137

James, John W., 168
jing (vital essence), 180–81, 187
joy, 239, 279

"foreboding," 241–42
within grief, 28, 244–45
performative, 238, 239
physiology, 243
as practice, 237
self-forgiveness and, 229
techniques for working with, 245–49
See also under grief and grieving
judgment, 55, 56, 66, 69, 172, 194–95, 196, 208

Keltner, Dacher, 269
kidney system, 180–81, 187, 191
Klass, Dennis, 46
Kok, Bethany E., 26
Kolk, Bessel van der; *The Body Keeps the Score*, 40
Kübler-Ross, Elisabeth, 52

A League of Their Own, 135
Lembke, Anna, 242
letting go, 58
in Compassionate Grieving, 12
cutting ties as, 45–48
finish line and, 51–54, 135
love's role in, 15
moving on as, 48–51
as practice, 44
as release, 54, 57
See also surrender
Lewis, C. S., 123
liver
qi, stagnation, 124–25, 126–27, 130
yin deficiency, 125–26
loneliness, 35, 41, 55, 66, 100, 101, 161, 211
losses
accumulated, 40
ambiguous, 39
naming, 38–39, 118–19, 242, 253
secondary, 41, 199
love, 13, 30, 221
and anger, relationship between, 127, 128
cultural narratives and, 43
embodiment of, 18
force of, 255
physiology of, 24
self-forgiveness and, 229
universal, 182
See also under grief and grieving
loving-kindness, 221, 232–33
lungs
ache in, 137–38
and heart, relationship of, 18–19, 28, 31, 140
kidneys and, 180–81
large intestine and, 115
qi depletion in, 137–38
in Traditional Chinese Medicine, 28, 78–79, 91, 188

medical care, need for, 139
memory/memories, 47–48, 248
autobiographical, 48–50
brain fog and, 75, 76, 77, 78
embracing, 53
energy for, 88
in grieving process, 48–49
numbness and, 163
qi and, 138
reconsolidation, 50
ritual and, 51
in Traditional Chinese Medicine, 79
writing and, 85
mind, 232
and body, relationship between, 14, 26–27, 81, 83
numbness and, 165
Sadhaka Pitta in, 29
sleep and, 101
softening, 152
steadying, 260
mind-body (Cartesian) dualism, 32, 41, 64
mindfulness, 60, 62, 68, 94, 183, 264–65
miscarriages, 33, 194–95, 210
mood, 102, 112, 192, 248, 259, 267
mortality, 228–29, 256
motivation, 20, 76, 138, 163, 168, 228, 256, 260
myth, 181–82, 279

narrative practices, 50, 119, 215, 222
nature, 22, 191–92, 220, 270, 280

Neimeyer, Robert, 244
nervous system, 239
  aliveness and, 267
  allostatic load and, 78
  attachments and, 46
  balancing, 43, 83, 92, 243
  breath and, 57
  caffeine and, 103
  calming, 13, 86, 97, 231
  compassion and, 11
  coregulating with others, 24
  embodiment and, 265
  fluctuations in, 23, 53
  joy and, 241–42
  numbness and, 163
  overwhelm, signs of, 147
  playfulness and, 244
  regulating, 71, 72, 153, 274
  sleep and, 101
  spine's role in, 93
  supporting, 82, 170
  suppression and, 42
  vibration and, 174
  See also autonomic nervous system
neuroscience, 229, 235, 260–61, 271
Nickman, Steven, 46
numbness, 17, 50, 60, 176, 242, 265
  anger and, 128
  cognitive effects, 163
  embodiment and, 62
  emotional effects, 162–63
  energy and, 87, 88
  from fear, 180
  physiology of, 161, 162
  as protection, 166–67, 168–69
  relational effects, 164
  from sadness, 138
  spiritual effects, 165–66
  techniques for working with, 169–75

O'Connor, Mary-Frances, 47
oxytocin, 24, 141, 144, 218, 244, 274

pain, 9–10
  allowing, 12, 54, 58
  body's natural relief chemistry, 137
  brain regions linked to, 78
  Cartesian view, 32
  as communication, 64
  cultural tendencies, 36–37, 251–52
  guarding, 239
  isolation and, 35
  layers of, 41
  regret and, 228
  in rituals, transforming, 51
  suppression and, 40, 41, 42
  unexpressed, 226
panic attacks, 151
parasympathetic nervous system
  activating, 21, 83, 98, 106, 152, 188, 218, 244, 246, 260
  awe and, 269
  crying and, 137
  enhancing, 185
  exhalation and, 155, 232
  influencing, 23
  role of, 20, 148–49
  and sympathetic, cycle between, 167
patience, 72, 80, 109, 128, 152, 226
perfectionism, 3, 37, 113, 114, 125, 208, 228, 229
performance, 3, 33, 37, 38, 77, 196, 238–39, 241
platitudes, 34–35, 59, 165
playfulness, 244, 247, 249, 275
Porges, Stephen W., 24, 268
post-traumatic growth, 215, 243, 256
post-traumatic stress, 38, 89
presence, 135, 254
  breath-based practices and, 138
  compassion and, 10, 15
  divine, 264–65
  embodiment and, 62, 69
  felt sense of, 267
  interoception and, 63
  love and, 17
  with one's own grief, 35
  of others, entrainment with, 23, 24, 25
  pausing and, 72
  remembering, 216
  restoring, 80–82, 157–58
  from self-protection, 168
  in terminal illness, 251
  in unscripted life, 257
pretending, 2, 35, 37–38, 69

productivity, 36, 37, 72, 77, 99, 167–68, 254, 271
professional guidance, when to seek, 73–74, 139, 206
proprioception, 63, 220
purpose, 254, 261
  complexity of, 251–52
  techniques for working with, 257–61

qi, 138
  and blood, relationship of, 28–29
  disrupting, 168
  flow of, reestablishing, 139–40, 240, 268, 274
  harmonizing, 259
  massage, 170–71
  moving, 91, 155, 175, 231
  plum-pit, 196
  stabilizing, 104
qigong, 28, 140, 153–54, 170–71, 186–87, 230–31, 257–58

regret
  acknowledging, 229–30
  error of omission, 228–29
  near end of life, 224–25
  techniques for working with, 230–35
  unrecognized, 227–28
regret-and-opportunity principle, 256
relationships
  fear in, 179–80
  grief-anxiety and, 147, 150–51
  numbness in, 164
  with those who have died, maintaining, 46–48, 84–85, 135
relaxation response, 21, 22, 26, 42, 116, 140
resentment, 51–52, 123, 127, 128, 131–32
rest. *See* sleep and rest
restorative practices, 126, 191
rhythm, 81, 154–55, 172–74
rituals, 53, 271
  evening, 101, 104
  grief altar, 143–44
  for grief and regret, 234–35
  healing, 135
  purpose, 51, 235
  tea, 98
rumination
  interrupting, 274
  quieting, 232, 269
  regret and, 229, 230
  releasing, 105, 233, 234–35
  shame and, 209, 214

Sadhaka Pitta, 29–30
sadness and sorrow, 28, 60, 134–35, 137, 144–45
  awe and, 269
  beauty and, 264
  energy and, 87
  grief and, 49
  guilt and, 195
  health and, 111
  honoring, 143
  inflammation and, 114
  jaw tension and, 106
  joy and, 245, 249
  releasing, 136–37
  sensations, noticing, 64
  suppressing, 136
  techniques for working with, 139–44
  unacknowledged, 212
  "wild edge," 181
Schut, Henk, 53
self-blame, 55, 78, 208, 226, 228–30, 233, 235
self-compassion, 143–44, 172, 205, 214, 229–30, 233
self-criticism, 2, 37, 41, 55, 209, 214
self-determination theory, 256
self-doubt, 38, 214, 229
self-forgiveness, 56, 215, 229, 235
self-judgment, 206, 221, 229, 230–31, 233
self-love, 221
self-punishment, 123, 226, 229, 233
self-soothing, 137, 141
self-worth, 198, 214
sensations, 63, 64–65, 68, 175
senses
  attuning, 264–65
  awakening, 191–92, 268–69
  focusing on, 157–58

sensitivity, 54, 265, 266–67, 272–73, 276
shame, 55, 56, 69, 262
  of comparison, 76
  gender identity and, 212–13
  and grief, relationship of, 208
  and guilt, distinctions in, 194, 195, 207–8, 209, 224, 235
  healing, 214–15
  narratives based on, 209–11, 213
  numbness and, 163
  releasing, 77, 118
  softening, 172
  techniques for working with, 215–22
  as universal, 207
Shen (spirit), 28, 168, 180–81, 187
Siegel, Daniel J., 167
sighing, 138
Sikh tradition, 182
Silverman, Phyllis, 46
sleep and rest
  anger and, 125, 126
  creating conditions for, 104
  difficulties with, 101–2
  guilt and, 195, 196, 206
  healing and, 101
  physiology, 102–3
  regret and, 227
  as sacred, 37
  techniques for working with, 105–9
social media, 12, 59, 168, 238
spiritual bypassing, 168
spirituality, 165–66, 168, 181–83, 188–90, 262–63
spoon theory, 91
stigma, 55, 56, 69, 123, 135, 144
stories
  acceptance, 52
  anger, 122–23
  anxiety, 146–47
  awakenings, 250–51, 252–53, 254
  body disconnection, 59–60
  brain fog, 75–76, 77, 80
  continuing bonds, 47
  creativity, 271–72
  cultural narratives, 33
  digestion, 110–11
  emotional buoyancy, 22
  fear, 177–78
  gender identity, 212–13
  guilt, 194–95
  heartbeat in, feeling, 19
  joy, absence of, 236–37, 239, 242, 243, 244
  joy within grief, 28
  letting go, 45
  losses, accumulated, 40
  memories, 50
  moving on, 48
  numbness, 160–61, 162–63
  oscillation, 53
  pain, physical, 46
  performance, 38
  Sadhaka Pitta, 29
  sadness, 134–35
  secondary grief, 89–90
  shame, 207
  sleeplessness, 100–101, 103
  vata imbalance, 150
stress
  in modern culture, 36
  reducing, 83, 94
  regret and, 227
  sleep and, 103
  suppression and, 42
  sympathetic nervous system and, 20
stress hormones, 75, 77, 112
stress response
  activating, 98, 235
  harmonizing, 97
  quieting, 218, 260
  reducing, 67, 133
  suppression and, 124–25
Stroebe, Margaret, 53
suffering, 239
  joy in easing, 243
  kindness in meeting, 10–11
  prolonging, 49, 240, 242
  shame and, 214
  witnessing others', 89
Sufism, 182
sugar, 112–13
suicide, 3, 137, 212–13, 236
suppression, 56, 135, 144, 211, 240, 279
  anger and, 124–25, 127–28

Ayurvedic understanding, 33
effects of, 137
embodiment and, 62, 65
energy drained in, 88–89
honesty and, 196
of joy, 239, 242, 245, 249
letting go and, 49, 50
normalizing, 212
physiology, 89
releasing tension from, 200
surrender, 14, 55–56, 182, 183–85, 257
swearing, 202
sympathetic nervous system
chronic activation, 21
influencing, 23
overactivation, 26, 168
and parasympathetic, cycle between, 167
role of, 20, 148–49
social disconnection and, 35
suppression and, 89
synchronization, 22–24, 26–27, 30, 31, 230

Takotsubo cardiomyopathy, 137
tears, 144, 161, 162
emotional and basal, 136
physiology, 88
as taboo, 135–36, 212
three P's, 72
throat, lump in, 196, 199–200
tone of being, 267
toxic positivity, 168, 238
Traditional Chinese Medicine, 16, 17, 191
anger in, 124–28, 130
avoidance patterns in, 168
dancing in, 274
digestion in, 114
energy in, 90–91, 92
fear in, 180–81, 187
grief fog in, 78–79
grief in, 188
heart in, 27–29
joy in, 240
lungs and large intestine in, 115
meridians in, 153–54
pulse breathing in, 140
sadness in, 137–38
sleep in, 104
See also jing; qi; Shen (spirit); yin and yang
trauma, 39, 210
small-*t*, 198
from sudden loss, 178
unhealed, 211–12
vicarious, 89

unscripted life, 229, 255–57, 260–61

vagal tone, 42, 115, 140, 149, 151–52
vagus nerve, 21, 26, 35, 42, 171, 188, 220, 246
ventral vagal state, 268

Ware, Bronnie; *Top Five Regrets of the Dying*, 225
Weller, Francis, 181
Western culture
acceptance in, 51–53
anger in, 124
emotions in, 32–33, 54
grief in, 36–38
values in, 36
See also cultural narratives and pressures
Western medicine, 27, 28, 29
Western science, 17, 24, 149, 188
whole-body yeses, 267–68, 273
Winnicott, Donald, 244
witnessing, 35, 89, 100, 195, 214, 224
words
power of, 209
unsaid, regretting, 226
See also platitudes
worthiness, 55, 56, 210, 216, 217–18, 220–21, 229

yin and yang, 27–29, 104
Yogic philosophy, 182

ABOUT THE AUTHOR

AmarAtma Singh Khalsa is a grief specialist, teacher, and board-certified chaplain who has spent more than fifteen years accompanying people through loss, uncertainty, and profound life transitions. His work bridges emotional care, somatic practices, and spiritual wisdom, offering a compassionate alternative to grief models that prioritize fixing, bypassing, or pathologizing pain.

Trained in both Traditional Chinese Medicine and ministry, AmarAtma integrates body-based approaches, mindfulness, and nervous system awareness to support grief as a lived, embodied experience. His work is informed by thousands of hours of clinical and spiritual care in hospitals, outpatient settings, retreats, and private practice, supporting adults, children, families, and caregivers navigating death, non-death losses, and existential grief.

AmarAtma is the CEO and founder of the Institute for Compassionate Grieving and the creator of the Compassionate Grieving model, which centers emotional safety, somatic relief, and the restoration of trust in the body's wisdom. He currently lives and teaches in the United States, offering classes, retreats, and educational programs devoted to helping people meet grief with tenderness, dignity, and depth.